Bake with Anna Olson

More than 125
Simple, Scrumptious, and Sensational Recipes
to Make You a Better Baker

appetite
by RANDOM HOUSE

Library and Archives of Canada Cataloguing in Publication
is available upon request.

ISBN: 9780147530219
eBook ISBN: 9780147530226

Book design by CS Richardson
Photography by Ryan Szulc and Mike McColl
Cake icon © er ryan, wheat icon © T-Kot; both Shutterstock.com

Printed and bound in China

Published in Canada by Appetite by Random House®,
a division of Penguin Random House Canada Limited

www.penguinrandomhouse.ca

10 9 8 7 6 5 4 3 2 1

Contents

Introduction

I'd like to ask you a little question: Do you like to bake?

You may have thought I was going to ask you something like "Do you like desserts?" or "Do you love breaking into a crusty, warm loaf of fresh bread?" But the most important question is, simply, "Do you like to bake?" because the answer is so important. Success stems from that simple "Yes."

Perhaps you're a seasoned baker, or maybe you've only ever dabbled in baking, having played with just a few recipes, or perhaps you consider yourself an intermediate baker and are feeling ready to expand your baking repertoire. Whatever your baking experience and skill level, I have some great new recipes for you to try in this book!

The art of baking is not about the end result (okay, maybe it is, just a little bit), but about the journey—the process of taking relatively basic ingredients and transforming them into something wonderful. We should all have some activity that makes us happy and fulfills us (or even distracts us) when we need it. Some people play golf as a hobby, others garden. But bakers know that it's about more than having an enjoyable pastime. Baking is about sharing: we bake not just for ourselves, but also for others. That act of sharing is an important part of the experience, and can even be the key motivator sometimes. And let's not ignore the personal sense of satisfaction you get when you've mastered a new recipe or technique, because baking is also about learning.

This book will allow you to find recipes by flavour and type, but you can also treat it a little like a textbook, seeking out recipes according to their required skill level—whether that means sticking to a level that you're comfortable with, or aiming for a level that might challenge you, allowing you to improve your baking skills and so become a better, more confident baker.

In a nutshell, your baking success will come from practice. You will continue to learn as you try new recipes and will improve your techniques by remaking your favourites. But ultimately, it is the sharing that will be your motivation—if you're in doubt about picking up your baking apron, just think of the smiles and nods of appreciation for your efforts that await you!

So, in answer to the little question I asked you before, I dearly hope the answer is "Yes!" And now, let's bake together!

Anna

About the Recipes

Simple, Scrumptious, and Sensational Recipes

In this book there are seven chapters, based on traditional recipe categories: cookies and bars, pies and tarts, cakes, other pastries, other desserts, breads, and sauces and décor. The chapters are divided into three sections according to the level of effort and ability required: Simple, Scrumptious, and Sensational. A Simple recipe such as Classic Chocolate Chip Cookies (page 17) requires few tools, no previous baking experience, and basic ingredients. The end result may be simple, but it will be fantastically delicious, too. A Scrumptious recipe like Pumpkin Crème Brûlée Tarts (page 88) involves a little planning and usually contains multiple elements; the result is more complex and showier than a Simple recipe. And if you're looking for a challenge, or looking to impress, then head straight to the Sensational recipes. The name says it all. These are the most complex recipes, with more challenging steps but also a glorious end result that will reflect the full extent of your efforts. A Croquembouche (page 199), a tower of cream-filled profiteroles, is a bold undertaking that is more than worthy of the description "Sensational"!

Please don't feel bound to match these categories strictly to your skill level, though. A novice baker can certainly take on a Sensational recipe. "Sensational" does not always mean more difficult; it may just be more involved, but all of the guiding steps are there for you to follow—just take your time. Equally, a seasoned baker need not turn up their nose at a Simple recipe. A classic Apple Tarte Tatin (page 72) may be simpler and require less effort than a "Blue Ribbon" Apple Pie (page 80), but it's still supremely tasty.

Foundation Recipes

Within all three recipe categories you will find some recipes or subrecipes that are flagged as "foundation." In a professional baking kitchen, foundation recipes are the basics from which many other recipes grow—sort of the way a good chicken stock is a foundation for countless types of soups and sauces. These are the recipes that are essential for any baker to master, as they are invaluable for extending and reinforcing your understanding of baking as a whole.

If you'd like to treat this cookbook as a bit of a baking textbook, then try your hand first at the foundation recipes themselves and the other recipes that use them. You'll quickly see how mastering the principles behind the foundation recipes improves your baking overall. And to make it even easier for you, here's a list:

Pastry Doughs

Chocolate Pastry Dough
(see Chocolate Slice Cookies, page 26)
Pâte Sablée Dough
(see Empire Cookies, page 49)
Pie Dough for Fruit Fillings (page 66)
Pie Dough for Fluid Fillings (page 67)
Puff Pastry Dough (page 170)
Danish Pastry Dough (page 172)
Basic Choux Paste (page 173)

Cakes

Ladyfingers (see Chocolate-Dipped
Ladyfingers, page 54)
Chocolate Cake (see Classic Devil's
Food Cake, page 114)
Sponge Cake
(see Victoria Sponge, page 126)
Carrot Cake (see Carrot Cake with
Cream Cheese Frosting, page 130)
Vanilla Cake (see Classic Vanilla Birthday Cake
with Caramel Pastry Cream, page 146)

Fillings and Frostings

Other Staples

Gluten-Free Recipes

There are a number of recipes in this book that are specifically designed to be free of wheat flour and other grains that contain gluten, and quite a few that are already inherently gluten-free. If you need to bake for someone who is avoiding gluten, you can choose from the following:

Essentials

Tools

There are essential tools for baking at any level. The following list lays out these tools, starting with the basics and moving on to tools that will make baking easier as your skills improve. Basic tools are the essentials that *every* baker needs. And while Sensational recipes can certainly be made without the Advanced set of tools, they will help you have a more enjoyable baking experience.

Basic Tools

If you're just getting into baking, here are the basics you need to get going:

Scale—professional bakers scale their ingredients (measure by weighing). The result is more precise and actually saves on dishes, since fewer scoops and bowls are required. Home-baking recipes in North America tend to express measurements in volume, but having a scale on hand is still important for things like butter and chocolate. You'll find it's a fairly inexpensive purchase and totally worth the money.

Measuring cups and spoons—for liquid measures, you'll want a glass measuring cup. If you like to measure your other ingredients by volume (using ¼ cup, ⅓ cup, ½ cup, and 1 cup measures) then use a reputable brand. The cutesy measuring cups you buy in gift shops may look nice, but they may not offer accurate measurements.

Baking pans—to cover most recipes in baking, you'll want to have:

- 2 x metal rimmed baking trays, any size
- 2 x metal square pans, 8-inch (20 cm) or 9-inch (23 cm)
- 2 x round metal baking pans, 8-inch (20 cm) or 9-inch (23 cm)
- 1 loaf pan, 9- x 5-inch (2 L)
- 1 muffin pan, 12-cup
- 1 glass pie plate, 9-inch (23 cm)

Cooling rack—allows baked goods to cool down quickly without damaging your countertops.

Electric beaters—a set of handheld beaters is relatively inexpensive and makes blending batters, whipping egg whites, and whipping cream a breeze.

Handheld whisk—to blend fluid ingredients or add volume.

Offset spatula (or palette knife)—this will become an extension of your hand as you bake. Use it to remove warm cookies from a tray, extract a perfect slice of cake, and spread frosting or meringue with ease, whether you're aiming for smooth and flat or for dimples and swirls.

Oven thermometer—you really get to know your oven when you bake, but why guess at the accuracy of temperatures when a thermometer will tell you not only when your oven is preheated, but also if it actually sits at 350°F when you set it to 350°F.

Rolling pin—a decent wooden rolling pin isn't a big investment. If you're not sure if you want to buy one, though, you can always roll pastry using a straight-sided wine bottle (empty or full is up to you!).

Silicone spatula—for mixing ingredients by hand, this is your most versatile option. The silicone head makes it heatproof, which makes it ideal for stirring fillings and sauces.

Intermediate Tools

A quick visit to a kitchen store or a store that carries cake decorating tools will get you stocked up with this next level of tools. These tools will help make your baking more efficient and polished.

Bench scraper—this straight metal scraper allows you to lift dough off your work surface with ease, and is great to use to clean your work surface too. The straight edge also makes it a handy tool for spreading an even, level layer of frosting onto the side of a cake.

Bowl scraper—this half-moon-shaped tool has a little flexibility to it and is used to scrape every last bit of batter out of your bowl. It can also be used to fold delicate ingredients together, like whipped cream into chocolate for mousse.

Butane kitchen torch—if you want to make crème brûlée, then this tool is definitely an essential. It is compact and safe and its intense flame melts and caramelizes sugar effortlessly.

Candy thermometer—once you start making cooked frostings (like Italian Buttercream, page 150) or anything with cooked sugar, you will find this tool is essential. Both battery-operated digital and classic glass versions are relatively inexpensive. You can even use this tool to precisely measure ingredient temperatures when necessary.

Cookie cutters—these come in an endless variety of shapes and sizes. Start your kit with a set of basic plain cutters and fluted round cutters, then work your way up into a collection of many shapes. Dainty small leaf and flower cutters are also useful in cake decorating, for cutting and shaping fondant decorations.

French rolling pin—a rolling pin with a tapered body and no handles. You'll find you have great control when you use one. Since your hands are over the pastry as you roll, you really get a sense of where you are, and the tapering allows you to curve and shape the dough with ease.

Ice cream scoop—getting serious about cookie or cupcake baking? These scoops will ensure evenly sized cookies. Multiple sizes of scoops are recommended when you really get serious, from small ones for mini muffins, truffles, or dainty cookies, to medium for regular cookies, and large for muffin and cupcake batter.

Pastry brushes—handy to use when dry to brush flour or icing sugar off baked goods or surfaces, and to evenly brush an egg wash or glaze onto goods to add shine and flair. A silicone pastry brush is easy to clean, but it often leaves streak marks when used to apply egg wash or glaze, so I prefer the fine bristles of a regular pastry brush. Make sure to handwash your brushes to keep them intact and prevent shedding.

Piping bags and tips—disposable piping bags are the most common these days and make for easy cleanup. You don't need too many piping tips to start (large and small plain and star tips will get you started) and they are inexpensive, as well. Some piping tips have numbers to indicate their size and style, but in this book I reference the size as simply small, medium, or large, and add a word about the shape (plain or star, for example).

Removable bottom tart pan—like the springform pan of the tart world, this two-part pan makes it easy to pop a tart out for display. The fluted edge adds visual appeal and also strength to a delicate tart. The pans come in an assortment of sizes and shapes.

Springform pan—essential for cheesecakes or for any cakes that have to set in a mould after assembly. The latch on the side of the pan makes the cake easy to extract.

Advanced Tools

If you're seriously committed to baking, these are the tools that will complete your inventory, especially if cakes and cake decorating are of particular interest.

Cake boards—simple cardboard rounds make it easy to lift cakes from your cake wheel to the fridge, or from the fridge to your cake stand or platter.

Cake wheel—a cake stand that spins not only makes getting polished sides on your cake a breeze, but also elevates the cake, so you don't put your back out leaning too far over to decorate. In a pinch, a lazy Susan will work.

Silicone baking mat—this heat-resistant baking mat is used on a baking tray in place of parchment paper when you're baking delicate cookies. It can be re-used hundreds of times. It should be handwashed and then stored rolled, not folded, so that it won't crack or fray.

Stand mixer—if you're baking regularly, the strong motor of a stand mixer takes the pressure off your electric beaters. Most stand mixers come with three attachments: a dough hook for bread doughs, a paddle for cookie and pastry doughs as well as many cake batters, and a whip for sponge cakes, meringues, and whipped cream.

More of everything—once you're truly baking obsessed, all the toys become appealing and collecting them is great fun: baking pans, cookie cutters, piping tips, dessert dishes, cake stands. Oh, what fun!

Pantry

You'll notice that the same basic ingredients appear in many baking recipes. Their quality really can affect the final product, so it's worth spending a little extra for good ingredients. Here are the essentials for a baker's pantry.

Butter—unsalted butter is a baker's choice, because it puts *you* in charge of the salt content. Recipe to recipe, salt requirements vary, as do butter requirements, and, brand to brand, the salt within butter can vary. By using unsalted butter, you control how much salt is added. Additionally, unsalted butter is sweeter and fresher-tasting, making a huge difference to the quality of your baked goods. The recipes in this book specify whether the butter should be softened to room temperature or used straight from the fridge. If it doesn't specify, you can safely presume that it doesn't matter. The simplest and quickest way to bring butter up to room temperature is to pull it from the fridge, cut it into small pieces, and place the pieces on a plate in a single layer (no need to cover). After 30 minutes the butter should be soft enough to use. I recommend always doing this in summer, as butter that sits out at room temperature in the hotter months can be too soft, even if you have air conditioning. Do not soften butter in the microwave, as it will do so unevenly.

Buttermilk—this thick, tangy, low-fat ingredient is key to many delicious cake and pastry recipes. I prefer using it in store-bought form as opposed to creating my own (by adding 2 tsp (10 mL) of lemon juice or vinegar to every 1 cup (250 mL) of milk), but if the alternative is not making the recipe at all, then substitute away!

Chocolate—baking chocolate, also known as couverture chocolate, is needed in all recipes that require the chocolate to be melted and worked into a batter, mousse, or frosting. The quality of couverture chocolate can vary and the quality of your chocolate desserts will reflect this, so do a little research: If the chocolate tastes good on its own, you will likely enjoy it in your treats (now that's my kind of research!). Chocolate chips can be used when they are stirred unmelted into a recipe and need to hold

their shape, as in chocolate chip cookies. Typically, semisweet and bittersweet chocolate (both forms of dark chocolate) can be used interchangably in a recipe (semisweet being a little milder and sweeter than bittersweet). Milk and white chocolate cannot be swapped for each other or for either of the dark chocolates. Unsweetened chocolate is also its own ingredient and should not be substituted for another type of chocolate—it has cocoa solids and cocoa butter in it, but no sugar or dairy like the other styles.

Cocoa powder—Dutch process cocoa powder is different from regular cocoa powder because it has been treated to remove some of its acidity, which results in a richly flavoured and richly coloured cocoa powder. Dutch process cocoa powder also reacts differently with leaveners, so if it's specified in one of the recipes, it should be used. When it's not specified, you can use it or any other type of cocoa powder.

Cream—for whipping cream, use 35% butterfat or higher.

Dried fruits—raisins, dried cranberries, dried apricots, and other dried fruits figure prominently in baking. They add a nice, natural sweetness and can be stored for months in an airtight container.

Eggs—all my recipes use large eggs. As with butter, I specify in each recipe if the eggs should be used straight from the fridge or at room temperature; if I don't specify either way you can assume it doesn't matter. Don't panic if you've forgotten to bring the eggs out ahead of time (or if you don't want to let the eggs sit out). It's easy to warm them up without letting them sit out too long: simply immerse the whole eggs, in their shells, in a bowl of hot tap water. Change the water after a minute, and in another minute, they will have warmed through and be ready to use.

Flours—I specify the type of flour needed in each recipe. For wheat flours, all-purpose is what I use most often, and you'll also see a lot of cake and pastry flour as well as bread flour. The difference between flours is primarily the protein content (the infamous gluten). Bread flour is high in gluten, which helps it hold in the carbon dioxide that yeast generates during fermentation when making bread. Cake and pastry flour has a lower gluten content, resulting in tender cakes and cookies. All-purpose flour sits right in the middle, and should be the primary wheat flour in your pantry. Baking without wheat flour has its own set of rules, and I find there is not a 1:1 substitution that fits all recipes. In the gluten-free recipes in this book, I call for particular flour replacements according to the specific needs of that recipe.

Fruits—desserts made with fresh fruits in season are always the best option, so do pay attention to what is at its peak when selecting a dessert to make in order to set yourself up for success. An apple pie made with autumn apples is just so fulfilling and a Fraisier Torte prepared with market-fresh local strawberries is truly divine.

Lemon juice and other citrus juices—fresh citrus is always best, especially when making a dessert where the citrus is the pronounced flavour, such as in Lemon Meringue Pie or Key Lime Cheesecake. When lemon juice is called for in small amounts for a different function (in a pie dough, for example, the acidity of the lemon juice allows the protein strands in the flour to stretch, resulting in an easy-to-roll and flaky pastry) then bottled is acceptable.

Milk—I test all of my recipes using 1% and 2% milk, so you can use either for successful results. Steer clear of skim milk in baking, as it is equivalent to baking with water, resulting in goodies that may taste dry or tough or be crumbly.

Nuts—freshness counts when you're using nuts in baking, since the oils in nuts can spoil faster than olive oil or other vegetable oils (this won't make you ill, but it will impart an acrid taste to your baking). Store nuts in an airtight container in the fridge or your pantry, or freeze them in an airtight container for up to a year.

Nut butters—whether I'm using almond or peanut butter, I prefer to use smooth nut butters. If it affects the recipe, I will specify if pure or conventional will work best.

Salt—for baking, fine salt is recommended since it can dissolve quickly; the choice between fine table salt and fine sea salt is yours. Salt is present in baking for the same reason it is in cooking: to heighten and balance flavours. If you would prefer to omit it, you can generally bake without salt without affecting the chemistry of your baking, other than when baking bread. In bread-baking, salt slows the fermentation of the yeast and draws out a better flavour and texture in the bread, so you do need it for proper results.

Sour cream, yogurt, and fresh cheeses—use full-fat unless otherwise specified.

Sugar—granulated sugar is the most common sweetening ingredient in baking; it's up to you if you use conventional or organic cane sugar. Regular golden and dark brown sugars are fully refined—they have molasses added back after refining to achieve their colour and moisture content. Icing sugar is finely ground and has added cornstarch to prevent clumping.

Vanilla—I always bake with pure vanilla products: beans, bean paste, or extract. It's a small ingredient but it makes a big impact on the final flavour. If you are using the seeds scraped from a vanilla bean, you need heat to extract their flavour, which is why you will see some recipes calling for the seeds to be steeped in milk. I only use vanilla beans or paste when the seeds will be visible in the final results—the effort vanilla seeds require is wasted on something like a chocolate cake, where vanilla extract will more than suffice. With vanilla bean paste the flavour is already extracted, so it can be added directly to the recipe.

Anna's Notes

Throughout the book I include many tips to help you maximize your chances of baking success or to explain a bit more about some of the ingredients or techniques in the recipe. Some of these tips may be specific to the recipe where they appear, and others are more general.

However, there are also some things that are good to know or do before you jump into baking.

Read your recipe. Before you jump right into cracking eggs and sifting flour, take a minute to read the recipe all the way through. Then read it again immediately. This will prevent any unpleasant surprises, such as discovering that you are one ingredient short or that the torte you are halfway through making must chill for 6 hours before slicing, but your guests are arriving in 40 minutes.

Measure carefully, since precision is the key to a successful end result in baking. Before you start, decide if you're going to measure by volume (cups, tablespoons) or by weight (grams) and stick to that one style throughout.

- **Dry ingredients**—use single-measure dry measuring cups (¼ cup, ⅓ cup, ½ cup, 1 cup). When measuring loose ingredients like flour, scoop after "fluffing" the ingredient first in the canister or spoon into the measure. Never shake the cup. Level it with a knife or your finger. Brown sugar should be packed into the measure. All ingredients should be measured before sifting.

- **Wet ingredients**—use a clear liquid measuring cup and eye the measurement as it rests on a level surface (if you lift it up to eye level, the cup could be on an angle).

- **Scaled ingredients**—place your mixing bowl on the scale and press "tare" to reach zero (deleting the weight of the bowl) and then add your first ingredient. Press "tare" after each ingredient to get a true, individual measure for each addition.

Ingredient temperatures count. When butter or eggs are called for at room temperature, it is for a good reason and for a better result. In very general terms, let your butter be your guide when it comes to determining what temperature your other ingredients should be. Ingredients of a like temperature incorporate more smoothly, so if the butter is listed as room temperature, then it's best to assume that your eggs, milk, etc., should be as well. If I don't specify temperature in my ingredients list, you can assume it won't affect the recipe.

Get to know your oven. The second we place our cakes and cookies in the oven we hand over full control to it, so it's a smart idea to really get to know it. What most people don't realize is that just because we may set our oven to heat to 350°F, it may not actually be at 350°F. Some ovens run hotter or cooler than their set temperature, and some even oscillate by up to 25°F (or by 15°C) above and below the set temperature. The best way to get to know your oven from the inside out is to buy an oven thermometer (see page 5). They're not expensive and you'll know how to better set your oven for optimal results (if it's WAY off, call in a repair person to calibrate it for you).

- **Fan or no fan?** Convection ovens are very common, and while they make for beautiful golden skin on a roasted chicken and crispy potato wedges, they're not so good for most baking recipes. The function of the fan is to move around hot air, and this can brown your cakes and cookies too much on the surface and accelerate leaveners so that your muffins peak in the middle. Delicacies like cheesecake and sponge cake can even bake crookedly because of the force of the fan. If you can't turn off the fan, then reduce your oven temperature by 25°F (or by 15°C).

- **Where in the oven?** Most recipes are best baked on the centre rack of your oven, for even heat circulation. Sometimes delicate cookies should be baked on an upper rack, since the heat source is usually at the bottom of the oven and can brown the bottoms of cookies too quickly. If no rack is specified in the recipe, you can assume that you use the centre rack.

- **If you're baking cookies in larger batches** on multiple trays, you may find it best to rotate your pans halfway through baking, switching the tray not only from the upper rack to a lower rack and vice versa, but also from the back of the oven to the front, or from left to right.

So, you've baked your goods and they look and smell tasty. Now what?

Cooling—all baked goods should be cooled on a cooling rack, so that the air can circulate fully around them to cool them quickly. If a cookie, for example, needs to be removed from the baking tray to cool, the recipe will specify this.

Chilling—frosted cakes can be initially chilled without being covered or wrapped; the frosting acts as a sealer, keeping moisture in. Most other desserts can be chilled uncovered, since anything (such as plastic wrap) touching the surface of the dessert might leave a mark. Once you've served your cake (and the "wow" moment has passed), you can cover the exposed side with a piece of plastic wrap or parchment to keep it from drying out.

Storing—each recipe states how the item is best stored and for how long.

Freezing—each recipe will state if it can be frozen and, if so, for how long. Generally, items with lots of sugar freeze less effectively than recipes with less sugar. Once frozen and then thawed, sugary cookies will turn soggy or soft, because the sugar in them stays fluid and can even seep out. Most unbaked doughs—cookie doughs, pie and tart doughs, and even bread doughs—can be frozen in an unbaked state. Thaw them in the fridge before baking according to the original recipe instructions.

Cookies
and Bars

There are no boundaries when it comes to cookies. A stack of chocolate chip cookies is just as appealing as (maybe more than?) fancily frosted cut-outs in a bakery window or a delicate chocolate-coated florentine cookie served with your espresso at the end of a Michelin-starred meal.

If you're a baker, cookies are your starting point. A cookie recipe often requires few tools and has a basic method that gets you comfortable with important but uncomplicated techniques. That said, making cookies can also challenge you as your confidence blossoms and you experiment with fillings, décor, and more.

Sometimes you make cookies because you crave a certain style, or even their smell as they bake. Whatever your motivation, though, never sell yourself short and say that you're "just" making cookies. Nothing made from scratch is a "just."

Simple

Scrumptious

Sensational

Classic Chocolate Chip Cookies

Warm chocolate chip cookies soothe the soul and can fix just about any small issue, whether it's a bad day at school or work or a defeat at soccer. They can turn an ordinary activity, like watching a movie, into something special. And they can be the perfect way to celebrate accomplishments, like completing a school project.

Makes about 2 dozen cookies • Prep 15 minutes plus chilling • Bake 18 minutes

**½ cup	115 g**	**unsalted butter, at room temperature**
**½ cup	100 g**	**packed light brown sugar**
**½ cup	100 g**	**granulated sugar**
**1	1**	**large egg, at room temperature**
**1 tsp	5 mL**	**pure vanilla extract**
**1 ¼ cups	180 g**	**all-purpose flour**
**1 Tbsp	8 g**	**cornstarch**
**½ tsp	2 g**	**baking soda**
**½ tsp	2 g**	**salt**
**1 ½ cups	240 g**	**chocolate chips (any type)**
**1 cup	100 g**	**lightly toasted, coarsely chopped pecans (optional)**

This chocolate chip cookie dough has two secrets for success. The first is the cornstarch, which holds in moisture and guarantees a soft-centred cookie. The second is chilling the cookies before baking—this ensures they all bake to the same shape and don't spread too much while baking.

• • • • • • • •

I like the delicate crunch of buttery pecans in my chocolate chip cookies, but they are completely optional and can be omitted.

1. Line a baking tray or large plate with parchment paper.

2. Cream the butter with the brown sugar and granulated sugar until well combined and a little fluffy. Beat in the egg and the vanilla.

3. In a separate bowl, sift the flour with the cornstarch, baking soda, and salt. Add this to the butter mixture and stir until blended. Stir in the chocolate chips and pecans (if using).

4. Using a small ice cream scoop or a tablespoon, scoop spoonfuls of dough (about 2 Tbsp/30 mL), shape them into a ball, and place them on a parchment-lined baking tray or a plate. Chill the scooped cookies for at least an hour. Once chilled, the cookies can be baked immediately or frozen for baking later.

5. Preheat the oven to 325°F (160°C). Line a second baking tray with parchment paper.

6. Divide the chilled scooped cookies equally between the parchment-lined baking trays, leaving 3 inches (7.5 cm) between the cookies. Bake for 15–18 minutes, until browned around the edges. Cool the cookies on the baking tray on a cooling rack. If you're baking cookie dough that has been frozen, arrange the frozen cookies on the baking tray and let them thaw for 20 minutes at room temperature before baking as above. The cookies will keep in an airtight container for up to 4 days.

Vanilla Bean Spritz Shortbread

Spritz cookies are piped into shapes, so the batter needs to be relatively soft.
This shortbread is fluffy, light, delicate, and delectably buttery, as a shortbread cookie should be.

Makes about 40 cookies • Prep 15 minutes plus chilling • Bake 25 minutes

1 ¼ cups | 285 g	unsalted butter, at room temperature
1 cup | 130 g	icing sugar, sifted
1 ½ tsp | 7 mL	pure vanilla bean paste or pure vanilla extract
1 ½ cups | 225 g	all-purpose flour
⅓ cup | 40 g	cornstarch
¼ tsp | 1 g	salt

I use a piping bag with a star tip to pipe these, but a cookie piping kit (if you have one) will work just as well. Shortbread cookies don't have egg or leaveners (baking soda or powder) in the batter, so the cookies will hold their piped shape nicely. The temperature of the butter is the only thing likely to affect the cookie shape—the specific room temperature and how long you allow the butter to soften will determine its temperature and hence texture. As I mention in the method, you can chill the cookies first before baking for a more defined shape, or bake them right after piping and have them spread a little (like in the photo).

1. Preheat the oven to 325°F (160°C). Line two baking trays with parchment paper.

2. Beat the butter and icing sugar until light and fluffy, about 3 minutes. Beat in the vanilla. It's important to beat the butter and sugar well together when making shortbread so that it holds together when baked. When you take a bite it will "snap" and then melt away. It also makes the batter nice and fluffy, so it is easy to pipe.

3. In a separate bowl, sift the flour, cornstarch, and salt. Add to the butter, mixing until well combined and soft. Spoon the dough into a piping bag fitted with a large star tip. Pipe the cookies into a spiral shape about 1 ½ inches (4 cm) across onto the prepared baking trays, leaving 1 inch (2.5 cm) between each cookie. If you want a flatter cookie that spreads, bake them right away. For a cookie that sits up and holds its shape, chill the piped unbaked cookies for 15 minutes before baking.

4. Bake for 20–25 minutes, until the cookies just begin to brown lightly on the bottom (gently lift a cookie with a spatula to check). Cool the cookies on the trays on a cooling rack. The cookies will keep for up to 1 week in an airtight container.

Classic Cranberry Almond Biscotti

Biscotti are very crunchy twice-baked cookies. Some are super crunchy and suitable for dunking in coffee or tea, but others, like the ones in this recipe, are crispy but still tender, yet will not disintegrate if dunked into your coffee.

Makes about 3 dozen biscotti • Prep 20 minutes plus cooling • Bake 55 minutes

¾ cup | 150 g	granulated sugar
½ cup | 125 mL	vegetable oil
2 | 2	large eggs
2 tsp | 10 mL	finely grated lemon zest
¾ tsp | 4 mL	pure almond extract
¾ cup | 120 g	whole raw almonds
½ cup | 70 g	dried cranberries
1 ¾ cups | 260 g	all-purpose flour
2 tsp | 6 g	baking powder
½ tsp | 2 g	salt
½ tsp | 2 g	ground nutmeg
1 | 1	egg, whisked with 2 Tbsp/30 mL water, for brushing

Slicing the biscotti log while it is still warm is the key to preventing it from crumbling. If an almond is close to the edge, it may pull away and crumble the biscotti a bit—but don't worry, that's to be expected. If the biscotti log cools too much, just pop the tray back in the oven for a minute or two before trying again.

1. Preheat the oven to 325°F (160°C). Line a baking tray with parchment paper.

2. In a large mixing bowl, whisk the sugar, oil, eggs, lemon zest, and almond extract together. Stir in the almonds and dried cranberries.

3. In a separate bowl, sift the flour, baking powder, salt, and nutmeg, add this to the wet mixture, and stir until completely blended. Shape the dough into two logs about 12 inches (30 cm) long, place them on the baking tray and pat down to flatten (you can flour your hands to prevent sticking), and brush with the egg mixture. Bake for about 35 minutes, until rich golden brown. Let the logs cool for about 15 minutes on the baking tray on a cooling rack, but only until they are still warm to the touch.

4. Using a serrated knife, slice the logs into cookies just over ½ inch (1.5 cm) thick. Place these back on the baking tray, leaving just a little space between them (you may need a second baking tray) and return them to the oven to bake at 325°F (160°C) for about 20 minutes, until lightly browned. Remove from the baking tray and place on a cooling rack to cool completely. The biscotti will keep in an airtight container for up to 3 weeks.

Langues de Chat

These delicate little cookies are named after their shape, little cats' tongues, but luckily that's where the resemblance ends! Crisp, tender, and sweet, these look lovely on a petits fours plate.

Makes about 6 dozen cookies • Prep 25 minutes • Bake 10 minutes

5 Tbsp | 75 g	unsalted butter, at room temperature
1 cup | 130 g	icing sugar, sifted
3 | 3	large egg whites
1 tsp | 5 mL	pure vanilla extract
⅔ cup | 100 g	all-purpose flour

This cookie is from the family of "batter cookies." French Tuile Cookies (page 38) and Classic Florentine Cookies (page 56) also fall into this category. They all share a few traits: they are thin and delicate, and their batter can be made days ahead and chilled in an airtight container, to be softened to room temperature and baked when needed.

1. Preheat the oven to 350°F (180°C). Line two baking trays with parchment paper. Use a marker pen to draw four parallel lines on the parchment paper, with 2 ½ inches (6.5 cm) of space between the first and second lines and between the third and fourth lines, so you have two evenly spaced sets of lines—this will help you to pipe cookies of a precise and equal length. Flip the parchment over so that the marker lines are on the underside.

2. Using electric beaters or in a stand mixer fitted with the paddle attachment, beat the butter with the icing sugar until smooth. Whisk the egg whites to loosen them and add half of them to the butter with the vanilla, beating well and scraping down the sides of the bowl (don't worry if the batter doesn't look smooth at this point). Add half of the flour and beat well, scraping down the bowl again. Add the remaining egg whites, beat well, and then finish by adding the remaining flour and beating until smooth.

3. Spoon the batter into a large piping bag fitted with a medium plain tip. Pipe lengths of batter between the sets of parallel lines, leaving 2 inches (5 cm) between each cookie (you will have to bake the cookies in batches). Bake the cookies for about 10 minutes until they brown just a little at the edges. Lift the entire sheet of parchment from the tray and place it on a cooling rack to cool the cookies on the paper for a minute, then lift the cookies off the paper to cool completely on the rack. Repeat with the remaining batter. The cookies will keep for up to 2 weeks in an airtight container.

Pfeffernüsse Cookies

These little gems have a lovely spicy character that comes not just from traditional baking spices, but also from black pepper. These are a great addition to a cookie tin mix.

Makes about 3 ½ dozen cookies • Prep 25 minutes • Bake 16 minutes

6 Tbsp | 110 g	honey
6 Tbsp | 75 g	granulated sugar
¼ cup | 50 g	packed dark brown sugar
¼ cup | 60 g	unsalted butter, melted
1 | 1	large egg
1 | 1	egg yolk
2 cups | 300 g	all-purpose flour
¾ tsp | 4 g	baking soda
½ tsp | 2 g	ground cinnamon
½ tsp | 2 g	ground cardamom
½ tsp | 2 g	anise seed
½ tsp | 2 g	ground allspice
½ tsp | 2 g	ground cloves
½ tsp | 2 g	ground black pepper
¼ tsp | 1 g	salt
	icing sugar, for rolling the baked cookies

1. Preheat the oven to 325°F (160°C). Line two baking trays with parchment paper.

2. In a large mixing bowl, whisk the honey with both sugars, the melted butter, egg, and egg yolk. Sift the flour, baking soda, spices, and salt over the sugar mixture and stir until evenly blended (the batter will be dense).

3. Use a small ice cream scoop or two teaspoons to scoop up the batter. Shape it into balls between the palms of your hands, place the balls on the prepared trays, leaving 2 inches (5 cm) between each, and bake for 14–16 minutes, until the cookies are lightly browned. Cool the cookies on the tray on a cooling rack and then roll them in icing sugar to coat them completely. The cookies will keep for up to 1 week in an airtight container or can be frozen for up to 3 months.

Ground anise seed really gives Pfeffernüsse cookies their distinctive taste and can usually be found at European food shops. If you don't have ground anise seed, you can leave it out. (I tried using crushed fennel seed in its place, but found it too strong-tasting.)

• • • • • • • •

I particularly love these cookies at holiday time (they are perfect to make ahead and freeze), and they get even better as they sit in the cookie tin, so try to resist the temptation to eat them immediately!

Chocolate Slice Cookies

These simple cookies are tasty on their own, but the recipe also doubles as a chocolate pastry crust for the Tarte au Chocolat (page 79) and Warm Chocolate Orange Tarts (page 98).

Makes about 2 dozen cookies • Prep 20 minutes plus chilling • Bake 12 minutes

Chocolate Pastry Dough

½ cup | 115 g	unsalted butter, at room temperature
½ cup | 65 g	icing sugar, sifted
3 | 3	large egg yolks
1 cup | 130 g	cake and pastry flour
¼ cup | 30 g	Dutch process cocoa powder
2 Tbsp | 15 g	cornstarch
½ tsp | 2 g	salt
	icing sugar, for dusting

Like Pâte Sablée, a sweet chocolate dough is an essential recipe for a baker, as it is used to make a base crust for any number of fillings. Once you become comfortable making and baking this dough, you'll grow to understand its multiple uses, and then you can really get creative as to how you'd like to fill the baked shell. You don't always have to fill it with a chocolate-based filling—try a pecan tart filling, or even a pumpkin custard filling (Pumpkin Crème Brûlée Tarts, page 88) if you wish.

• • • • • • • •

A basic chocolate slice cookie is a style to add to a cookie tin. The dough can be made ahead of time, so you can get a head start on preparing for special occasions. After you've shaped the dough into a log, wrap it, and freeze up to 3 months ahead, then thaw in the fridge before slicing and baking as per the method above. The dough can also be rolled and cut into shapes and then decorated.

1. Beat the butter and icing sugar until smooth, then add all three egg yolks at once and beat until well combined.

2. In a separate bowl, sift the flour, cocoa powder, cornstarch, and salt. Add this to the butter mixture and stir until evenly combined. Shape the dough into a log about 2 inches (5 cm) in diameter, wrap in plastic wrap, and chill at least 2 hours or until ready to use.

3. Preheat the oven to 325°F (160°C). Line two baking trays with parchment paper.

4. Cut the dough into slices about ⅛ inch (3 mm) thick and arrange them on the prepared baking trays. Bake for about 12 minutes, until they are no longer shiny. Cool on the baking trays on a cooling rack. Once cooled, dust the cookies with icing sugar. The cookies will keep for up to 4 days in an airtight container.

Granola Bars

*These are school-safe (nut-free) granola bars that use very little fat,
making them much better than the store-bought, processed versions.*

• • • • • • • •

*To make this recipe gluten-free, use quinoa flakes rather than any of the other listed options
and check that the oats are gluten-free (not all oats are certified gluten-free).*

Makes 12 to 16 bars • Prep 15 minutes • Bake 30 minutes plus cooling

1 ½ cups | 150 g	rolled oats (not instant or quick cook)
1 cup | 100 g	quinoa flakes (or spelt, or barley flakes, or additional rolled oats)
½ cup | 150 g	honey
¼ cup | 45 g	virgin coconut oil
	zest of 1 orange
1 tsp | 5 mL	pure vanilla extract
½ tsp | 2 g	ground cinnamon
	pinch salt
½ cup | 60 g	unsalted, roasted shelled pumpkin seeds
¼ cup | 30 g	unsalted, roasted sunflower seeds
½ cup | 70 g	dried cranberries
½ cup | 75 g	raisins

Orange zest is my signature addition to my homemade granola. I find that it fits in here beautifully. Feel free to tailor your granola bars to your own tastes. The seeds can be replaced with nuts, and additions like dried apricots or cherries can be used in the same measure (you can even sneak in a handful of chocolate chips if you wish).

• • • • • • • •

Virgin coconut oil is handy in this recipe since it is in a solid state at room temperature, which helps prevent the granola bars from crumbling once cooled and sliced. If coconut is an allergy-sensitive ingredient, you can use unsalted butter in its place in the same measure.

1. Preheat the oven to 350°F (180°C). Line a baking tray with parchment paper. Grease an 8-inch (20 cm) square pan and line it with parchment paper so that it comes up and over the sides of the pan.

2. Spread the oats and quinoa flakes (or other flakes) on the baking tray and toast for about 12 minutes, stirring once, until lightly browned. While the grains are toasting, heat and stir the honey, coconut oil, orange zest, vanilla, cinnamon, and salt in a saucepan over low heat until the coconut oil has melted.

3. Place the pumpkin seeds, sunflower seeds, dried cranberries, and raisins in a large mixing bowl. Pour the toasted grains over the seeds and dried fruit and add the warm honey mixture. Stir well to fully coat everything with the honey mixture.

4. Scrape the granola mixture into the prepared pan. Press it VERY firmly into the pan (using a flat dish to press down on it stops your hands from sticking) so the bars will hold together when sliced. Bake for about 15 minutes, until lightly browned at the edges. Cool the granola bars in the pan before slicing. The granola bars will keep for 1 week, well wrapped in plastic wrap and stored at room temperature (either individually wrapped or packed together), or they can be frozen up to 1 month.

Fudge Brownies

*Delectable and rich, these brownies are a real crowd-pleaser, and
will actually improve if you let them sit for a day. (But I'm afraid I don't have
any tips for how to help you keep eager hands away from the pan.)*

Makes 12 brownies • Prep 30 minutes • Bake 20–25 minutes plus cooling

Salt-Roasted Pecans

1 Tbsp	15 g	unsalted butter
1 cup	100 g	pecan halves
½ tsp	2 g	sea salt

Brownies

4 oz	120 g	unsweetened chocolate, chopped (any kind)
1 ¼ cups	285 g	unsalted butter, cut into pieces
1 cup	200 g	granulated sugar
¾ cup	150 g	packed light brown sugar
3	3	large eggs, at room temperature
2 tsp	10 mL	pure vanilla extract
1 cup	150 g	all-purpose flour
¼ cup	30 g	Dutch process cocoa powder, sifted

1. Preheat the oven to 350°F (180°C). Grease a 12-square brownie pan or 8-inch (20 cm) square pan.

2. For the salt-roasted pecans, melt the butter in a sauté pan over medium heat and add the pecans and salt. Toast the pecans, stirring them frequently, for about 8 minutes, until they have a pleasant nutty aroma (the salt will not dissolve, but adds a nice crunch). Remove the pan from the heat and let cool while you prepare the brownies.

3. For the brownies, place the chocolate with the butter in a medium saucepan over medium-low heat, stirring until melted. Remove the saucepan from the heat, add both sugars, and whisk them into the melted chocolate. Whisk in the eggs one at a time, then whisk in the vanilla. Stir in the flour and cocoa powder until evenly combined.

4. Count out 12 pecan halves and set them aside. Roughly chop the remaining pecans and stir them into the brownie batter.

5. Divide the batter into the brownie pan, or spread it evenly in the square pan, and arrange the reserved pecan halves on top. Bake for about 20 minutes, until the tops of the brownies lose their shine. If you're using an 8-inch (20 cm) pan, bake for an additional 5 minutes. Cool the brownies for 1 hour in the pan on a cooling rack before removing from the pan (and slicing, if necessary). The brownies will keep for up to 5 days in an airtight container.

Toasting the pecans in butter and salt really takes these brownies over the top but can be omitted if you need to keep them nut-free.

• • • • • • • • •

Walnuts are a classic brownie inclusion, and you can use them in place of the pecans, but I still recommend toasting them with the butter and salt to add richness and contrast to the sweet brownie.

I like to use the brownie pan (as pictured) because I like the contrast of the crispy exterior with the soft, fudgy centre—and the fudgy centre tends to stay nice and soft. If you're baking them in a square pan and cutting them into portions, be sure your storage container for them is absolutely airtight.

Oatmeal Raisin Sandwich Cookies

A peanut butter filling turns these classic oatmeal cookies into something special.
This particular cookie is nice and chewy, so when you bite into it, the filling won't ooze out.
Of course, you can enjoy the oatmeal cookies on their own if you're not a fan of peanut butter.

Makes about 18 sandwich cookies • Prep 25 minutes • Bake 10 minutes plus cooling

Cookies

1 cup | 225 g	**unsalted butter, at room temperature**
1 cup | 200 g	**granulated sugar**
½ cup | 100 g	**packed dark brown sugar**
2 | 2	**large eggs, at room temperature**
1 tsp | 5 mL	**pure vanilla extract**
1 ¼ cups | 180 g	**all-purpose flour**
2 Tbsp | 15 g	**cornstarch**
½ tsp | 2 g	**baking soda**
½ tsp | 2 g	**ground cinnamon**
½ tsp | 2 g	**ground ginger**
¼ tsp | 1 g	**ground allspice**
¼ tsp | 1 g	**salt**
2 ¼ cups | 225 g	**regular rolled oats (not instant)**
1 cup | 150 g	**raisins**

Filling

¾ cup | 190 g	**smooth peanut butter**
¼ cup | 60 g	**unsalted butter, at room temperature**
½ cup | 65 g	**icing sugar, sifted**

I use regular oats, not instant oats, in my baking. Instant oats are steamed further and more finely ground than regular rolled oats, and I find that they swell up too quickly in my batters, making the results crumbly or stodgy. The added perk is that regular rolled oats have a slightly higher fibre content than instant.

1. Preheat the oven to 375°F (190°C). Line two baking trays with parchment paper.

2. For the cookies, cream the butter, granulated sugar, and brown sugar together by hand until smooth and light. Add the eggs one at a time, beating well after each addition. Stir in the vanilla.

3. In a separate bowl, stir the flour, cornstarch, baking soda, cinnamon, ginger, allspice, and salt together. Add this to the butter mixture and stir to blend. Stir in the oats and then add the raisins. Drop the cookies by tablespoonfuls (or use a small ice cream scoop), leaving at least 2 inches (5 cm) between the cookies. Bake the cookies for 10 minutes (the cookies may look underdone, but will set up to be nice and chewy once cooled) and allow them to cool on the baking tray on a cooling rack.

4. For the filling, beat the peanut butter, butter, and icing sugar until smooth. Spread a layer of the filling on the bottom of one cookie and sandwich with a second cookie. The cookies will keep for 3 days (filled or unfilled) in an airtight container.

Scottish Pan Shortbread

This shortbread is the style that is pressed into a pan and then scored while still warm so that it can be easily snapped into its wedge-shaped portions.

Makes one 9-inch (23 cm) fluted pan • Serves 16 • Prep 15 minutes • Bake 1 hour

¾ cup | 180 g	**unsalted butter, at room temperature**
½ cup | 100 g	**packed light brown sugar**
1 ¼ cups | 180 g	**all-purpose flour**
¼ cup | 35 g	**brown rice flour**
½ tsp | 2 g	**salt**

Shortbread is a prime example of where baking with unsalted butter is key. It puts you in control of the salt balance (you never know how much salt is in salted butter) and the pure buttery taste really comes through.

• • • • • • • •

Docking the shortbread is essential to its successful baking. Piercing the dough with a fork allows the heat to get through the dense dough evenly, so you don't get a soft or unbaked centre.

• • • • • • • •

Pan shortbread is best after it "cures" for a few days in a cookie tin. After cooling just after baking, you may find it a little crispy, but give it a day or two in a tin and the shortbread softens just enough to make it tender but still with a little "snap."

1. Preheat the oven to 300°F (150°C). Grease a 9-inch (23 cm) removable-bottom fluted tart pan and place it on a baking tray.

2. Beat the butter and brown sugar vigorously by hand, with electric beaters, or in a stand mixer fitted with the paddle attachment until pale and fluffy, about 3 minutes. It's important to beat the butter and sugar well together when making shortbread so that it holds together when baked. When you take a bite it will "snap" and then melt away.

3. In a separate bowl, sift both flours and the salt. Add this to the butter and mix until blended. Using floured hands, press this into the prepared pan. Use a fork to dock the shortbread right through to the bottom and bake for 1 hour, until just lightly browned. As soon as you remove the shortbread from the oven, slice it into 16 wedges, then cool completely in the pan on a cooling rack. This shortbread improves over a few days. It will keep for up to 10 days in an airtight container or can be frozen for up to 3 months.

Chocolate Pistachio Cantucci

Biscotti and cantucci (or cantuccini, for smaller ones) are the long, tender biscuits that you would spot in a jar in a coffee shop. Biscotti and cantucci are essentially interchangeable terms, although I find cantucci are a little lighter in texture than biscotti.

Makes about 2 dozen cantucci • Prep 20 minutes • Bake 1 hour plus cooling

4 | 4	large eggs, at room temperature
1 | 1	large egg yolk
1 ¼ cups | 250 g	granulated sugar
2 tsp | 10 mL	pure vanilla extract
2 cups | 300 g	all-purpose flour
½ cup | 60 g	cocoa powder
1 ½ tsp | 7 g	baking soda
½ tsp | 2 g	salt
1 ¼ cups | 170 g	shelled unsalted pistachios
1 cup | 150 g	chopped dark chocolate chunks or chips

This version of biscotti makes seriously large cookies that look impressive wrapped up for gift giving. Dipping them in chocolate would take them to the next level.

• • • • • • • •

I like how the tender pistachios in this recipe pair with the crisp yet tender texture of the cookie itself. Other rich and tender nuts such as pine nuts or pecans would also work in place of the pistachios.

1. Preheat the oven to 350°F (180°C). Line a baking tray with parchment paper.

2. Using electric beaters or in a stand mixer fitted with the whip attachment, whip the eggs, egg yolk, sugar, and vanilla on high speed until the mixture holds a ribbon when the beaters are lifted, about 3 minutes.

3. Sift the flour, cocoa powder, baking soda, and salt into a bowl and fold them into the whipped eggs until fully incorporated (the mixture will deflate a little and will look like a cake batter in consistency). Stir in the pistachios and chocolate chunks, spoon the mixture onto the prepared baking tray, and spread it into the rough shape of a single log, the length of your baking tray and about 8 inches (20 cm) wide. The batter will be soft, so don't worry if the shape isn't too precise. Bake for about 35 minutes, until a tester inserted in the centre of the cantucci log comes out clean. You may have to test in a few places because of the chocolate chunks. Allow the log to cool on the pan on a cooling rack for about 20 minutes.

4. Reduce the oven temperature to 300°F (150°C). Line two baking trays with parchment paper.

5. Move the cantucci log to a cutting board and use a serrated knife to slice it width-wise into cookies ½ inch (1 cm) thick. Arrange these on the prepared baking trays, leaving just ½ inch (1 cm) between them and bake for 12 minutes. Remove the trays from the oven, flip the cantucci over, and return them to the oven to bake for another 12 minutes. Cool the cantucci on the tray. If you find that the cantucci aren't crunchy all the way through after cooling, you can return them to the oven to bake for a few more minutes. The cantucci will keep for up to 2 weeks in an airtight container.

French Tuile Cookies

Tuiles translates from French as "tiles." The curves of these classic thin, sweet cookies, shaped after baking while still warm and pliable, are meant to resemble the tiles found on French rooftops.

Makes 5 to 6 dozen cookies • Prep 30 minutes plus chilling • Bake 6 minutes

5 Tbsp | 75 g	**unsalted butter, at room temperature**
½ cup | 65 g	**icing sugar, sifted**
2 Tbsp | 40 g	**honey**
1 | 1	**egg white**
⅔ cup | 100 g	**all-purpose flour**

1. Using electric beaters or in a stand mixer fitted with the paddle attachment, beat the butter with the icing sugar and honey until smooth. Beat in the egg white (the mixture may look curdled—that's okay). Sift in the flour and stir until the batter is smooth. Transfer to an airtight container and chill the batter until firm, about 2 hours.

2. Preheat the oven to 350°F (180°C). Line a baking tray with a silicone-coated liner (parchment paper doesn't work here because it can wrinkle). Prepare a template by cutting out a shape from the centre of a flat piece of plastic (a yogurt container lid with the edges trimmed away is ideal). The template can be just about any shape or size. The classic French *tuile* is a square, but a teardrop, leaf, or heart are also common. Place a small rolling pin or other curved tool on or against something to steady it so that it doesn't move—resting the warm cookies on this will give them their curve.

3. Place the template on the silicone liner and, using an offset spatula, spread an even layer of batter into the template, smoothing as necessary. Lift the template carefully, scrape off any excess batter, place it next to the first cookie, and repeat until the tray is filled. Bake the cookies for 5–6 minutes, until they brown at the edges. Stay near the oven, since 30 seconds can make a big difference in this recipe.

4. Remove the baking tray from the oven and immediately and carefully start lifting the warm cookies and placing them on the rolling pin to curl and cool. If the cookies cool before you can get them to the rolling pin, you can return the tray to the oven for 10–15 seconds to soften up the cookies again. Repeat until you have as many tuiles as you need (making a few extra is wise, since they are delicate and can break easily). The remaining batter will keep, refrigerated, for up to 2 weeks, or can be frozen for up to 3 months. The tuiles will keep for up to 2 days in an airtight container (but only 1 day if conditions are humid). Avoid stacking the cookies when storing them as, again, they break easily.

These cookies are wafer-thin, and pastry chefs like to use them to garnish desserts. They also happen to be susceptible to humidity, so bake them the day you plan to use them. Luckily, the batter can be made ahead of time and chilled or frozen.

Pumpkin Spice Cake Cookies

Soft and spiced, these pumpkin cookies will get snapped up in a hurry. It's hard to eat just one!

Makes 30 cookies • Prep 30 minutes • Bake 20 minutes plus cooling

Cookies

½ cup | 115 g	unsalted butter, at room temperature
1 cup | 200 g	granulated sugar
½ cup | 100 g	packed light brown sugar
1 | 1	large egg
1 cup | 250 g	pure pumpkin purée (page 45)
2 ½ cups | 375 g	all-purpose flour
1 tsp | 3 g	baking powder
½ tsp | 2 g	baking soda
½ tsp | 2 g	salt
1 tsp | 3 g	ground ginger
½ tsp | 2 g	ground cinnamon
¼ tsp | 1 g	ground nutmeg

Frosting

½ cup | 115 g	unsalted butter, at room temperature
½ cup | 125 g	cream cheese, at room temperature
2–3 cups | 260–390 g	icing sugar, sifted
1 tsp | 5 mL	pure vanilla extract
	ground cinnamon, for sprinkling

These are a favourite cookie of mine in the fall. The aromas of the spices with the pumpkin are homey and comforting, and you feel like you're eating a cupcake when you bite into one of these.

1. Preheat to the oven to 350°F (180°C). Line two baking trays with parchment paper.

2. For the cookies, beat the butter and both sugars together (by hand or with electric beaters) until smooth and then beat in the egg. Add the pumpkin purée and stir in to combine.

3. In a separate bowl, sift the flour, baking powder, baking soda, salt, and spices. Add this to the pumpkin batter, stirring until evenly mixed. Using a medium ice cream scoop, scoop dough onto the baking trays, leaving 2 inches (5 cm) between each one. Bake the cookies for 17–20 minutes, until they lift easily from the tray. Allow the cookies to cool on the trays on a cooling rack before frosting them.

4. For the frosting, beat the butter and cream cheese together until smooth and then add 1 cup (130 g) of the icing sugar, beating well. Add the vanilla and an additional 1 cup (130 g) of icing sugar, beating until fluffy and adding additional icing sugar until the frosting is a spreadable consistency.

5. Pipe or spread the frosting onto each cookie and sprinkle a bit of cinnamon over top. The cookies will keep for 1 day in an airtight container. They can be refrigerated for 3 days, but are best enjoyed at room temperature.

Nanaimo Bars

*The definitive Nanaimo Bar was created by Joyce Hardcastle in 1985.
Hers was the winning recipe in a contest hosted by the mayor of Nanaimo, British Columbia,
to find the ultimate Nanaimo Bar. It has now become a truly Canadian staple treat.
My version of this has a thicker, exceptionally smooth custard filling, and isn't quite as sweet.*

Makes one 8-inch (20 cm) square pan • Serves 18
Prep 20 minutes • Bake 12 minutes plus chilling

Crust

1 cup	125 g	graham cracker crumbs
3 Tbsp	22.5 g	cocoa powder
½ tsp	2 g	salt
1 cup	100 g	sweetened flaked coconut
½ cup	50 g	walnut pieces
6 Tbsp	90 g	unsalted butter, melted
1	1	large egg, lightly beaten

Filling

½ cup	125 g	unsalted butter, at room temperature
2 cups	260 g	icing sugar, sifted
2 Tbsp	30 g	vanilla custard powder
	pinch salt
3 Tbsp	45 mL	milk
1 tsp	5 mL	pure vanilla extract

Topping

4 oz	120 g	semisweet couverture/baking chocolate, chopped
2 Tbsp	30 g	unsalted butter
	sea salt, for sprinkling (optional)

You may notice by the photo that I like a Nanaimo Bar with a LOT of custard filling. If you've never had a Nanaimo Bar before, then disregard this note—they are just as they should be ;)

• • • • • • • •

The challenge in slicing a Nanaimo Bar is how to cut through the hard chocolate topping without cracking it. I find that if I first score the chocolate with a serrated knife and then switch to a chef's knife to cut through my markings, the topping stays intact, making perfect bars.

1. Preheat the oven to 350°F (180°C). Lightly grease an 8-inch (20 cm) square pan and line it with parchment paper so that it comes up and over the sides of the pan.

2. For the crust, combine the graham crumbs with the cocoa powder and salt, then add the coconut and walnut pieces. Stir in the melted butter and the egg until blended. Press this into the bottom of the prepared pan and bake for 12 minutes. Cool the crust completely in the pan before preparing the filling.

3. For the filling, beat the butter by hand with 1 cup (130 g) of the icing sugar, the custard powder, and a pinch of salt until smooth. Add the milk and vanilla and beat them in (don't worry if it doesn't look smooth at this point—it will smooth out). Beat in the remaining 1 cup (130 g) of icing sugar. Do not overbeat—the filling should be smooth but not fluffy. Spread this evenly over the cooled crust.

4. For the topping, melt the chocolate and butter in a metal bowl placed over a saucepan of barely simmering water, stirring gently with a spatula until melted. Cool the chocolate slightly and then pour it evenly over the filling. If you wish, sprinkle the top with a little sea salt. Chill in the pan for about 2 hours before slicing into bars (3 rows of 6 rectangular bars each). The bars can be stored, refrigerated, for up to 1 week.

Pumpkin Swirl Cheesecake Squares

Craving pumpkin cheesecake, but need something easy to pick up and eat?
This is the square for you.

Makes one 8-inch (20 cm) square pan • Serves 16
Prep 30 minutes • Bake 50 minutes plus chilling

Crust

1 cup	150 g	all-purpose flour
¼ cup	50 g	packed light brown sugar
⅓ cup	75 g	cool unsalted butter, cut into pieces

Pumpkin Cheesecake

½ cup	125 g	cream cheese, at room temperature
¾ cup	150 g	granulated sugar
1 cup	250 g	pure pumpkin purée
2 Tbsp	17 g	all-purpose flour
½ tsp	2 g	baking powder
½ tsp	2 g	ground cinnamon
1	1	egg, at room temperature
1	1	egg yolk

Cheesecake Swirl

¼ cup	60 g	brick cream cheese, at room temperature
1 ½ Tbsp	18 g	granulated sugar
1	1	egg yolk
½ tsp	2 mL	pure vanilla extract

1. Preheat the oven to 350°F (180°C). Grease an 8-inch (20 cm) square pan and line it with parchment paper so that it comes up and over the sides of the pan.

2. For the crust, use a food processor to pulse the flour and brown sugar together, then cut in the butter until evenly blended (the mixture will be dry and crumbly). Alternatively, this base can be made by hand, blending the butter into the flour and sugar with a pastry cutter. Press this into the prepared pan and bake for about 18 minutes, until it turns just a little brown at the edges. Cool while making the filling.

3. Beat the cream cheese to soften it and then beat in the sugar. Add the pumpkin and stir until smooth. Switch to a whisk and add the flour, baking powder, and cinnamon. Whisk in the egg and egg yolk and set aside.

4. For the cheesecake swirl, beat the cream cheese until smooth and then beat in the sugar. Stir in the egg yolk and vanilla until smooth.

5. Pour the pumpkin cheesecake onto the cooled crust. Either spoon or pipe the cheesecake swirl on top and use a bamboo skewer to create pretty swirls. Bake for about 30 minutes until, like a cheesecake, the filling is set at the edges but still has a little jiggle at the centre. Cool to room temperature and then chill in the pan, uncovered and on a cooling rack, for at least 2 hours before slicing into squares. The squares will keep, refrigerated, for up to 3 days.

I keep the spice character of these squares pretty simple (cinnamon only).
The filling tastes more like cheesecake than pumpkin pie this way.

• • • • • • • •

When baking with pure pumpkin purée (which is different from pre-sweetened and pre-spiced pumpkin pie filling), you can used canned purée, or make your own from fresh pie pumpkins. To prepare your own, cut a pie pumpkin in half, scoop out the seeds, and place, cut side down, onto a parchment-lined baking tray. Pierce the skin with a fork or knife and roast at 350°F (180°C) for about 30 minutes, until tender. Cool, peel off the skin (it will peel away easily), and purée the pumpkin until smooth. Store this in an airtight container or a resealable bag in the fridge for up to 5 days, or freeze for up to 3 months.

Blueberry Almond Linzer Cookies

Linzer cookies are classic sandwich cookies—almond cookies filled with jam, with a window cut into the top cookie to show off that glistening filling. Raspberry jam is traditional in a linzer cookie, but I use blueberry here just to switch things up.

Makes about 3 dozen sandwich cookies • Prep 45 minutes plus chilling • Bake 17 minutes

1 cup | 225 g	unsalted butter, at room temperature
1 ½ cups | 195 g	icing sugar, sifted, plus extra for dusting
4 | 4	large egg yolks
1 tsp | 5 mL	finely grated lemon zest
1 tsp | 5 mL	pure vanilla extract
¼ tsp | 1 mL	pure almond extract
¾ cup | 90 g	ground almonds
3 cups | 390 g	cake and pastry flour
¼ tsp | 0.75 g	baking powder
¼ tsp | 1 g	salt
¾ cup | 180 mL	blueberry jam

Any jam will work with these, just so long as it has a nice set. A thin jam may run out the sides, and a fruit spread could possibly soak into the cookie, making it go soft.

1. Beat the butter and icing sugar until light and fluffy. Beat in the egg yolks and then add the lemon zest and vanilla and almond extracts. Beat in the ground almonds.

2. In a separate bowl, sift the flour with the baking powder and salt and add this to the butter mixture, stirring until blended. Shape the dough into two discs (the dough will be soft), wrap in plastic wrap, and chill until firm, at least 1 hour.

3. Preheat the oven to 350°F (180°C). Line two baking trays with parchment paper.

4. Knead the dough a little to soften it (this will help prevent it from cracking when rolled). Roll out the first disc on a lightly floured surface and cut out cookies using a 2-inch (5 cm) teardrop cutter. Place them on one baking tray, re-rolling the dough as necessary. Roll out the second disc, cut out cookies using the same cutter, and then cut a hole in the centre of each of these using a cutter ½-inch (1 cm) smaller. Place these on the second tray. Repeat with any remaining dough, making sure you have the same number of tops and bottoms. Bake the cookies with holes for about 15 minutes and the intact cookies for 17 minutes. Cool the cookies on the tray on a cooling rack before filling.

5. Sift icing sugar over the cookies *with* the holes. Stir the jam to soften it and spread a teaspoonful over the bottom of each base cookie. Gently press a dusted cookie on top and continue with the other bases and tops. Let them set for about 1 hour. The cookies will keep for up to 3 days in an airtight container.

Empire Cookies

Empire cookies are just so pretty and inviting. These jam-filled sandwich cookies are topped with a vanilla glaze and decorated with a little piece of candied cherry. Who could resist?

Makes about 2 dozen sandwich cookies • Prep 1 hour plus chilling • Bake 12 minutes

Pâte Sablée Dough

10 Tbsp | 145 g	unsalted butter, at room temperature
10 Tbsp | 80 g	icing sugar, sifted
1 | 1	yolk from a large hard-boiled egg
1 | 1	large raw egg yolk
½ tsp | 2 mL	pure vanilla extract
1 ¾ cups | 225 g	cake and pastry flour, sifted
¼ tsp | 1 g	salt

Icing and Assembly

⅓ cup | 80 mL	raspberry jam
1 cup | 130 g	icing sugar, sifted
1–2 Tbsp | 15–30 mL	warm water
¼ tsp | 1 mL	pure almond or vanilla extract
6–8 | 6–8	glacé (candied) cherries, each chopped into 6

1. For the dough, beat the butter and icing sugar together until smooth. Push the hard-boiled egg yolk through a sieve and stir the raw egg yolk and vanilla into it. Add this to the butter mixture and stir until blended.

2. Add the flour and salt to the butter mixture and stir until blended. Shape this into a disc (it will be soft), wrap in plastic wrap, and chill until firm, about 2 hours.

3. Preheat the oven to 325°F (160°C). Line two baking trays with parchment paper.

4. On a lightly floured surface, gently knead the dough just to soften it slightly. Roll it out to ¼ inch (0.5 cm) thick, cut out cookies using a 2-inch (5 cm) fluted cookie cutter, and place on the baking trays, with ½ inch (1 cm) of space between them.

5. Bake the cookies for 10–12 minutes, until just lightly browned around the edges. Cool the cookies completely on the trays on a cooling rack before assembling.

6. Stir the raspberry jam to soften it. Spread just over ½ tsp (2 mL) on a cookie bottom and sandwich a second cookie on top, pressing gently to secure. Repeat with the remaining cookies.

7. For the icing, whisk the icing sugar with 1 Tbsp (15 mL) of the water and the almond or vanilla extract, adding some of the remaining water if necessary, until it is a thin icing consistency.

8. Spread a thin layer of icing over each cookie, top with a piece of glacé cherry, and set on a cooling rack to dry. Allow about 3 hours for the icing to dry. The cookies will keep for up to 3 days in an airtight container.

This dough is more than just for cookies. It is also known as pâte sablée, a classic French pastry dough that is used as a sweet base for a number of tarts, and an excellent recipe for bakers to master. I use this same recipe as a base for Pumpkin Crème Brûlée Tarts (page 88) and Peach and Raspberry Custard Tart (page 96).

• • • • • • • •

The addition of a cooked egg yolk to this dough is the secret behind not only its tender texture but also, and very importantly, its ease of handling when being rolled out.

Decorated Chocolate Shortbread Cut-Out Cookies

This chocolate shortbread is tender and delicate and has a nice chocolate intensity. The colour of these cookies is deeply dark and rich and, even though the measurement of the cocoa powder may seem small, the chocolate flavour is huge!

Makes about 18 cookies • Prep 90 minutes plus chilling • Bake 15 minutes

Chocolate Shortbread

½ cup | 115 g	unsalted butter, at room temperature
¼ cup | 50 g	granulated sugar
¼ cup | 32 g	icing sugar, sifted
¾ cup | 110 g	all-purpose flour
2 Tbsp | 15 g	Dutch process cocoa powder
¼ tsp | 1 g	salt

Standard Royal Icing

3 Tbsp | 45 mL	meringue powder
4 cups | 520 g	icing sugar, sifted
6 Tbsp | 90 mL	warm water
	food colouring paste (optional)

1. For the shortbread, beat the butter with both sugars until light and fluffy, about 3 minutes. It's important to beat the butter and sugar well together when making shortbread so that it holds together when baked. When you take a bite it will "snap" and then melt away. It also makes the batter nice and fluffy, so it is easy to pipe.

2. In a separate bowl, sift together the flour, cocoa powder, and salt. Add this to the butter mixture and stir until evenly blended. Shape the dough into a disc, wrap in plastic wrap, and chill until firm, about 1 hour.

3. Preheat the oven to 325°F (160°C). Line a baking tray with parchment paper.

4. Unwrap the dough and knead it a little just to soften it, making it easier to roll. Roll the dough out on a lightly floured work surface until it is just over ⅛ inch (3 mm) thick. Cut out cookies using a 2 ½-inch (5 cm) fluted cutter and place them carefully on the baking tray, re-rolling the dough if needed. Bake the cookies for 13–15 minutes, until they come off the parchment easily when lifted with a spatula. Cool the cookies on the tray on a cooling rack.

5. For the royal icing, mix all the ingredients in a stand mixer fitted with the paddle attachment and beat until everything comes together and is fluffy, about 5 minutes.

6. To make a "flood" style of icing—one that spreads over the surface of the cookie—add just a little more water until it is a consistency that spreads on its own to completely cover the cookie. (You want it thicker than a glaze.) Adjust by adding more water or icing sugar, as needed. Add food colouring paste in small amounts, as desired.

7. Spoon the icing into a piping bag with a small plain tip or into a parchment paper cone. Pipe an outline on the cookie and then fill it in with icing, or pipe dots and use a toothpick to swirl the colours. Allow 2–3 hours for the icing to dry. The cookies will keep for up to 5 days in an airtight container.

Meringue powder is dried egg white used mainly for specialized things such as making royal icing, so that you don't have to work with raw egg whites. The powder whips up to the same volume as fresh egg whites and dries even quicker.

• • • • • • • •

While I use the "flood" version of royal icing to cover these cookies, you can make a royal icing for piping from the same recipe. Just add more icing sugar as you are beating the ingredients, until you get a thicker icing that holds its shape when the beaters are lifted. Tint as desired and then put into piping bags for decorating.

For instructions on how to make a parchment paper cone for piping, please refer to Piped Chocolate Garnishes (page 288). I like using parchment cones for quick tasks, like piping "Happy Birthday" on top of a cake, when only a little melted chocolate or icing is needed.

Chocolate Peanut Butter Whoopie Pies

These sandwiched cake cookies actually have nothing to do with pie.
In fact, they seem more closely related to cupcakes, and their frosting-like
filling makes them simple and easy to eat!

Makes 8 to 10 large whoopie pies • Prep 40 minutes • Bake 15 minutes

Cookies

1 ¾ cups | 260 g	all-purpose flour
1 cup | 200 g	granulated sugar
¾ cup | 90 g	Dutch process cocoa powder
½ tsp | 1.5 g	baking powder
½ tsp | 2 g	baking soda
½ tsp | 2 g	salt
½ cup | 115 g	cool unsalted butter, cut into pieces
1 | 1	large egg
¾ cup | 180 mL	milk, at room temperature
½ cup | 125 g	sour cream
2 tsp | 10 mL	pure vanilla extract

Filling

1 cup | 225 g	unsalted butter, at room temperature
1 cup | 250 g	pure, smooth peanut butter
2 cups | 260 g	icing sugar, sifted
1 tsp | 5 mL	pure vanilla extract

1. Preheat the oven to 375°F (190°C). Line two baking trays with parchment paper. Place the trays in the oven to warm right before making the cookie dough (this step will help the cookies bake with smooth curved tops).

2. For the cookies, sift the flour, sugar, cocoa powder, baking powder, baking soda, and salt into a large mixing bowl or the bowl of a stand mixer fitted with the paddle attachment. Add the butter and mix on medium-low speed to cut it in until the pieces are barely visible.

3. In a separate bowl, whisk together the egg, milk, sour cream, and vanilla. Add to the flour mixture and mix on low speed to incorporate then increase to medium-high and beat for about 2 minutes, until the batter is fluffy and holds its structure. Use a medium ice cream scoop to scoop out 16–20 portions onto the now-hot, prepared baking trays, leaving 3 inches (7.5 cm) between them. Bake the "pies" for about 15 minutes, until the tops spring back when gently pressed. Cool the "pies" on the baking trays before filling.

4. For the filling, beat the butter to lighten it and then beat in the peanut butter. Add 1 cup (130 g) of the icing sugar and beat in. Stir in the vanilla and then beat in the remaining 1 cup (130 g) of icing sugar until fluffy. Fill a piping bag fitted with a large star tip, pipe filling onto one of the "pies," and top with a second "pie," pressing gently. Repeat with the remaining pies. They will keep in an airtight container, or on a plate covered in plastic wrap, for up to 3 days—no need to refrigerate.

Try serving these cookies as a plated dessert alongside my Bananas Foster sauce (page 285). Peanut butter, banana, chocolate, AND a warm caramel sauce—you'll be channelling your inner Elvis!

Chocolate-Dipped Ladyfingers

*We most often think of ladyfingers as an element of a larger,
grand dessert such as tiramisù or my Elegant Raspberry Lemon Torte (page 152),
but they are a lovely, tender, and light biscuit (cookie doesn't seem the appropriate
term for these, somehow) that can be enjoyed all on their own.*

Makes about 3 dozen biscuits • Prep 40 minutes • Bake 8 minutes

Ladyfingers

½ cup | 75 g	**all-purpose flour**
5 Tbsp | 38 g	**cornstarch**
3 | 3	**eggs, separated and at room temperature**
9 Tbsp | 115 g	**granulated sugar**
½ tsp | 2 g	**cream of tartar**

For dipping

5 oz | 150 g	**bittersweet couverture/baking chocolate, chopped**

*If you would prefer to fully prepare the ladyfingers
ahead of time (dipping and all), then you will have
to temper the dipping chocolate first, rather than
just melting it. Tempered chocolate sets differently
and holds for a long time at room temperature. See
my notes on tempered chocolate on page 61.*

• • • • • • • •

*This is a foundation recipe since, although the
batter itself is similar in method to a genoise
sponge cake batter, the ladyfinger batter can be
piped and baked in different shapes and used as a
component of other desserts, like tiramisù or
Elegant Raspberry Lemon Torte (page 152).
Once you've mastered the sponge batter and the
piping technique, you'll never have to buy
ladyfinger biscuits in the store again.*

1. Preheat the oven to 400°F (200°C). Line two baking trays with parchment paper.

2. For the ladyfingers, sift the flour and cornstarch together and set aside. Whip the egg yolks with 3 Tbsp (40 g) of the sugar until they are thick and pale and hold a ribbon when the beaters are lifted.

3. In a separate bowl, whip the egg whites with the cream of tartar until foamy, then slowly add the remaining 6 Tbsp (75 g) of sugar as you whip. Continue whipping until the whites hold a medium peak when the beaters are lifted.

4. Fold the whites into the yolk mixture using a whisk, then fold in the flour until just incorporated. Fill a piping bag fitted with a large plain tip with the batter and pipe 4-inch (10 cm) long ladyfingers onto the prepared trays, 1 inch (2.5 cm) apart (they will spread a little once piped). Bake for about 8 minutes, until the fingers are an even golden brown. Allow the fingers to cool completely on the trays on a cooling rack before removing them from the trays.

5. For dipping, melt the chocolate in a metal bowl placed over a saucepan of barely simmering water, stirring until smooth. Freshly line two baking trays with parchment paper. Dip each ladyfinger one-third of the way into the chocolate and place on baking trays to set (chill for a little bit, if necessary). The dipped ladyfingers should be enjoyed the day they are dipped, but undipped ladyfingers can be stored for up to 5 days in an airtight container at room temperature; do not refrigerate or freeze them.

Classic Florentine Cookies

These wafer-thin almond cookies are so delicate that they need a layer of chocolate to give them strength (and it doesn't hurt that the chocolate-almond combination is always a magical one!). You may think, with their name, that they are an Italian cookie, but they are a French creation. This recipe involves tempering chocolate, a technique well worth the effort of mastering (see my notes on this on page 61).

Makes about 4 dozen cookies • Prep 50 minutes • Bake/Cook 12 minutes

1 ½ cups | 150 g	sliced almonds
10 Tbsp | 130 g	granulated sugar
¼ cup | 75 g	honey
⅓ cup | 80 mL	whipping cream
5 oz | 150 g	bittersweet couverture/baking chocolate, chopped

1. Preheat the oven to 350°F (180°C). Line a baking tray with a silicone-coated liner or parchment paper.

2. Place the sliced almonds in a resealable bag and crush them a little using a rolling pin or even your hands. Set aside.

3. Place the sugar and honey in a small saucepan with the cream and bring to a full boil while stirring. Continue to boil and stir until the mixture reaches 244°F (118°C) on a candy thermometer. Remove the saucepan from the heat, stir in the almonds, and transfer to a bowl to cool for about 15 minutes.

4. Have a bowl of cool water on hand as well as a 2 ½-inch (6.5 cm) round cookie cutter. Drop small teaspoonfuls of the almond batter onto the prepared baking tray, leaving at least 3–4 inches (7.5–10 cm) between each to allow for spreading. With wet fingers, press down the almond batter a little. Bake the Florentines for about 12 minutes, until they have flattened and have browned evenly (you may find that rotating the pans halfway through baking promotes even browning).

5. Let the Florentines sit for 30–90 seconds to set a little (but not fully). Dip the cookie cutter in the cool water and press it into each cookie to cut a precise circle. Now allow the cookies to fully cool on the tray on a cooling rack. Use a palette knife to carefully lift them off the tray, carefully pulling away the trimmings, and set onto a baking tray lined with fresh parchment paper. Repeat with the remaining batter (keep the scraps—they make an excellent topping for ice cream or can be stirred into a cheesecake batter).

6. Once the Florentines have fully cooled, prepare the chocolate. To temper the chocolate, you will need a marble board (or a granite or other stone countertop; a stainless steel counter will also do). Place all of the chopped chocolate in a metal bowl and set this over a saucepan of barely simmering water (no bubbles visible), stirring gently until melted and the temperature reaches 113–122°F (45–50°C). Pour two-thirds of the chocolate onto your marble surface and set the bowl with the remaining chocolate off to the side on a towel (away from the heat and not on the marble).

7. Using two putty knives, or a palette knife and bench scraper, spread out the chocolate into a thin layer and use your tools to push the chocolate back into the centre of the board, scraping your tools to clean them of the chocolate at each push. This action of moving the chocolate plus the cooling property of the marble will lower the temperature of the chocolate. Regularly check the temperature of your chocolate using a thermometer and keep repeating this process until a temperature of 81–82°F (27–28°C) is achieved.

8. Stir your reserved chocolate and check its temperature—it should have cooled to 104–113°F (40–45°C). Now add the marble-cooled chocolate back to the bowl and stir vigorously for about 30 seconds before checking the temperature again—it should be between 88°F and 90°F (31–32°C). It is now tempered. To double-check, dip a piece of parchment into the chocolate and set the paper on your marble—the chocolate should start setting within a minute or two.

9. Use a pastry brush to brush an even layer of the chocolate onto the back of each Florentine and place them on a parchment-lined baking tray to set. Pop the tray in the fridge for 3–5 minutes, just for a final "cure," or set, but then remove to store them. The Florentines will keep for up to 1 week in an airtight container in a cool, dry place. Do not refrigerate them.

As a decorative option, you can place the Florentines chocolate-side down on cocoa butter transfer sheets (found at stores that carry cake decorating supplies). Chill the Florentines as above, then peel off the transfer sheet, revealing a lovely, shiny design.

Chocolate-Covered Caramel Bars

These are a true "candy bar"—a tender cookie base topped with caramel and completely enrobed in chocolate. You will need a candy thermometer for the caramel and a good probe or instant read thermometer for the melted chocolate.

Makes 30 bars • Prep 45 minutes plus cooling • Bake/Cook 35 minutes

Base

½ cup | 115 g	unsalted butter, at room temperature
½ cup | 100 g	granulated sugar
1 | 1	large egg yolk
1 ¼ cups | 190 g	all-purpose flour
	pinch salt

Caramel and Assembly

⅓ cup | 80 mL	water
¾ cup | 150 g	granulated sugar
⅓ cup | 100 g	sweetened condensed milk
⅓ cup | 80 mL	white corn syrup
¼ cup | 60 g	unsalted butter, at room temperature
1 tsp | 5 mL	pure vanilla extract
½ tsp | 2 g	salt
1 lb | 450 g	milk couverture/baking chocolate, chopped

1. Preheat the oven to 350°F (180°C). Grease an 8-inch (20 cm) square pan and line it with parchment paper so that it comes up and over the sides of the pan.

2. For the base, beat the butter and sugar by hand and beat in the egg yolk. Add the flour and salt and stir until the mixture becomes rough and crumbly (it will not come together like a dough). Press this crumble into the prepared pan and bake for about 15 minutes, until it browns a little at the edges. Cool in the pan while you make the caramel layer (the base does not have to be completely cooled for this).

3. For the caramel, have all your other ingredients measured and on hand. Place the water, sugar, and condensed milk in a medium saucepan. Bring the sugar mixture up to a boil on high heat, stirring constantly with a silicone spatula. Once it reaches a boil, add the corn syrup and reduce the heat to medium, stirring constantly (this is to prevent the sugars from boiling over) until it reads 230°F (110°C) on a candy thermometer, about 7 minutes (the caramel will just be starting to colour a bit). At this point, stir in the butter (the temperature will drop by at least 5°F/3°C), and then stir constantly, still on medium heat, until the caramel reaches 240°F (115°C), 3–4 minutes—at this point the caramel will be a pale brown (lighter than peanut butter colour). Stir in the vanilla and salt and pour this over the shortbread base. Let this cool completely, about 3 hours.

4. Line two baking trays with parchment paper.

5. Prepare the bars for dipping into chocolate. Lift the base out, holding the parchment. Peel away the parchment, cut the square into three strips, and cut each strip into 10 bars. Arrange these on the prepared baking trays.

Continued . . .

6. To temper the chocolate, you will need a marble board (or a granite or other stone countertop, or a stainless steel counter will also do). Place all of the chopped chocolate in a metal bowl and set this over a saucepan of barely simmering water (no bubbles visible), stirring gently until melted and the temperature reaches 104–113°F (40–45°C). Pour two-thirds of the chocolate onto your marble surface and set the bowl with the remaining chocolate off to the side on a towel (away from heat and not on the marble).

7. Using two putty knives, or a palette knife and bench scraper, spread out the chocolate into a thin layer and use your tools to push the chocolate back into the centre of the board, scraping your tools to clean them of the chocolate at each push. This action of moving the chocolate plus the cooling property of the marble will lower the temperature of the chocolate. Regularly check the temperature of your chocolate using a thermometer and keep repeating this process until a temperature of 81–82°F (27–28°C) is achieved.

8. Stir your reserved chocolate and check its temperature—it should have cooled to just below 104–109°F (40–43°C). Now add the marble-cooled chocolate back to the bowl and stir for about 30 seconds before checking the temperature again—it should be between 84°F and 86°F (29–30°C). It is now tempered. To double-check, dip a piece of parchment into the chocolate and set the paper on your marble—the chocolate should start setting within a minute or two.

9. Using truffle forks or a pair of small or narrow tongs, dip each cookie finger in the chocolate to completely coat it, shake vigorously to remove any excess chocolate, and place back on the baking trays to set. Pop the tray in the fridge for 3–5 minutes, just for a final "cure," or set, but then remove to store them. The bars will keep for up to 1 week in an airtight container in a cool, dry place. Do not refrigerate them.

Tempering Chocolate

The process of tempering chocolate is important when the completed recipe needs to be stored at room temperature (for example the Florentines on page 56 can't be refrigerated because the sugar would dissolve, turning them into syrupy puddles). When chocolate is melted, cooled, and then gently warmed again, in combination with being moved around, a bonding develops that allows the chocolate to set up quickly and hold its shape at room temperature. Without this step, the chocolate would eventually set, but would be brittle and have a dull finish.

. . . .

Reaching the precise temperature listed in the recipe is critical when tempering chocolate, so an instant read thermometer is an invaluable tool here. Keep in mind that the temperatures you need to achieve when tempering milk chocolate are different than for dark chocolate, so follow the recipe method carefully to match the chocolate you are using. When I am tempering chocolate, I write down the three temperatures I need to reach on a little piece of paper, in the order I need to reach them, and then I check each one off when reached.

. . . .

For the Chocolate-Covered Caramel Bars you need to use good-quality couverture milk chocolate. Milk chocolate chips and grocery store chocolate bars will not work for tempering. If you cannot find couverture milk chocolate then you can use couverture dark chocolate, which is a little easier to source—but be certain to temper it to the temperatures listed for dark chocolate (Classic Florentine Cookies, page 56).

The tempering method discussed in the recipe is called "tabling," and you'll need a flat surface such as marble or even smooth granite or stainless steel (not wood) and two putty knives that can be easily found at a hardware store.

. . . .

If you don't hit the right temperatures on your first try, don't panic. Let the chocolate cool right down to room temperature and then start the process again. Like any skill, such as riding a bike or speaking another language, tempering chocolate takes practice. It can take a few tries to get the hang of it, but once you do, your confidence will grow quickly. And just like bike-riding or speaking another language, if you haven't done it in a while, you may be rusty and have to give it a few tries before getting back on top of your game.

. . . .

The final step in tempering chocolate is the "cure"—chilling it for just a few minutes to set those beautifully bonded (tempered) chocolate molecules together. You don't want to chill the chocolate for longer than 5 minutes, otherwise a bloom may develop on the chocolate once you pull it from the fridge. A bloom is that white dust or streakiness you may have seen on chocolate. It isn't mould, it is cocoa butter that has risen to the surface of the chocolate, and is a sign that the chocolate has gone through a quick temperature change (perhaps being improperly stored) or wasn't tempered effectively. The chocolate is still fine to use and to eat; it just doesn't look the nicest.

Pies and Tarts

This collection of pie and tart recipes covers a full range in terms of taste as well as technique—all the major categories of flavour combinations from classic to inventive are covered. What makes a pie or tart so gratifying is that complexity of delicate pastry combined with a cream or fruit filling (and often a topping, too).

Making a pie or a tart is a time commitment. The pastry base often needs to be chilled and even pre-baked before it is filled, and then it needs to chill again after it's baked. But there's something immensely satisfying about that combination of crisp pastry crust topped with something fruity or creamy or rich (or all three!) that makes the effort worth it. When I decide to make a pie or a tart, it's often not because I'm in the mood to eat it, but because I'm in the mood to MAKE it. I find making a tart an immensely gratifying task, and your level of knowledge grows exponentially with each tart you make.

Simple

Scrumptious

Sensational

Pie Dough for Fruit Fillings

Fruit pies are a distinctive dessert category, and deserve a customized pie dough recipe. The pie dough delivers on flakiness and tenderness but doesn't get soggy, due to the addition of a little vegetable oil before the butter gets worked in.

Makes enough for one double-crust pie • Prep 15 minutes plus chilling

2 ½ cups | 375 g	all-purpose flour
1 Tbsp | 12 g	granulated sugar
1 tsp | 5 g	salt
3 Tbsp | 45 mL	vegetable oil
1 cup | 225 g	cool (does not have to be ice-cold) unsalted butter, cut into pieces
¼ cup | 60 mL	cool water
2 tsp | 10 mL	lemon juice or white vinegar

1. Stir the flour, sugar, and salt together in a bowl or in the bowl of a stand mixer fitted with the paddle attachment. Add the oil and cut it in using a pastry cutter (or blend on low speed) until the flour looks evenly crumbly in texture. Add the butter and cut in (or blend) again until rough and crumbly but small pieces of butter are still visible.

2. Stir the water with the lemon juice or vinegar and add this to the flour mixture all at once, mixing just until the dough comes together. Shape the dough into two discs (unless otherwise directed by the pie recipe you are following), wrap in plastic wrap, and chill until firm, at least 2 hours. The dough can be made up to 2 days ahead and stored in the fridge. Alternatively, it can be frozen for up to 3 months and thawed in the fridge before rolling.

If you are building your knowledge as a baker, then making a fruit pie is an essential on your to-do list. Fruit pies are always a favourite dessert, and a masterful pie pastry-making skill is enviable. Mastering this pie dough recipe is the first step toward success.

• • • • • • • •

The benefits of adding the vegetable oil to a pie dough is a recent discovery of mine. I find that the oil evenly coats all of the flour, so when you work in the cool butter, the butter doesn't fully get absorbed by the flour. As the pie bakes, the butter melts and the water within the butter turns to steam, pushing up the flour layers around it, making the flakiness that we want and expect.

• • • • • • • •

I find that working with butter that is cool but not ice-cold is fine when making pie dough. If butter is too cold, it shatters and breaks into uneven pieces, and it takes longer to work into the dough, risking overdevelopment of the proteins in the flour, and so risking a tough crust. Slightly softer butter works in evenly and quickly.

• • • • • • • •

The lemon juice or vinegar that you add to a pie dough is a small measure, but it makes a difference. The acidity allow the proteins in the flour to become elastic, ensuring not only a tender crust but also one that does not spring back or shrink when you roll and bake it.

Pie Dough for Fluid Fillings

This dough is designed for pies that have a wet filling,
such as coconut cream pie or butter tarts.
It holds together but is also tender.

Makes enough for one double-crust pie • Prep 15 minutes plus chilling

2 ¼ cups | 295 g	cake and pastry flour
2 Tbsp | 25 g	granulated sugar
¾ tsp | 4 g	salt
1 cup | 225 g	cool (does not have to be ice-cold) unsalted butter, cut into pieces
6 Tbsp | 90 mL	cool water
1 Tbsp | 15 mL	lemon juice or white vinegar

1. Stir the flour, sugar, and salt together in a bowl or in the bowl of a stand mixer fitted with the paddle attachment. Cut in the butter by hand with a pastry cutter (or blend on low speed), just until small pieces of butter are still visible and the mixture as a whole just begins to take on a pale yellow colour (indicating that the butter has been worked in sufficiently).

2. Stir the water with the lemon juice or vinegar and add this to the flour mixture all at once, mixing just until the dough comes together. Shape the dough into two discs (unless otherwise directed by the pie recipe you are following), wrap in plastic wrap, and chill until firm, at least 2 hours. The dough can be made up to 2 days ahead and stored in the fridge. Alternatively, it can be frozen for up to 3 months and thawed in the fridge before rolling.

Try using this foundation pie dough for any of your pies that have a fluid filling—it is tender and flaky with a unique density, thanks to the use of cake and pastry flour. Cake and pastry flour is milled to a finer texture and has a lower protein (gluten) content than all-purpose flour, so it produces a pie dough that has a delicate texture, but also a density that keeps it more watertight than some other pie doughs.

Whole Wheat Pie Dough

I find that whole wheat pie dough makes a crust that browns nicely and stays crispy under heavy fillings, like with my Pumpkin Pie (page 82). This pie crust method stands apart from the previous two recipes as it suits using a food processor; the others I prefer to make by hand or in a stand mixer.

Makes enough for one single-crust pie • Prep 15 minutes plus chilling

¾ cup | 105 g	whole wheat flour (all-purpose)
¾ cup | 100 g	cake and pastry flour
1 Tbsp | 12 g	granulated sugar
½ tsp | 2 g	salt
10 Tbsp | 145 g	unsalted butter, cut into pieces and then frozen for 10 minutes
1 | 1	large egg yolk
3 Tbsp | 45 mL	cold water
1 Tbsp | 15 mL	lemon juice

1. In a food processor, pulse the flours, sugar, and salt to combine (the dough can also be prepared by hand or in a stand mixer fitted with the paddle attachment). Add the butter and pulse it in quick pulses just until small pieces of butter are visible and the mixture as a whole just begins to take on a pale yellow colour (indicating that the butter has been worked in).

2. Stir the egg yolk, water, and lemon juice together and add this to the dough all at once. Pulse until the dough barely comes together (it should look like a dough for a crumble). Shape the dough into a disc (unless otherwise directed by the pie recipe you are following), wrap in plastic wrap, and chill until firm, at least 2 hours. The dough can be made up to 2 days ahead and stored in the fridge. Alternatively, it can be frozen for up to 3 months and thawed in the fridge before rolling.

You might find that you like this whole wheat crust recipe so much that you use it for all of your fruit pies!

Pecan Butter Tarts

Butter tarts are a classic Canadian sweet treat. Feel free to use other additions in place of the pecans, such as raisins or walnut pieces—or simply leave the butter tarts plain.

Makes 12 butter tarts • Prep 30 minutes • Bake/Cook 25 minutes

1 | 1	recipe Pie Dough for Fluid Fillings (page 67), shaped into 2 logs and chilled
½ cup | 115 g	unsalted butter
1 cup | 200 g	packed dark brown or demerara sugar
2 | 2	large eggs
½ cup | 125 mL	pure maple syrup
1 Tbsp | 15 mL	lemon juice
1 tsp | 5 mL	pure vanilla extract
¼ tsp | 1 g	salt
½ cup | 50 g	lightly toasted pecan pieces

1. Preheat the oven to 400°F (200°C). Lightly grease a 12-cup muffin pan. Pull the chilled dough from the fridge 20 minutes before you are ready to roll it.

2. Cut each log of chilled pie dough into six. Roll each piece out on a lightly floured work surface to just under ¼ inch (0.5 cm) thick and use a 4 ½-inch (12 cm) round cookie cutter to cut each into a circle. Line each muffin cup with the pastry—it should be about ½ inch (1 cm) higher than the muffin pan. Chill the pastry in the pan while you prepare the filling.

3. Melt the butter and brown sugar in a saucepan over medium heat, stirring until the mixture is fully bubbling. Remove the saucepan from the heat.

4. In a bowl, whisk the eggs with the maple syrup, lemon juice, vanilla, and salt and slowly pour in the hot sugar mixture, whisking constantly until incorporated.

5. Remove the muffin pan from the fridge. Sprinkle a few pecan pieces into the bottom of each tart shell and ladle or pour in the filling.

6. Bake the tarts for 10 minutes at 400°F (200°C), then reduce the oven temperature to 375°F (190°C) and bake for an additional 10–15 minutes, until the filling is bubbling and the crust edges have browned evenly. Leave the tarts in the pan on a cooling rack. After about 5 minutes, carefully twist them around in the pan to prevent sticking. Keep them in the pan until completely cooled. The butter tarts should be refrigerated but are best served at room temperature. The tarts can be stored for up to 3 days in an airtight container in the fridge.

I like to have my butter tart crusts just a little higher than the top of the muffin pan to hold in the gooey filling.

· · · · · · · ·

It's important to whisk the butter tart filling by hand, rather than using electric beaters. If you mix too much or too vigorously, you risk aerating the eggs, which will cause them to rise with the heat of the oven and then collapse once cooled, leaving your butter tarts with sunken centres.

Twisting the baked tarts in the pan after they've cooled just a few minutes is key to getting them out easily, since the filling can sometimes spill out and caramelize (which tastes fantastic, by the way, but makes removing them a little tricky).

Apple Tarte Tatin

This classic French apple tart is baked upside down, with the fruit at the bottom and the puff pastry baked on top. Once inverted, the glossy, caramelized apples are revealed. Gorgeous!

Makes one 9-inch (23 cm) tart • Serves 6 • Prep 20 minutes • Bake/Cook 1 hour

1 sheet | 225 g	store-bought butter puff pastry, thawed but chilled
2.6 lb | 1.2 kg	cooking apples (about 5), such as Honeycrisp or Spartan
6 Tbsp | 90 g	unsalted butter, divided
10 Tbsp | 125 g	granulated sugar
1 Tbsp | 15 mL	lemon juice

You can make this tarte using good-quality, store-bought butter puff pastry, but to turn it from Simple to Sensational, make the puff pastry from scratch (page 170).

• • • • • • • •

Firm apple varieties are needed for this recipe, so that they don't collapse under the weight of the pastry as it bakes upside down. Honeycrisp, Spartan, Mutsu, or even Granny Smith work well.

• • • • • • • •

I like to use a cast iron skillet for an apple tarte tatin because the pan can go from stovetop to oven and the cast iron holds the heat well.

1. Preheat the oven to 375°F (190°C).

2. On a lightly floured surface, roll the pastry out into a circle just over 9 inches (23 cm) in diameter and just over ¼ inch (0.5 cm) thick. Use the ring of a 9-inch (23 cm) fluted pan to cut it into a circle and create a lovely edge for the pastry. Dock this with a fork and chill until ready to use.

3. Peel, halve, and core the apples. Melt 2 Tbsp (30 g) of the butter and pour this over the apples, tossing with 2 Tbsp (25 g) of the sugar to coat. Set aside.

4. Place a 9-inch (23 cm) ovenproof skillet (or other round pan that can go from the stovetop to the oven) over medium-high heat and add the remaining ¼ cup (60 g) of butter, ½ cup (100 g) of the sugar, and the lemon juice and stir to combine. Once the liquid is bubbling at the edges, add the apples, arranging them so the curved outside of the apples are at the bottom and they are overlapping slightly, to pack them in. Increase the heat to high and cook for 2–3 minutes, until the liquid is bubbling vigorously at the edges. Place the pan of apples in the oven to bake for 15 minutes.

5. Pull the pan from the oven and place the chilled puff pastry on top of the apples, tucking it in a little around the edges. Make sure the pastry is between the apples and the inside edge of the pan. Return the pan to the oven and bake for 30–35 minutes, until the pastry is golden brown. Let the tarte cool in the pan for 20–30 minutes. Use a palette knife to loosen any apples that might be sticking to the sides of the pan. Place a large plate over the pan, use a tea towel or oven gloves to protect your hands, and invert the pan so the plate is on your countertop. Lift up the pan to reveal the tarte. The tarte tatin can be served warm or at room temperature and enjoyed the day it is baked.

Apple Cinnamon Galettes

A galette is a single-crust, free-form tart—very rustic and pretty.
These are individual tarts, and take less time to make than a traditional apple pie.

Makes 6 individual galettes • Prep 30 minutes • Bake 25 minutes

1 | 1	**recipe Pie Dough for Fruit Fillings (page 66), shaped into 2 logs and chilled**
½ cup | 125 g	**sour cream**
10 Tbsp | 125 g	**packed dark brown or demerara sugar**
½ tsp | 2 mL	**pure vanilla extract**
4 cups | 800 g	**peeled and thinly sliced Granny Smith, Cortland, or other tart apple (about 3 apples)**
1 tsp | 3 g	**ground cinnamon**
2 Tbsp | 30 g	**unsalted butter, divided**
1 | 1	**egg, whisked with 2 Tbsp (30 mL) water, for brushing**
	turbinado sugar, for sprinkling

I like the little bit of sour cream filling that hides under the apples in this recipe. It adds almost a custard-like element to the galette.

• • • • • • • •

When folding your galette pastry over your fruit filling, be sure to leave a gap in the centre so the fruit is visible—no need to hide it.

1. Pull the pie dough from the fridge 20 minutes before you are ready to roll it. Preheat the oven to 375°F (190°C). Line two baking trays with parchment paper.

2. Slice each log into three pieces and roll each piece out on a lightly floured work surface into circles just under ¼ inch (0.5 cm) thick and 8 inches (20 cm) in diameter. Place three circles on each baking tray and chill while you prepare the filling.

3. Stir the sour cream, 2 Tbsp (25 g) of the brown sugar, and the vanilla together in a bowl. In another bowl, toss the apples with the remaining ½ cup (100 g) brown sugar and the cinnamon.

4. Spoon equal amounts of sour cream into the centre of each circle of dough and top with apple slices. Place 1 tsp (5 mL) of the butter on the top of each tart. Fold the dough over the apples, making five or six overlapping creases so that the apples are almost fully covered, but not quite. Brush the pastry with the egg wash and sprinkle generously with turbinado sugar.

5. Bake the galettes for about 25 minutes, until the pastry is a rich golden brown colour. Let them cool on the baking trays on cooling racks for at least 20 minutes before serving warm, or cool completely and serve at room temperature. The galettes will keep for up to 3 days in the fridge, but should be served warm or at room temperature.

Frosted Raspberry Hand Pies

At first glance, these individual pies look like turnovers, but are made using pie dough rather than the puff pastry. This thinner pie dough allows more room for the filling, which means they definitely qualify as pies. Once the glaze sets, they are easy to pick up and eat, making them perfect for a picnic.

Makes 6 hand pies • Prep 30 minutes • Bake 25 minutes

½ | ½	recipe Pie Dough for Fruit Fillings (page 66), chilled for at least 2 hours
2 cups | 500 mL	fresh raspberries
½ | ½	medium tart apple, peeled and coarsely grated
¼ cup | 50 g	granulated sugar
	pinch ground cinnamon
1 | 1	egg, whisked with 2 Tbsp (30 mL) water, for brushing
	turbinado sugar, for sprinkling

Glaze

1 cup | 130 g	icing sugar, sifted
1 ½ Tbsp | 22 mL	milk or water
½ tsp | 2 mL	pure vanilla extract

1. Preheat the oven to 375°F (190°C). Line a baking tray with parchment paper.

2. Slice the chilled pie dough into six pieces and roll each piece out to a circle about 6 inches across and just under ¼ inch (0.5 cm) thick. Use a 6-inch (15 cm) round cookie cutter to trim away the rough edges on each and make perfect circles.

3. Use a fork to combine the raspberries, apple, sugar, and cinnamon, gently crushing the raspberries a little as you mix.

4. Spoon the raspberry filling evenly among the dough circles. Brush the outside edge halfway around with a little of the egg wash and fold in half to make a semi-circle. Pinch the edges of each hand pie in the same style as you would the edge of a traditional pie, fluting the edges. Place the hand pies on the prepared baking tray, brush the tops with egg wash, and sprinkle with turbinado sugar. Snip a few holes into the pies with a pair of scissors so the steam can escape.

5. Bake the hand pies for about 25 minutes, until the pie dough is a rich golden brown. Cool the pies on the tray on a cooling rack before glazing.

6. For the glaze, whisk the icing sugar, milk, and vanilla together until smooth and still fluid (add more icing sugar or liquid, if necessary). Using a fork, drizzle the glaze over the pies. Let the glaze set for at least 1 hour before serving. The pies are best enjoyed the day they are baked.

When I use fresh raspberries in a pie filling, I like to also add grated apple. The grated apple absorbs not only the berry flavour, but also the juice that cooks out of the berries, keeping the pie from being too runny.

Crushing the berries a little as you make your filling releases some of the pectin that is in the seeds, which will help thicken up the sauce a bit.

Tarte au Citron

*I love a classic lemon tart after a rich meal. A slender slice, with its
tart-sweet creamy filling and sweet crust, is beautifully balanced in taste and in texture.*

Makes one 9-inch (23 cm) tart • Serves 8 to 10
Prep 30 minutes • Bake 30 minutes plus chilling

1 | 1	recipe Pâte Sablée Dough (page 49), chilled
3 | 3	whole eggs
3 | 3	egg yolks
¾ cup | 150 g	granulated sugar
1 Tbsp | 15 mL	lemon zest
⅔ cup | 160 mL	fresh lemon juice
⅔ cup | 150 g	unsalted butter, cut into pieces
½ cup | 125 g	sour cream

1. On a lightly floured work surface, gently knead the dough just a little to soften it, then roll it out to a circle about 12 inches (30 cm) across and ¼ inch (0.5 cm) thick. Carefully lift it onto a 9-inch (23 cm) removable-bottom fluted tart pan, press it into the bottom and sides, and trim away any excess dough. Dock the pastry with a fork and then chill the tart shell for 30 minutes.

2. Preheat the oven to 325°F (160°C).

3. Place the chilled tart shell on a baking tray and dock the bottom of the pastry with a fork. Bake the tart shell for about 20 minutes, until the edges just begin to brown. Cool in the pan on a cooling rack to room temperature while you prepare the filling.

4. For the filling, whisk the eggs, egg yolks, sugar, lemon zest, and lemon juice together in a metal bowl and place the bowl over a saucepan of gently simmering water. After 1 minute, add the butter and continue to whisk until the curd has thickened, about 5 minutes. Remove the curd from the heat, strain through a fine mesh sieve into a clean bowl, and whisk in the sour cream. Pour the warm curd into the cooled tart shell and chill, uncovered, until set, about 2 hours. The tart is best served the day it is baked, but it will keep, refrigerated, for 1 day. Do not cover it, as plastic wrap will mark the surface of the tart.

*This tart is made with the dough from Empire Cookies (page 49),
known as Pâte Sablée (literally, sandy dough, in English). It is tender and sweet,
but has a density to it that makes it perfect for a fluid filling like this lemon curd.*

• • • • • • • •

*This tart's filling is cooked before it goes into the baked tart shell, so that all it
needs to do is chill before serving. To get a level and shiny tart, you need to
pour the curd into the shell while the filling is still hot and fluid.*

Tarte au Chocolat

They may look similar, but in contrast to the Tarte au Citron (page 78),
with its sweet and tart characteristics, this slender chocolate tart, with its
chocolate pastry and thin layer of ganache filling, is ultra-rich and decadent.

Makes one 9-inch (23 cm) tart • Serves 8 to 10
Prep 30 minutes • Bake 30 minutes plus chilling

½ | ½	recipe Chocolate Pastry Dough (page 26), chilled
½ cup | 125 mL	whipping cream
¼ cup | 60 g	unsalted butter, cut into pieces
8 oz | 240 g	bittersweet couverture/baking chocolate, chopped
¼ cup | 50 g	granulated sugar
½ cup | 125 mL	hot, strongly brewed coffee
2 | 2	large eggs, at room temperature
1 tsp | 5 mL	pure vanilla extract

1. Knead the chocolate pastry dough once or twice on a lightly floured work surface to soften it, then roll it out to a circle just less than ¼ inch (0.5 cm) thick. Carefully lift it onto a 9-inch (23 cm) removable-bottom fluted tart pan, press it into the bottom and sides, and trim away any excess dough. Dock the pastry with a fork. Chill the tart shell for at least 20 minutes.

2. Preheat the oven to 350°F (180°C).

3. Place the chilled tart shell on a baking tray and bake it for about 18 minutes, until you see that the pastry has an even, dull finish. Cool to room temperature while you prepare the filling.

4. For the filling, place the cream and butter in a medium saucepan over medium heat and bring to just below a simmer. Place the chocolate in a large bowl and pour the hot cream mix over top, letting it sit for just a few seconds. Gently stir the mixture with a spatula until the chocolate melts, then whisk in the sugar and the coffee. Lightly beat the eggs in a small dish and add them to the chocolate, along with the vanilla, whisking gently until incorporated. Pour this into the cooled tart shell and bake (still at 350°F/180°C) for 12 minutes. Allow the tart to cool in the pan on a cooling rack to room temperature, and then chill uncovered for at least 2 hours before serving. The tart can be stored for up to 2 days in the fridge. Do not cover it, as plastic wrap will mark the surface of the tart.

This tart is definitely for chocolate-lovers—especially because of the coffee.
The coffee doesn't add a distinctive coffee taste, but intensifies the taste of the chocolate.
For a milder version, use hot water or tea instead of coffee.

• • • • • • • •

Take care to only bake the filled tarte for 12 minutes to set the egg.
Any more and the filling will taste grainy, not silky smooth.

"Blue Ribbon" Apple Pie

This apple pie will be sure to win you the "blue ribbon" first prize at the next apple pie contest.

Makes one 9-inch (23 cm) pie • Serves 8 • Prep 40 minutes • Bake 1 hour plus cooling

1 | 1	**recipe Pie Dough for Fruit Fillings (page 66), chilled**
6 cups | 1.2 kg	**peeled and sliced (½-inch (1 cm) thick), mixed apples (such as Mutsu, Granny Smith, Royal Gala, Honeycrisp, or Cortland) about 5 medium apples**
1 Tbsp | 15 mL	**fresh lemon juice**
½ cup | 100 g	**granulated sugar**
⅓ cup | 70 g	**packed light brown sugar**
1 tsp | 3 g	**ground cinnamon**
¼ tsp | 1 g	**ground allspice**
¼ tsp | 1 g	**ground nutmeg**
2 Tbsp | 12 g	**rolled oats**
2 Tbsp | 30 g	**unsalted butter**
1 | 1	**egg, whisked with 2 Tbsp (30 mL) water, for brushing**
	granulated sugar and ground cinnamon, for sprinkling

1. Pull the dough from the fridge 15–30 minutes before you are ready to roll it. Preheat the oven to 400°F (200°C). Line a baking tray with parchment paper or aluminum foil.

2. Toss the sliced apples with the lemon juice in a large non-reactive bowl. Leave half the apples in the bowl. Place the other half in a sauté pan or saucepan and heat on medium until some of the juices cook out and the apples soften, about 10 minutes. Remove the apples from the pan with a slotted spoon and stir with the uncooked apples to cool.

3. In a separate bowl, stir both the sugars with the cinnamon, allspice, and nutmeg to blend. Stir this into the apples and set aside.

4. On a lightly floured surface, roll out the first disc of dough into a circle just less than ¼ inch (0.5 cm) thick. Dust a 9-inch (23 cm) pie plate with flour and line the bottom and sides of the plate with the pastry so that it hangs over the edge of the plate a little. Sprinkle the bottom of the shell with the oats (this will help absorb any excess juices). Spoon the apple filling into the shell and dot with the butter. Roll out the remaining disc of dough to ¼ inch (0.5 cm) thick and place over the apples. Trim off any excess dough and pinch the edges of the crust together, creating a fluted edge. Brush the pastry with the egg wash. Stir a little sugar and cinnamon together and sprinkle generously over top. Use scissors to snip an opening in the top crust to allow steam to escape.

5. Place the pie on the prepared baking tray and bake for 10 minutes. Reduce the oven temperature to 375°F (190°C) and continue to bake for another 40–50 minutes, until the crust is golden brown and the filling is bubbling. Cool the pie in the pan on a cooling rack for at least 2 hours before serving.

Pulling your pie dough out of the fridge up to half an hour before you roll it out saves you stress. The dough will roll more easily, with less cracking, and the flakiness and tenderness are not at all compromised, as you may have been warned about when making pie dough. I find a dough ice-cold from the fridge cracks more and takes more effort—why create a headache when it can be prevented simply by pulling out the dough a little bit ahead?

I like to cook half of the apples to allow some of the excess juices to cook away. This not only concentrates the flavour but also ensures I won't get a gap between the fruit and the top crust as the pie bakes. I only cook half of them, though, since I do want some juiciness and fresh apple flavour.

Pumpkin Pie

What appeals to me about pumpkin pie is that it's really pumpkin custard baked into a pie shell, and that contrast of creamy filling with flaky, buttery pastry is so fulfilling. The subtly nutty taste of the whole wheat pie dough used for this recipe really works well with the fall filling.

Makes one 9-inch (23 cm) pie • Serves 8
Prep 50 minutes • Bake 50 minutes plus chilling

1 | 1	**recipe Whole Wheat Pie Dough (page 68), chilled**
2 cups | 500 g	**pure pumpkin purée**
½ cup | 100 g	**packed light brown sugar**
3 | 3	**large eggs**
¾ cup | 180 mL	**full-fat evaporated milk**
1 ½ tsp | 7 mL	**finely grated fresh ginger**
¾ tsp | 2.5 g	**ground cinnamon**
⅛ tsp | 0.5 g	**ground cloves**
⅛ tsp | 0.5 g	**salt**
1 | 1	**egg, whisked with 2 Tbsp (30 mL) of water, for brushing**

1. Pull the dough from the fridge 30 minutes before you are ready to roll it. Preheat the oven to 400°F (200°C). Line a baking tray with parchment paper or aluminum foil.

2. On a lightly floured work surface, roll out the dough to just under ¼ inch (0.5 cm) thick. Lightly dust with flour a 9-inch (23 cm) pie plate and line the bottom and sides of the plate with the pastry. Trim the pastry off right to the edge of the pie plate and press it down gently to secure. Reserve any remaining dough for trim and chill it and the pie shell while you prepare the filling.

3. Whisk the pumpkin purée, brown sugar, and eggs together, then whisk in the evaporated milk, ginger, cinnamon, cloves, and salt. Pour this into the chilled pie shell.

4. To create the trim, roll out the remaining pie dough into a long rectangle and cut it into strips about ⅓ inch (0.8 cm) wide. Braid three strips together, gently pulling the dough a little to stretch it as you braid. You may have to make a few braids to cover the complete edge of where the pie dough is visible. Lightly brush the edge of the pie dough and place the braided dough over top, lightly pressing down. Brush the braid(s) with egg wash.

5. Place the pie on the prepared baking tray and bake for 10 minutes at 400°F (200°C), then reduce the oven temperature to 375°F (190°C) and bake for another 35–40 minutes, until the pumpkin filling is set but still has a little jiggle to it in the centre. Cool the pie in the pan on a cooling rack to room temperature, then chill completely, uncovered, about 4 hours, before serving. The pie is best served chilled, and can be stored, uncovered in the fridge, for up to 2 days.

Since I prepare this pie shell in a food processor, I freeze the butter for the dough for a few minutes before using to compensate for the heat from the friction of the processor blades. Of course, if you make this recipe by hand or in a mixer, you don't need to freeze the butter.

· · · · · · · ·

For the pie filling, you can use canned pure pumpkin purée (but not pre-sweetened or pre-spiced pumpkin pie filling), or make your own. For tips on making your own, see Pumpkin Swirl Cheesecake Squares (page 44).

I used to always use whipping cream in my filling, but have found that can be a little rich for some tastes. I now use evaporated milk instead, which adds richness without the added fat.

Mincemeat Pie

A spiced, wintry mix of apples and dried fruits with a generous sprinkling of spices make this a festive treat.

Makes one 9-inch (23 cm) pie • Serves 8
Prep 1 hour • Bake 50 minutes plus cooling

1 | 1	recipe Pie Dough for Fruit Fillings (page 66), chilled
2 | 2	medium apples (any type), peeled and coarsely grated
1 cup | 150 g	golden or Thompson raisins
1 cup | 160 g	currants
½ cup | 70 g	dried cranberries
¼ cup | 25 g	finely diced crystallized ginger
½ cup | 100 g	packed dark brown sugar
⅓ cup | 100 g	honey
¼ cup | 60 mL	brandy (optional)
2 Tbsp | 30 mL	lemon juice
1 Tbsp | 15 mL	finely grated orange zest
2 tsp | 10 mL	finely grated lemon zest
½ tsp | 2 g	ground allspice
½ tsp | 2 g	ground nutmeg
¼ tsp | 1 g	ground cloves
¼ cup | 60 g	unsalted butter, melted
1 | 1	egg mixed with 2 Tbsp water, for brushing
	turbinado or granulated sugar, for sprinkling

1. Toss the grated apple, raisins, currants, dried cranberries, and candied ginger with the brown sugar, honey, brandy, lemon juice, orange and lemon zests, and spices. Cover and chill for at least 2 hours, up to 24 hours.

2. Pull the dough from the fridge 30 minutes before you are ready to roll it. Preheat the oven to 400°F (200°C). Line a baking tray with parchment paper or aluminum foil.

3. On a lightly floured surface, roll out the first disc of dough into a circle just less than ¼ inch (0.5 cm) thick. Dust a 9-inch (23 cm) pie plate with flour and line the bottom and sides of the plate with the pastry. Trim away the excess dough and pinch the edges to create a fluted design.

4. Stir the melted butter into the mincemeat filling and spoon this into the pie shell, using the back of a spoon to level it out. Roll out the second disc of dough to the same thickness and use a cookie cutter to cut out shapes of your choosing. Arrange the cut-outs over the mincemeat filling, placing them closely together over the entire surface of the pie. Brush the pastry with egg wash and sprinkle lightly with sugar.

5. Place the pie on the prepared baking tray and bake for 10 minutes at 400°F (200°C), then reduce the oven temperature to 375°F (190°C) and bake for about another 40 minutes, until the crust is golden brown. Cool the pie in the pan on a cooling rack for at least 2 hours before serving. If you want to serve it chilled, refrigerate for at least 3 hours before serving. The pie can be stored, refrigerated and uncovered, for up to 2 days.

Feel free to make this filling and spoon it into smaller tart shells for individual mince pies. The grated apple holds in the moisture and keeps the texture of the filling fine and delicate.

Strawberry Cream Tarts

The classic pastry cream is the standout element in these simple tarts.
The graham cracker crust and fresh berry on top are there merely to
accentuate the smooth, creamy texture of a well-made custard.

Makes 24 mini tarts • Prep 30 minutes • Bake 10 minutes plus chilling

Pastry Cream

1 cup | 250 mL	milk
½ | ½	vanilla bean, seeds only, or 1 ½ tsp (7 mL) vanilla bean paste
3 | 3	large egg yolks
3 Tbsp | 36 g	granulated sugar
2 Tbsp | 15 g	cornstarch
2 Tbsp | 30 g	unsalted butter, cut into pieces

Crust

1 cup | 150 g	all-purpose flour
1 cup | 125 g	graham cracker crumbs
4 tsp | 16 g	granulated sugar
¼ tsp | 1 g	salt
½ cup | 115 g	unsalted butter, melted
30 | 30	fresh strawberries, stems removed

Once you wash and hull a strawberry, it should
be used and eaten fairly soon afterwards.
To avoid last-minute work, you can prepare
the crust and pastry cream filling a day ahead,
and then assemble your tarts a few hours
before you plan on serving them.

• • • • • • • •

This recipe uses a classic pastry cream filling,
which can be used for any number of tart
recipes. It makes about 1 ½ cups (375 mL) in
total and can be refrigerated for up to
4 days in an airtight container.

1. For the pastry cream, heat the milk with the vanilla bean seeds or paste in a medium saucepan over medium heat until just below a simmer.

2. In a bowl, whisk together the egg yolks, sugar, and cornstarch.

3. Place the butter in a separate bowl, with a sieve resting over the bowl.

4. Gradually whisk the hot milk into the egg mixture and then return the mixture to the saucepan. Whisk this constantly (switching to a spatula now and again to get into the corners) over medium heat until thickened and glossy, about 2 minutes. Pour this immediately through the sieve, whisking it through if needed, and stir in the butter. Place a piece of plastic wrap directly on the surface of the custard, cool to room temperature, and then chill completely until ready to use.

5. For the crust, preheat the oven to 350°F (180°C). Lightly grease a mini muffin pan.

6. Combine the flour, graham cracker crumbs, sugar, and salt in a bowl. Add the melted butter and mix until you have an even, crumbly texture. Spoon about 1 Tbsp (15 mL) of the mixture into each muffin cup and press it into the bottom and all of the way up the sides of each muffin cup. Bake for 10 minutes, then cool in the pan on a cooling rack before filling.

7. Use a skewer to gently remove each tart shell from the pan. Stir the pastry cream to soften, spoon or pipe the filling into each cup, and then arrange a strawberry on top of each. Chill until ready to serve. The tarts should be enjoyed within a few hours of assembling.

Pumpkin Crème Brûlée Tarts

These tarts are a blend of two of my favourite desserts—pumpkin pie and crème brûlée—and are perfect for a fancy, festive gathering.

Makes 8 individual tarts • Prep 50 minutes • Bake 35 minutes plus chilling

1 | 1	recipe Pâte Sablée Dough (page 49), shaped into a log and chilled
¾ cup | 180 g	cream cheese, at room temperature
¾ cup | 150 g	packed dark brown sugar
6 | 6	large egg yolks
¾ cup | 190 g	pure pumpkin purée (page 45)
1 tsp | 5 mL	finely grated fresh ginger
½ tsp | 2 g	ground cinnamon
3 Tbsp | 45 mL	brandy (optional)
	granulated sugar, for brûléeing

Where crème brûlée is made to be served in the dish in which it is baked, a sweet dough replaces the need for a dish. The bit of cream cheese in the filling helps give it body, making it thicker than a crème brûlée filling, which keeps it from sinking into the baked crust.

• • • • • • •

Don't "torch" the tops of the tarts until you are ready to serve them. If this was done ahead of time and the tarts were chilled until needed, the crunchy sugar top would liquefy after an hour or two.

1. Unwrap the chilled dough and slice it evenly into eight. On a lightly floured work surface, first lightly knead each piece to soften and then roll out into a circle that is just under ¼ inch (0.5 cm) thick. Use each pastry circle to line the bottom and sides of ungreased 4-inch (10 cm) removable-bottom fluted tart shells, pressing the dough into the shell and trimming away any excess. Chill the tart shells for 30 minutes or until firm.

2. Preheat the oven to 325°F (160°C).

3. Place the tart shells on a baking tray, dock the bottom of each shell with a fork, and bake for about 18 minutes, until the edges begin to brown a little. Leave the oven on. Cool the shells to room temperature on the baking tray on a cooling rack before filling.

4. For the filling, combine the cream cheese and brown sugar using a blender or immersion blender. Add the egg yolks, pumpkin purée, ginger, cinnamon, and brandy (if using) and blend until smooth. Pour this filling into the cooled tart shells and return to the oven to bake for about 16 minutes, until the filling has set around the edges, but still has a little jiggle in the centre. Cool the tarts on the tray on a cooling rack to room temperature and then chill, uncovered, until set, at least 3 hours.

5. To serve, remove the tarts from the metal tart shells, sprinkle the top of each tart with a little sugar, and use a butane kitchen torch to melt and caramelize the sugar. Serve immediately. Before brûléeing, the tarts can be stored, refrigerated and uncovered, for up to a day.

Lemon Meringue Pie

Lemon meringue pie is a perennial favourite.
I've included a list of tips with this recipe to guarantee your success!

Makes one 9-inch (23 cm) pie • Serves 8 • Prep 75 minutes • Bake/Cook 1 hour plus chilling

⅓ | ⅓		**recipe Pie Dough for Fluid Fillings (page 67), chilled**
1 | 1		**egg white, lightly whisked with a fork**

Lemon Curd Filling

1 cup	200 g	granulated sugar
¼ cup	30 g	cornstarch
1 cup	250 mL	cold water
6	6	large egg yolks
½ cup	125 mL	fresh lemon juice
2 Tbsp	30 g	unsalted butter

Meringue

4	4	large egg whites, at room temperature
½ tsp	1.5 g	cream of tartar
⅓ cup	70 g	granulated sugar
3 Tbsp	24 g	icing sugar, sifted

1. Pull the chilled pie dough from the fridge 30 minutes before you wish to roll it. Roll out the disc of dough on a lightly floured work surface into a circle that is just under ¼ inch (0.5 cm) thick. Lightly dust a 9-inch (23 cm) pie plate with flour. Press the dough into the bottom and sides of the pie plate, trim away any excess dough, pinch the edges to create a fluted pattern, and chill for 30 minutes.

2. Preheat the oven to 400°F (200°C).

3. Line the chilled pie shell with aluminum foil and fill the foil with dried beans, raw rice, or pie weights. Bake the pie shell for 20 minutes, then carefully remove the foil and weights and bake the crust for 8–10 minutes more, until the centre of the pie shell is dry-looking and just starts to brown a little. Immediately after removing the pie shell from the oven, brush the hot crust with a little of the whisked egg white. This will create a barrier to keep the crust crispy once filled. Reduce the oven temperature to 325°F (160°C). Cool the pie crust in the pan on a cooling rack.

4. For the filling, have all your ingredients measured and nearby. Whisk the sugar and cornstarch together in a medium saucepan, then whisk in the cold water. Bring the sugar mixture up to a full simmer over medium-high heat, whisking as it cooks, until the mixture is thick and glossy, about 5 minutes.

Continued . . .

5. Combine about 1 cup (250 mL) of this thickened filling with the egg yolks while whisking. Return to the saucepan, still over medium heat, and whisk for just 1 minute more. Whisk in the lemon juice and cook until the filling just returns to a simmer. Remove the saucepan from the heat, whisk in the butter, and then immediately pour the hot filling into the cooled pie shell (the filling will seem very fluid, but it will set up once chilled). Directly cover the surface of the filling with plastic wrap to keep it hot. Immediately prepare the meringue topping.

6. Whip the egg whites with the cream of tartar using electric beaters or in a stand mixer fitted with the whip attachment. Whip on medium speed until foamy, then increase the speed to high and gradually pour in the granulated sugar and icing sugar and continue whipping just until the whites hold a medium peak when the beaters are lifted.

7. Remove the plastic wrap from the hot lemon filling, then dollop half of the meringue directly onto the filling (the filling will still be very soft, so work gently). Be sure to spread the meringue with an offset spatula so that it completely covers the lemon filling and connects with the outside crust, then use a bamboo skewer or paring knife to swirl the meringue just a touch (this will secure it to the lemon curd). Dollop the remaining meringue onto the pie and use the back of your spatula to lift up the meringue and create spikes. Bake the pie for about 20 minutes at 325°F (160°C), until the meringue is nicely browned. Cool the meringue completely to room temperature on a cooling rack before chilling for at least 4 hours.

Adding the lemon juice at the end of cooking the curd filling ensures that it retains its fresh flavour, and also reduces the contact with the cooking cornstarch (its thickening power is reduced in the presence of an acid).

· · · · · · · ·

It is critical that the filling is hot when you spread the meringue over it. If it cools, the meringue will sweat, creating a liquid layer in between the filling and the meringue itself, causing the meringue to loosen and slide off the filling.

Be sure to spread the meringue so that it joins with the crust. This will also help to prevent a moisture layer from forming, which will prevent the meringue from shrinking as it cools and sliding off the filling.

· · · · · · · ·

If a meringue sweats or "beads" on top it can be a sign that the whites have been over-whipped or overbaked—or sometimes merely a sign of a humid day. The whipped whites should hold a medium peak when the beaters are lifted and should still appear glossy. Once baked, the meringue should be a light brown, but with a few white patches still visible.

Individual Coconut Cream Pies

*When I visit a diner or restaurant that is known for its homemade pies,
I usually order the coconut cream pie, to really put their pie-making skills to the test!
A homemade coconut filling is essential for success, and this one is a real winner.*

Makes 6 individual pies • Prep 1 hour • Bake/Cook 30 minutes plus chilling

1 | 1	recipe Pie Dough for Fluid Fillings (page 67), shaped into 2 logs and chilled

Coconut Cream Filling

1 | 1	398 mL can full-fat coconut milk
2 tsp | 10 mL	pure vanilla extract or vanilla bean paste
5 | 5	large egg yolks
⅓ cup | 70 g	granulated sugar
5 Tbsp | 48 g	cornstarch
3 Tbsp | 45 g	unsalted butter, at room temperature
1 Tbsp | 15 mL	rum (optional)
⅔ cup | 65 g	sweetened flaked coconut

Topping and Assembly

2 cups | 500 mL	whipping cream
3 Tbsp | 36 g	granulated sugar
2 Tbsp | 8 g	instant skim milk powder
1 tsp | 5 mL	pure vanilla extract
	lightly toasted sweetened flaked coconut, for garnish

1. Pull the dough from the fridge 20 minutes before you are ready to roll it. Slice each log into three and roll each piece out on a lightly floured work surface to just under ¼ inch (0.5 cm) thick. Lightly dust six 5-inch (12 cm) individual metal pie pans with flour and line the bottom and sides of each with pie dough, trimming the edges completely. Chill the pie shells for 20 minutes.

2. Preheat the oven to 400°F (200°C). Line a baking tray with parchment paper.

3. Remove the pie shells from the fridge, dock the bottom of each with a fork, and place an empty 5-inch (12 cm) metal pie pan inside each shell. Turn upside down and place on the prepared baking tray. (If you do not have spare pie pans, line each pie shell with aluminum foil and fill it with uncooked rice to weigh it down as it bakes.) Bake the shells for 8 minutes at 400°F (200°C), then reduce the oven temperature to 375°F (190°C) and bake for another 8–10 minutes until golden. Flip the pie shells right side up, remove the top pie pan, and let the shells cool in the original pans on a cooling rack.

4. For the coconut cream filling, heat the coconut milk and vanilla in a saucepan over medium heat until just below a simmer. Whisk the egg yolks, sugar, and cornstarch in a bowl and then slowly pour the hot coconut milk over them while whisking. Return the mixture to the saucepan and whisk over medium heat until the custard is thick and glossy, about 5 minutes. Pour this custard through a fine mesh sieve into a large bowl. Stir in the butter and rum (if using), then stir in the coconut. Place a sheet of plastic wrap directly on the surface of the custard, cool to room temperature on a cooling rack, then chill, still covered, until set, at least 3 hours.

5. To assemble, whip the cream to a soft peak and then whip in the sugar, skim milk powder, and vanilla.

6. Stir the coconut cream filling to soften (it will be quite firm) and then fold in ¾ cup (180 mL) of the whipped cream. Spoon this into the cooled tart shells and spread to level. Pipe or dollop the remaining whipped cream onto each pie and sprinkle each one with a little toasted coconut. Chill until ready to serve. The pies can be stored, refrigerated, for up to 2 days.

The technique of pre-baking pie shells by placing another pie plate on top, and then baking the shell upside down, is a professional baker's secret. If you have to bake 24 pies at a time, you likely don't have time to fuss with foil and raw rice, and you always have extra pie plates on hand. Baking the shells upside down when using glass pie plates also means that you can easily see when the bottom is baked and browned.

. . . .

Coconut milk makes a delicious base for this custard filling and means you don't need to use coconut extract (which I find reminds me more of suntan lotion than dessert!).

The skim milk powder stabilizes the whipped cream, so you can whip and decorate these pies up to two days ahead of time, and the whipped cream won't weep or collapse when you take your first bite.

. . . .

This recipe makes six cute individual pies, but the filling and topping will also fill a standard 9-inch (23 cm) pie, made with a single pie crust (half a recipe of the pie dough).

Blueberry Lattice-Top Pie

If you are really into making fruit pies, mastering a lattice-top pie should be on your to-do list. There's something about a lattice-top pie that somehow seems more personal—it shows it was made with love.

Makes one 9-inch (23 cm) pie • Serves 8 • Prep 50 minutes • Bake/Cook 65 minutes plus chilling

1 | 1	recipe Pie Dough for Fruit Fillings (page 66), chilled
4 cups | 1 L	fresh blueberries
1 | 1	medium tart apple, peeled and coarsely grated
1 cup | 200 g	granulated sugar
1 Tbsp | 15 mL	lemon or lime juice
1 tsp | 5 mL	lemon or lime zest
¼ tsp | 1 g	ground cinnamon
2 ½ Tbsp | 24 g	cornstarch
1 | 1	egg, whisked with 2 Tbsp (30 mL) water, for brushing
	turbinado or granulated sugar, for sprinkling

1. In a medium saucepan over medium heat, bring the blueberries, apple, sugar, citrus juice and zest, and cinnamon up to a simmer, stirring occasionally, until the blueberries are soft and tender, about 10 minutes. Whisk the cornstarch with a few tablespoons (30–45 mL) of cold water and add this to the blueberry filling, returning to a simmer while stirring until the filling has thickened and is glossy. Set aside to cool to room temperature. If making ahead, chill the filling, but bring it up to room temperature before baking into the pie.

2. Pull the dough from the fridge 15–30 minutes before you are ready to roll it. Preheat the oven to 400°F (200°C). Line a baking tray with parchment paper or aluminum foil.

3. On a lightly floured surface, roll out the first disc of dough into a circle just less than ¼ inch (0.5 cm) thick. Dust a 9-inch (23 cm) pie plate with flour and line the bottom and sides of the plate with the pastry, leaving the edges untrimmed. Spoon the blueberry filling into the crust.

4. Roll out the second disc of pastry slightly thinner than the bottom crust, about ⅛ inch (3 mm), and in more of a square shape. Use a knife or pastry wheel to cut long strips about ½ inch (1 cm) wide (you should have between 12 and 18 strips). Lay half of the strips over the blueberry pie filling, leaving a ½-inch (1 cm) gap between them. Gently lift alternating strips of pastry, folding them halfway back. Place a new strip of pastry perpendicular against where the strips are folded back, then fold those pieces over the newly laid strip. Now lift the opposite alternating strips and fold them back as far as they can go (to the edge of that newly laid strip) and place a second perpendicular strip beside them. Repeat this technique, moving toward one side of the pie shell, and then repeat toward the other side, until the top has a complete lattice top. Trim away the excess pastry and pinch the edges to create a fluted design. Brush the lattice top with the egg wash and sprinkle with sugar.

5. Place the pie dish on the prepared baking tray. Bake the pie for 10 minutes at 400°F (200°C), then reduce the oven temperature to 375°F (190°C) and bake for about another 40 minutes, until the pastry is golden brown. Cool the pie on a cooling rack to room temperature and then chill until ready to serve. The pie can be stored, refrigerated and uncovered, for 2 days.

Always place your fruit pies on a baking tray lined with parchment or foil when you bake them. You can never tell how juicy or drippy your pie will be, and I have yet to meet a person who enjoys scraping burned fruit and sugar from the bottom of their oven.

• • • • • • •

A cooked fruit filling like this one is popular in pie-making because pre-cooking and thickening the fruit before adding it to the pie crust ensures a consistent filling that isn't runny. Which means it will not seep through and ruin your beautiful flaky pastry crust.

Peach and Raspberry Custard Tart

*Most pastry shops have a version of this classic tart. A sweet dough is
topped with a pastry cream and fresh, colourful fruit. A glaze of melted jelly seals
in the fruit and adds that professional sparkle.*

Makes one 9-inch (23 cm) tart • Serves 8 • Prep 75 minutes • Bake/Cook 40 minutes plus chilling

1 | 1	recipe Pâte Sablée Dough (page 49), chilled
1 cup | 250 mL	milk, divided
1 tsp | 5 mL	pure vanilla extract
1 tsp | 5 mL	finely grated orange zest
2 Tbsp | 30 g	unsalted butter, at room temperature
3 | 3	large egg yolks
¼ cup | 50 g	granulated sugar
3 Tbsp | 36 g	cornstarch
1 Tbsp | 15 mL	orange liqueur or brandy (optional)
2 | 2	fresh peaches
1 cup | 250 mL	fresh raspberries
¼ cup | 60 mL	apple jelly

1. On a lightly floured work surface, gently knead the chilled dough just a little to soften, then roll it out to a circle about 12 inches (30 cm) across and ¼ inch (0.5 cm) thick. Carefully lift the pastry and line the bottom and sides of a 9-inch (23 cm) removable-bottom fluted tart pan. Press it into the pan, and trim away any excess dough. Chill the tart shell for 30 minutes.

2. Preheat the oven to 325°F (160°C). Line a baking tray with parchment paper or aluminum foil.

3. Place the chilled tart shell on the prepared baking tray and dock the bottom of the pastry with a fork. Bake the tart shell for about 20 minutes, until the edges just begin to brown. Cool the tart shell in the pan on a cooling rack to room temperature.

4. For the custard filling, bring all but 2 Tbsp (30 mL) of the milk, the vanilla, and the orange zest to just below a simmer in a medium saucepan over medium heat.

5. Place the butter in a large bowl and set a fine mesh sieve over the bowl, ready for when the custard has thickened.

6. In a separate bowl, whisk the egg yolks with the sugar, cornstarch, and remaining 2 Tbsp (30 mL) of milk. Slowly pour the hot milk into the egg mixture while whisking and then pour the entire mixture back into the saucepan. Whisk this over medium heat until the custard just comes to a boil, thickens, and becomes glossy, about 5 minutes. Remove the saucepan from the heat, strain the custard through the sieve, and stir until the butter is melted into the mixture. Add the liqueur (if using) and then cover with plastic wrap so that the wrap sits directly on the surface of the custard. Cool to room temperature, then chill, still covered, for at least 2 hours.

7. To assemble the tart, whisk the custard to soften it and then spread it evenly over the bottom of the cooled tart shell (leave the tart shell in the pan). Peel and slice the peaches and arrange them and the raspberries over the custard.

8. Melt the apple jelly in a small saucepan over medium-low heat, whisking until smooth. Brush the peaches and raspberries with the melted apple jelly and chill, uncovered, until ready to serve. Carefully remove the tart from the pan and place it on a serving platter before slicing. The tart is best served the day it is made, but can be stored, refrigerated, for up to 1 day.

Any fruit at its peak can be used to top this tart. What is important to keep in mind is that the fruits should be relatively tender and of a similar texture, so that when you slice the tart, it cuts easily without crushing through the custard and crust. You should also pick fruits that don't oxidize (brown) when cut. Think berries, peaches, pineapple, kiwi, mango, or even poached fruits (pears, apricots).

If your peaches are very firm, you may find them a challenge to peel. To remove the skins easily, blanch the peaches in hot water and then shock them in a bowl of ice water before peeling.

• • • • • • • •

Apple jelly works well as a glaze because it's clear and sets up nicely, with great shine. Alternatively, you could use currant or raspberry jelly for an all-berry tart, or heat and strain the pieces from apricot jam instead.

Warm Chocolate Orange Tarts

Imagine a soft but fluffy chocolate mousse–like filling, lightly scented with orange and baked into a delicate, crisp chocolate pastry. Hungry? Well, it's time to get baking, then!

Makes 8 individual tarts • Prep 45 minutes plus chilling • Bake/Cook 30 minutes

1 | 1	**recipe Chocolate Pastry Dough (page 26), shaped into a disc and chilled**
1 | 1	**egg white, lightly whisked**
3 | 3	**large eggs, separated**
½ cup | 100 g	**granulated sugar, divided**
1 tsp | 5 mL	**pure vanilla extract**
2 tsp | 10 mL	**finely grated orange zest**
¼ cup | 30 g	**Dutch process cocoa powder, sifted**
3 oz | 90 g	**bittersweet couverture/baking chocolate, melted (but still warm)**
2 Tbsp | 30 mL	**orange liqueur or orange juice**

1. Knead the chilled chocolate pastry dough once or twice on a lightly floured work surface to soften, then roll out the dough to a circle just less than ¼ inch (0.5 cm) thick. Cut circles of the pastry to line the bottom and sides of eight 4-inch (10 cm) fluted tart shells (removable-bottom shells are ideal), pressing the dough into the shells and trimming away any excess. Dock the pastry with a fork. Chill the tart shells for at least 20 minutes.

2. Preheat the oven to 350°F (180°C).

3. Place the chilled tart shells on a baking tray and bake them for about 18 minutes, until you see that the pastry has an even, dull finish. As soon as the tart shells come out of the oven, brush the surface of each shell with lightly whisked egg white (this creates a seal to prevent the filling from seeping in and making the crust soggy). Allow to cool while you prepare the filling. Leave the oven on.

4. For the filling, whip the remaining three egg whites until foamy then slowly add ¼ cup (50 g) of the sugar, whipping on high speed until the whites hold a soft peak when the beaters are lifted. Set aside.

5. Whip the three egg yolks with the remaining ¼ cup (50 g) of sugar, the vanilla, and orange zest by hand until pale and thick. Fold the egg whites into this yolk mixture. Gently whisk in the cocoa powder by hand, then whisk in the warm melted chocolate and orange liqueur (or juice). Pour this into the cooled tart shells and bake for about 8 minutes at 350°F/180°C, until the tarts just begin to lose their shine around the edges but the centre is still dark and glossy. Allow the tarts to cool in the pan on a cooling rack for 2 minutes before carefully removing them from their shells to serve warm.

6. Alternatively, you can prepare the filling, fill the tarts, and chill them, uncovered, until you're ready to bake. Simply add an additional 2–3 minutes to the baking time.

This is definitely the type of dessert you would see on a restaurant dessert menu. Try serving these with a sauce on the side: Crème Anglaise (page 286), Caramel Sauce (page 285), and Espresso Chocolate Sauce (page 284) all work well.

• • • • • • • •

I really like that you can fully assemble these tarts ahead of time and chill them until you're ready to bake. It's impressive to serve a freshly baked dessert at a dinner party, and here you get to take care of all of the work well ahead of time.

White Chocolate Cranberry Mousse Tart

This is a festive favourite of mine. A cranberry filling is nestled in a fluffy, white chocolate mousse set in a chocolate crumb crust. This is definitely one that will impress.

Makes one 9-inch (23 cm) tart • Serves 8 to 10
Prep 50 minutes • Bake/Cook 35 minutes plus chilling

Cranberry Compote

2 cups | 500 mL	fresh or frozen cranberries
½ cup | 125 mL	water
⅔ cup | 140 g	granulated sugar
2 tsp | 10 mL	finely grated orange zest
2 Tbsp | 30 mL	brandy (optional)
1 tsp | 5 mL	pure vanilla extract

Chocolate Crust

1 ½ cups | 185 g	chocolate cookie crumbs
¼ cup | 60 g	unsalted butter, melted

White Chocolate Mousse

8 oz | 240 g	chopped white couverture/baking chocolate
2 Tbsp | 30 g	unsalted butter
1 ¼ cups | 310 mL	milk
3 | 3	large egg yolks
3 Tbsp | 36 g	granulated sugar
2 Tbsp | 15 g	cornstarch
2 tsp | 3.5 g	unflavoured gelatin powder, softened in 3 Tbsp (45 mL) cold water
1 cup | 250 mL	whipping cream

Instead of making a tart, you could use this recipe to build beautiful cranberry and white chocolate mousse parfaits. Prepare and chill both the mousse and the cranberry compote, layer them in parfait glasses, and chill again until serving time.

· · · · · · · ·

The cranberry compote can also be used as a side with a slice of gingerbread cake (page 107) or baked onto brie or served on a cheese board.

1. For the cranberry compote, simmer the cranberries with the water, sugar, and orange zest in a medium saucepan over medium heat, stirring occasionally, for about 20 minutes, until the cranberries are tender and have "popped." Remove the saucepan from the heat, stir in the brandy and vanilla, and then cool to room temperature before chilling until ready to use.

2. Preheat the oven to 350°F (180°C).

3. For the crust, stir the cookie crumbs and butter together and press this mixture into an ungreased 9-inch (23 cm) fluted, removable-bottom tart pan. Bake the shell for 10 minutes and then cool.

4. For the white chocolate mousse, place the white chocolate and butter into a large bowl, and place a fine mesh sieve over top, then set aside. Heat the milk in a medium saucepan over medium heat to just below a simmer. In a separate bowl, whisk the egg yolks, sugar, and cornstarch together. Pour the hot milk into the egg mixture gradually, whisking constantly. Return the liquid to the saucepan and continue to whisk over medium heat until a glossy and thickened custard is created, about 4 minutes. Remove the pan from the heat and stir in the softened gelatin. Pour the custard mixture into the fine mesh sieve and strain over the white chocolate and butter. Whisk together until the chocolate and butter have melted completely into the custard. Cool to room temperature.

5. Whip the cream until it holds a soft peak and then fold it into the cooled chocolate mixture to create your chocolate mousse. Cover with plastic wrap and chill the mousse until set slightly but still soft, about 90 minutes.

6. To assemble the tart, spread half of the mousse over the bottom of the tart shell. Stir the chilled cranberry compote to loosen it and spoon it over the centre of the tart, spreading gently right to the edges. Spoon the remaining half of the mousse into a piping bag fitted with a large star tip and pipe it around the edge of the tart, creating a scalloped pattern. Chill the tart until ready to serve. The tart will keep, refrigerated, for up to 3 days.

Cakes

There is a reason this chapter has the most recipes. Cake is the cornerstone of a dessert kitchen, and as much fun and fulfillment comes from making them as eating them.

Perhaps you are someone who prefers to focus your attention on the outside of a cake with its decoration, and to challenge yourself with new techniques to develop your creativity and style. Or perhaps you are someone who is determined to master the richest chocolate cake or fluffiest angel food cake, or to combine a cake with fillings and frostings for a sumptuous result. Whatever your cake wish, you can make it happen here.

As with all of the chapters, the Simple recipes aren't just meant for beginner bakers, although if this is your first time making a cake from scratch, it is a smart place to start. These basic cakes are foundation recipes where the effort goes into the cake itself, rather than into fancy combinations of fillings and decoration. If a cake is frosted in this section, it will be a straight-forward process.

The Scrumptious cakes have a little more panache and are a little more challenging, and you will need to budget your baking time accordingly. These cakes build on some of the techniques from the Simple repertoire, so a novice baker should take some time to review those recipes before diving right in.

The Sensational cakes are showpieces, and ideal for a celebration when you really want to make the recipient feel special. They may take more time to make and assemble, but you will be rewarded with "ooh's" and "aah's" and the roar of applause as you present them at the table.

Simple

Scrumptious

Sensational

Zucchini Loaf with Orange

Zucchini is a bit of a chameleon in the kitchen.
Its neutral taste and soft texture help it to absorb other flavours.
It is one of only a few vegetables that can move easily from the savoury to the sweet kitchen.

Makes one 9- x 5-inch (2 L) loaf • Serves 12 to 16 • Prep 20 minutes • Bake 1 hour

½ cup | 125 mL	vegetable oil
2 | 2	eggs
1 cup | 200 g	granulated sugar
2 tsp | 10 mL	finely grated orange zest
1 tsp | 5 mL	pure vanilla extract
1 ½ cups | 225 g	all-purpose flour
1 tsp | 3 g	baking powder
¼ tsp | 1 g	baking soda
¼ tsp | 1 g	salt
1 ½ cups | 240 g	loosely packed, coarsely grated zucchini
½ cup | 90 g	chocolate chips (any kind) (optional)

1. Preheat the oven to 350°F (180°C). Grease a 9- x 5-inch (2 L) loaf pan and line it with parchment paper so that it comes up and over the sides.

2. Whisk the oil, eggs, sugar, zest, and vanilla together by hand in a large bowl.

3. In a separate bowl, sift the flour, baking powder, baking soda, and salt. Stir in the zucchini to coat it with the flour and add this to the wet mixture, stirring until blended. Stir in the chocolate chips (if using) and scrape the batter into the prepared pan.

4. Bake the loaf for 50–60 minutes, until a tester inserted in the centre comes out clean. Cool the loaf completely in the pan on a cooling rack before turning it out to slice. The loaf will keep, in an airtight container or wrapped in plastic wrap, for up to 3 days, and can be frozen for up to 3 months. Do not refrigerate.

Lemon and orange zests are interchangeable in recipes like this, where they are used as accent flavours. The choice is yours.

• • • • • • • •

Loaf cakes are part of a family called "quick cakes and breads" and they share a common method: the wet ingredients are combined in one bowl, dry ingredients are combined in another, and then the two are mixed together.

Classic Gingerbread Cake

This moist, fragrantly spiced cake is a fall staple for me. Since it doesn't have a frosting or filling, the best way to serve it is plated with a dollop of whipped cream.

Makes one 13- x 9-inch (33 x 23 cm) cake • Serves 18 to 24
Prep 20 minutes • Bake 45 minutes

1 cup | 225 g	unsalted butter, at room temperature
1 cup | 200 g	packed dark brown sugar
¾ cup | 195 g	fancy molasses
2 | 2	eggs, at room temperature
2 Tbsp | 30 mL	lemon juice
2 Tbsp | 30 mL	finely grated fresh ginger
2 ¼ cups | 335 g	all-purpose flour
½ tsp | 2 g	ground cinnamon
½ tsp | 2 g	ground cloves
½ tsp | 2 g	ground nutmeg
½ tsp | 2 g	ground allspice
½ tsp | 2 g	salt
½ cup | 125 mL	boiling water
½ tsp | 2 g	baking soda
2 Tbsp | 12 g	finely chopped crystallized ginger
	icing sugar, for dusting
	lightly sweetened whipped cream, for serving

Fancy molasses is a lighter, milder style of molasses that bakers prefer for cakes and cookies. Blackstrap molasses is darker in colour and is stronger, leaning toward bitter, and is used mostly in bread making.

1. Preheat the oven to 350°F (180°C). Grease a 13- x 9-inch (33 x 23 cm) baking pan.

2. Beat the butter and brown sugar by hand or using electric beaters until light and fluffy. Beat in the molasses, then add the eggs one at a time, beating well after each addition. Stir in the lemon juice and then the fresh ginger.

3. In a separate bowl, sift the flour with the spices and the salt. Add this to the butter mixture and stir until combined. Stir the boiling water into the baking soda and add this quickly to the batter, stirring well, and then stir in the crystallized ginger (the batter will be fluid). Scrape the batter into the prepared pan and bake for 45 minutes, until a tester inserted in the centre comes out clean. Cool the cake completely in the pan on a cooling rack and cut into squares to serve with a dusting of icing sugar and a dollop of whipped cream. The cake will keep, in an airtight container or wrapped in plastic wrap, for up to 3 days. Do not refrigerate.

Angel Food Cake

Whipped egg whites give angel food cake its angelic airiness. This is a fantastic make-ahead cake, since it stays moist for days. The simplicity of this cake is not only because it is presented without a filling or frosting, but also because of its technique. It is the perfect recipe for a novice baker to practise whipping egg whites, without other technical distractions.

Makes one 10-inch (25 cm) tube cake • Serves 12 to 16 • Prep 25 minutes • Bake 35 minutes

1 cup | 130 g	**cake and pastry flour**
1 cup | 200 g	**granulated sugar**
8 | 8	**egg whites, at room temperature**
½ tsp | 2 g	**cream of tartar**
⅛ tsp | 0.5 g	**salt**
½ cup | 65 g	**icing sugar, sifted**
½ tsp | 2 mL	**pure vanilla extract**
	whipped cream and berries, to serve

It may seem counterintuitive to not grease a cake pan, but an ungreased pan is very important for angel food cake. As the cake bakes and rises, the batter clings to and climbs the sides of the pan. If the pan were greased, the batter would slide down and the end result would be anything but angelic.

· · · · · · · · ·

Sifting the flour and sugar twice ensures that the flour will fold easily into the whipped egg whites without any lumps. The granulation of the sugar sifted with the flour keeps the flour from clumping together.

· · · · · · · ·

Cooling angel food cake upside down in its pan is key to its fluffy, light texture. When the cake is warm it is fragile. If left to cool upright, the cake would sink and collapse a little. When it is cooled upside down, the whipped egg whites are stretched downward so they hold their volume.

1. Preheat the oven to 325°F (160°C).

2. Sift the flour and granulated sugar twice into a large bowl and set aside.

3. Whip the egg whites with the cream of tartar and salt in a separate bowl, using electric beaters or in a stand mixer fitted with the whip attachment on high speed until foamy, then gradually add the icing sugar as you whip, whipping until the whites hold a medium peak when the beaters are lifted. Stir in the vanilla.

4. Add the flour to the whipped whites in two additions, using a handheld whisk to fold in the flour evenly and easily. Scrape the batter into a 10-inch (25 cm) ungreased tube pan, spread the batter to level it out, and bake for 30–35 minutes, until the cake springs back when gently pressed (try not to open the oven before 25 minutes).

5. Turn the cake pan upside down to cool the cake on a cooling rack, but do not remove the cake from the pan until completely cool to the touch. To remove, run an offset spatula carefully around the inside edge of the pan and very gently around the inner tube (so you do not tear the cake), invert the pan, and tap it on the counter until the cake comes out. Serve with whipped cream and berries, if you wish. The cake will keep, in an airtight container or wrapped in plastic wrap, for up to 4 days. Do not refrigerate.

Green Tea Genoise Sponge Cake

This classic sponge cake has the tasty addition of Matcha green tea powder to add a lovely flavour. You can frost it if you wish, but I think it is delectable on its own or with my Mango Coconut Salad (page 287): the airy texture melts on the tip of your tongue, leaving just a hint of green tea to savour.

Makes one 9-inch (23 cm) cake • Serves 12 to 16 • Prep 20 minutes • Bake 45 minutes

6	6	eggs
2	2	egg yolks
1 cup	200 g	granulated sugar
1 ¼ cups	180 g	all-purpose flour
1 Tbsp	15 mL	Matcha green tea powder
	pinch salt
¼ cup	60 g	unsalted butter, melted
1 tsp	5 mL	pure vanilla extract
	icing sugar, for dusting

Warming the eggs before whipping them increases their volume.

• • • • • • • •

To keep a sponge cake from drying out overnight, place a slice of bread on top of it, under the plastic wrap—just like you add bread to a canister of brown sugar to keep it soft and moist.

1. Preheat the oven to 350°F (180°C). Line the bottom of a 9-inch (23 cm) springform pan with parchment paper, but do not grease the pan.

2. Warm the eggs in their shells in hot tap water for about 5 minutes (change the water once halfway through warming). Whip the whole eggs and egg yolks with the sugar using electric beaters or in a stand mixer fitted with the whip attachment on high speed until the mixture is pale and holds a ribbon when the beaters are lifted, about 5 minutes. You can't overwhip whole eggs, so if in doubt, keep whipping!

3. Sift the flour, green tea powder, and salt together into a small bowl. Add the flour to the eggs gradually while whipping on medium-low speed. In a bowl, spoon a generous dollop of the batter into the melted butter, add the vanilla, and stir it all together (don't worry if it deflates a little). Add this buttered batter to the main batch of batter and fold it in by hand. Scrape the batter into the prepared pan and spread to level. Bake the cake for 40–45 minutes, until it is an even golden brown on top and springs back when gently pressed. The cake may dome a little at the end of its baking, but it will settle into a level state once it starts to cool. Cool the cake completely in its pan on a cooling rack.

4. To serve, run an offset spatula carefully around the inside edge of the pan to loosen the cake and remove the ring. Peel away the parchment from the bottom of the cake and place the cake on a platter. Dust with icing sugar. The sponge cake will keep, in an airtight container or wrapped in plastic wrap, for up to 3 days, or can be frozen up to 2 months. Do not refrigerate.

Classic Lemon Pound Cake

Pound cake is not at all heavy or dense, as its name implies. It is buttery and rich, but also tender and moist. Lemon is the classic pound cake, but you can take the lemon zest out of this recipe and skip the glaze to create an incredible vanilla pound cake instead.

Makes one 9- x 5-inch (2 L) loaf • Serves 16 • Prep 20 minutes • Bake 70 minutes

Cake

1 cup | 225 g	unsalted butter, just cooler than room temperature (60–65°F/15–18°C)
1 ½ cups | 300 g	granulated sugar
1 Tbsp | 15 mL	finely grated lemon zest
5 | 5	eggs, almost at room temperature
⅓ cup | 85 g	sour cream
1 ½ tsp | 7 mL	pure vanilla extract
1 cup | 150 g	all-purpose flour
½ cup | 65 g	cake and pastry flour
½ tsp | 2 g	salt

Glaze

3 Tbsp | 45 mL	fresh lemon juice
2 Tbsp | 30 mL	water
⅓ cup | 70 g	granulated sugar

1. Preheat the oven to 325°F (160°C). Grease a 9- x 5-inch (2 L) loaf pan.

2. Beat the butter, sugar, and lemon zest using electric beaters or in a stand mixer fitted with the paddle attachment on high speed until light and fluffy, about 3 minutes. In a separate bowl, lightly whisk the eggs with a fork and add them to the batter in a few additions, beating well and scraping down the bowl in between each addition. Stir the sour cream and vanilla together and beat this into the batter.

3. In a separate bowl, sift both flours and the salt. Add this to the batter, mixing until fully incorporated—scrape down to the bottom of the bowl to ensure this. Scrape the batter into the prepared pan and tap it a few times to make the batter level and allow any air bubbles to escape. Bake the cake for 65–70 minutes, until a tester inserted in the centre of the cake comes out clean. Remove the cake from the oven and prepare the glaze while the cake is still warm.

4. For the glaze, heat the lemon juice, water, and sugar in a small saucepan over medium heat until the sugar has dissolved. Poke holes in the warm pound cake using a bamboo skewer and brush the warm glaze over the cake. Let the cake cool completely in the pan (the glaze will set once the cake is cool) before removing to serve. The cake will keep, in an airtight container or wrapped in plastic wrap, for up to 3 days. Do not refrigerate.

A well-made pound cake is fluffy, yet with
a fine texture, tender, but not crumbly.
The keys to achieving this are having the butter
just cooler than room temperature and not
skimping on the initial step of beating the butter
and sugar—those 3 minutes on high speed
ensure a good structure to your cake.

If you are fond of making fancy, decorated
cakes that involve carving the cake to get curves
and details (almost like a sculpture), try using this
recipe. The cake isn't prone to crumbling and
because of its dense (but rich and tasty!)
texture, you can stack it quite high.

Classic Devil's Food Cake

To qualify as a devil's food cake (the antithesis to an angel food cake, page 108),
the cake should be very dark and rich in chocolate taste but still have a delicate, moist texture.
This cake meets all of those qualifications. More specifically, a devil's food cake
needs to include cocoa powder, baking soda, and hot coffee or water.

Makes one 2-layer 8-inch (20 cm) cake
Serves 10 to 12 • Prep 1 hour • Bake/Cook 30 minutes plus chilling

Chocolate Cake

1 ½ cups | 195 g	cake and pastry flour
1 ⅓ cups | 300 g	superfine (quick-dissolve) sugar
½ cup | 60 g	Dutch process cocoa powder
¾ tsp | 4 g	baking soda
¼ tsp | 1 g	salt
½ cup | 115 g	cool unsalted butter, cut into pieces
½ cup | 125 mL	hot, strongly brewed coffee
½ cup | 125 mL	milk
1 tsp | 5 mL	pure vanilla extract
2 | 2	eggs, at room temperature

Fudge Frosting

12 oz | 360 g	semisweet couverture/baking chocolate, chopped
1 ¾ cups | 440 mL	whipping cream
½ cup | 125 g	sour cream
½ tsp | 2 mL	pure vanilla extract
	pinch salt

1. Preheat the oven to 350°F (180°C). Grease two 8-inch (20 cm) cake pans and line the bottoms with parchment paper. Dust the sides of the pans with flour, tapping out any excess.

2. For the cake, sift the flour, sugar, cocoa powder, baking soda, and salt into a large mixing bowl. Using electric beaters or in a stand mixer fitted with the paddle attachment, cut in the butter, starting on low speed and gradually increasing to medium speed until the mixture is a fine crumble (like the texture of fine breadcrumbs) and no large pieces of butter are visible.

3. Stir the hot coffee, milk, and vanilla together and add them all at once to the flour mixture, mixing until smooth. Break the eggs into a small dish, stir them with a fork to break the yolks, and then add them to the batter, mixing on medium speed just until smooth (the batter will be very fluid). Divide the batter evenly between the prepared pans and tap them on the counter to eliminate any air bubbles.

4. Bake the cakes for about 30 minutes, until a tester inserted in the centre of the cake comes out clean. Cool the cakes for 20 minutes in their pans on a cooling rack, then tip them out onto the rack to cool completely to room temperature. The cakes can be baked a day ahead and stored, in an airtight container or wrapped in plastic wrap, at room temperature before frosting.

5. For the frosting, place the chocolate and cream in a metal bowl and place it over a saucepan of barely simmering water. Stir the chocolate and cream occasionally and gently until all the chocolate has melted and the mixture is smooth. Remove the bowl from the heat and whisk in the sour cream, vanilla, and salt. Let the mixture cool completely to room temperature, stirring occasionally (you can chill the mixture for just a few minutes to start it setting, then let it continue to cool naturally at room temperature). Once cooled to a thicker consistency, whisk by hand to thicken just into a spreadable consistency (do not whip it vigorously or with electric beaters).

6. Place the first cake layer on your serving plate and, if necessary, trim it to level it. Spread a generous layer of the frosting over the top of the cake. Trim the second cake, if necessary, and place it on top of the first layer. Spread the frosting over the top and then the sides of the cake, using a swirling motion with your spatula to create a nice design. Chill the cake for at least 2 hours before serving. The cake will keep, refrigerated in an airtight container, for up to 3 days.

A rich, moist chocolate cake is an excellent foundation recipe for bakers to master because of its universal appeal and versatility. You can switch up the fillings and frostings to suit your tastes, or those of the person you are making it for.

. . . .

I find that using superfine sugar (also called fruit sugar or caster sugar) works well for this cake recipe, making it come out fine and delicate, with little crumbling. If you don't have superfine sugar on hand, don't panic (or run out to the store just for that) as you can pulse granulated sugar in a food processor to make it finer.

. . . .

To keep this frosting dense and fudgy, take care not to overmix it, but if you are looking for more of a classic, whipped chocolate frosting, then do beat it well. It will turn lighter in colour, however, losing its "devilishly" dark intensity.

Classic Raspberry Jelly Roll

A jelly roll cake is a flexible sponge cake that has a filling and is rolled up. You do need a jelly roll pan for this. It is a baking tray with at least a ½-inch (1 cm) lip to hold in the cake batter. The key to jelly roll success is to roll up the cake while it is warm and flexible, so that it holds its shape and does not crack when unrolled to be filled.

Makes one 10-inch (25 cm) jelly roll cake • Serves 12 to 16
Prep 35 minutes plus cooling • Bake 12 minutes

4 | 4	eggs, separated and at room temperature
¼ cup | 30 g	icing sugar, sifted, plus extra for dusting
1 tsp | 5 mL	pure vanilla extract
⅛ tsp | 0.5 g	salt
2 Tbsp | 25 g	granulated sugar
¾ cup | 100 g	cake and pastry flour
⅔ cup | 160 mL	raspberry jam

1. Preheat the oven to 350°F (180°C). Line the bottom of a 15- x 10-inch (38 x 25 cm) jelly roll pan with parchment paper.

2. Whip the egg yolks and icing sugar using electric beaters or in a stand mixer fitted with the whip attachment on high speed until the yolks have doubled in volume and hold a ribbon when the beater is lifted, about 4 minutes. Whip in the vanilla.

3. In a separate bowl, whip the egg whites with the salt on low speed until foamy. Increase the speed to high and pour in the granulated sugar, whipping until the whites hold a medium peak.

4. Sift half of the flour into the yolk mixture and fold in using a handheld whisk. Fold in half of the whipped egg whites. Repeat with the remaining flour, and then change to a spatula to fold in the last of the whites until evenly incorporated. Spread the batter into the prepared pan, taking time to ensure the batter is level.

5. Bake the cake for about 12 minutes, until the cake springs back when gently pressed in the centre. Let the cake cool for about 2 minutes in the pan on a cooling rack, then loosen the sides with a spatula. Sift a layer of icing sugar over the surface of the cake and cover with a clean tea towel. Place a second pan (it can be any pan or even a cutting board of similar size to the jelly roll pan) over the towel and quickly invert it, removing the pan it was baked in. Peel off the parchment paper and dust the exposed surface with icing sugar. Roll the cake up from the short side, using the towel to help you, and let it cool completely (cooling it in its rolled position sets its "memory" so the cake won't crack once filled).

6. Stir the raspberry jam to soften it. Unroll the cake and spread an even layer of jam over the cake. Roll the cake back up again and dust the top with icing sugar. Cover and store at room temperature until ready to serve. The cake can be prepared up to a day in advance and stored in an airtight container or wrapped in plastic wrap. Do not refrigerate.

The flexibility in a jelly roll (also called Swiss roll) cake is all due to the eggs. Whipped eggs are very flexible while they're warm, so they can be rolled and moulded easily.

• • • • • • •

Raspberry jam is the classic jelly roll filling, but of course other jam flavours can be used, such as strawberry, apricot, or even marmalade. If your jam has bits of fruit in it, purée it a little before spreading it onto the cake so that it spreads evenly.

Classic New York Cheesecake

New York–style cheesecake is decadently rich in taste, but fluffy in texture.
It is also distinguished by the generous amount of sour cream used in the recipe.

Makes one 9-inch (23 cm) cheesecake • Serves 12 to 16
Prep 25 minutes • Bake 85 minutes plus chilling

Crust

1 cup | 125 g	graham cracker crumbs
2 Tbsp | 25 g	granulated sugar
¼ cup | 60 g	unsalted butter, melted, plus extra for greasing the pan.

Cheesecake

4 cups | 1 kg	cream cheese, at room temperature
1 ⅓ cups | 270 g	granulated sugar
3 Tbsp | 22 g	cornstarch
2 tsp | 10 mL	pure vanilla extract
2 tsp | 10 mL	finely grated lemon zest
3 | 3	eggs
1 | 1	egg yolk
1 ½ cups | 375 g	sour cream, divided
2 tsp | 10 mL	fresh lemon juice

1. Preheat the oven to 350°F (180°C).

2. For the crust, stir the graham crumbs, sugar, and melted butter in a bowl until evenly combined, then press them into the bottom of an ungreased 9-inch (23 cm) springform pan. Bake for 10 minutes, then cool. Brush the insides of the pan with a little melted butter.

3. For the cheesecake, increase the oven temperature to 400°F (200°C). Beat the cream cheese using electric beaters or in a stand mixer fitted with the paddle attachment on high speed until light and fluffy. Add 1 ¼ cups (250 g) of the sugar a little at a time, beating well between each addition and scraping the sides and bottom of the bowl often. Beat in the cornstarch, vanilla, and lemon zest. Beat in the eggs one at a time, on a lower speed, scraping down the bowl after each addition, then beat in the yolk. Still on low speed, beat in half of the sour cream. Scrape this over the cooled crust.

4. Bake the cheesecake for 10 minutes. Reduce the oven temperature to 225°F (105°C) and bake for 35 more minutes. Turn off the oven and leave the cheesecake in there for 1 hour, cracking the oven door after 30 minutes. While the cheesecake is baking, prepare the sour cream layer.

5. Stir the remaining sour cream with the remaining sugar and the lemon juice. Spread this over the top of the cheesecake as soon as it has come out of the oven. Allow the cheesecake to cool completely to room temperature, then carefully run a spatula around the outside of the cheesecake to loosen it from the pan and chill the cheesecake for at least 6 hours, or overnight, before slicing and serving. The cheesecake will keep, refrigerated, for up to 4 days.

For a cheesecake that doesn't crack,
two steps are key:

1. When adding the eggs, be sure to mix them
in on a low speed, so as not to aerate them.

2. Make sure the cheesecake is cooled completely to room temperature before chilling. The gradual
temperature change will keep the cheesecake from getting "shocked" and contracting.

That said, the special step of a finishing layer of sweetened sour cream spread on top of the cake would
hide any cracks that might develop. No one will know (and I won't tell a soul!).

Blood Orange Syrup Cake

*Cornmeal and ground almonds give this cake its structure and great texture
without the use of wheat flour. Soaking the cornmeal in hot milk plumps it up,
so there isn't the coarseness you might find in a traditional cornmeal-based cake.*

Makes one 9-inch (23 cm) cake • Serves 12 • Prep 20 minutes • Bake/Cook 45 minutes

Cake

1 cup | 250 mL	milk
½ cup | 115 g	unsalted butter
1 cup | 165 g	cornmeal
1 cup | 200 g	granulated sugar
4 | 4	eggs, at room temperature
2 tsp | 10 mL	finely grated blood orange zest
1 cup | 120 g	ground almonds
2 tsp | 6 g	baking powder (gluten-free, if necessary)
¼ tsp | 1 g	salt
	pinch ground cinnamon

Syrup

½ cup | 125 mL	blood orange juice (about 2 oranges)
½ cup | 100 g	granulated sugar

*I do enjoy cornmeal cakes and cornbread, but it's
a recent trick of mine to let the cornmeal soak in a
liquid first for a few minutes. It really does make
a difference in terms of a nicely textured cake
and also one that holds together.*

• • • • • • • •

*You'll be impressed by how moist and light
this cake is—and with no crumbling. I like to
serve a slice of it on its own, or with a dollop of
whipped cream and some fresh fruit.*

1. Preheat the oven to 350°F (180°C). Grease a 9-inch (23 cm) springform pan.

2. Heat the milk and butter in a saucepan over medium-low heat until the butter has melted. Place the cornmeal in a large mixing bowl and pour the milk-butter mix over it, whisking by hand as you add it (it will thicken up quickly). Whisk in the sugar and add the eggs one at a time, whisking after each addition. Stir in the zest.

3. In a separate bowl, stir the ground almonds with the baking powder, salt, and cinnamon and add this to the batter, stirring until blended. Pour the batter into the prepared pan and bake for about 45 minutes, until a tester inserted in the centre of the cake comes out clean.

4. To make the syrup, bring the blood orange juice and sugar to a full boil over medium-high heat. While the cake is still hot from the oven, poke holes in it with a bamboo skewer and then spoon the syrup over it (the syrup will soak in quickly). Allow the cake to cool to room temperature in the pan on a cooling rack before serving. The cake will keep, in an airtight container or wrapped in plastic wrap, at room temperature for 3 days. Do not refrigerate.

Citrus Madeleines

*Madeleines are lovely shell-shaped individual sponge cakes.
A properly made madeleine has a little bump in its centre, called "la bosse."
I've included a few easy techniques in the method to help you achieve this.
To make this recipe, you will need two madeleine pans, available at most kitchen stores.*

Makes 24 madeleines • Prep 20 minutes plus chilling • Bake/Cook 17 minutes

3 | 3	eggs, at room temperature
¾ cup | 150 g	granulated sugar
2 tsp | 10 mL	finely grated orange or lemon zest
1 tsp | 5 mL	pure vanilla extract
1 cup | 150 g	all-purpose flour
2 tsp | 6 g	baking powder
½ cup | 115 g	unsalted butter, melted (still warm)
¼ cup | 60 mL	milk
1 Tbsp | 15 mL	vegetable oil

The aroma of madeleines baking is truly something to be experienced. Because they are individual cakes, the surface area of the pan browns the cakes, emanating a brown butter scent that wafts through the house, enticing everyone to come to the kitchen. If I am making these for a dinner party, I prepare the batter a day ahead and then bake them right before I plan to serve them.

• • • • • • • •

Whereas a ladyfinger recipe also uses a sponge batter, bakes up more like a biscuit or cookie (and you can find the recipe in the cookie chapter, page 54), and can be used in other recipes, a madeleine maintains its identity. It is a soft, buttery cake and is enjoyed just as it is.

1. Whip the eggs with the sugar, zest, and vanilla using electric beaters or in a stand mixer fitted with the whip attachment on high speed until the eggs are thick and pale and hold a ribbon when the beaters are lifted, about 3 minutes.

2. Sift the flour and baking powder together and add this to the eggs while beating on medium-low speed, mixing until combined. In a separate bowl, whisk the butter, milk, and oil together. Spoon about 1 cup (250 mL) of the batter into the butter and whisk it in. Add all this back to the base batter and fold in until blended. Cover and chill the batter for 2 hours to set the butter.

3. Preheat the oven to 375°F (190°C). Lightly grease and flour two madeleine pans, tapping out any excess flour.

4. Stir the chilled madeleine batter gently to deflate it slightly (this is key to getting the little bump that a well-made madeleine has) and with an ice cream scoop or a piping bag fitted with a plain tip, fill the madeleine moulds three-quarters full. Bake the madeleines for 10 minutes, then bang the pans down (again, for the bump) before returning to the oven for another 5–7 minutes, until the madeleines are golden brown at the edges. Remove the madeleines from the pan immediately and enjoy warm or at room temperature. Madeleines are best enjoyed the day they are baked.

Warm Maple Almond Chiffon Cakes

These chiffon cakes can be made ahead and served at room temperature, but they are really something special when plated and served warm with a little warm Espresso Chocolate Sauce (page 284).

Makes 8 individual cakes • Prep 20 minutes • Bake/Cook 30 minutes

4 | 4	egg whites, cold
½ cup | 125 mL	pure maple syrup
⅓ cup | 70 g	packed light brown sugar
¼ cup | 60 mL	vegetable oil
3 | 3	egg yolks
1 tsp | 5 mL	pure vanilla extract
1 cup | 120 g	ground almonds
3 Tbsp | 22 g	tapioca starch (available at bulk and health food stores)
¼ tsp | 1 g	salt
	icing sugar, for dusting

1. Preheat the oven to 325°F (160°C). Place eight ungreased 10-ounce (300 mL) ramekins or other similar baking dishes on a baking tray.

2. Whip the egg whites using electric beaters or in a stand mixer fitted with the whip attachment on high speed until foamy.

3. In a saucepan over high heat, boil the maple syrup until it reaches 240°F (115°C), about 2 minutes. Remove the saucepan from the heat and carefully pour the syrup into the whites while whipping them on medium speed (pour the syrup down the side of the bowl to avoid splashing), then increase the speed to high and whip the whites until they hold a stiff peak. Set aside.

4. Whip the brown sugar, oil, egg yolks, and vanilla in a separate bowl using electric beaters or in the clean bowl of a stand mixer fitted with the whip attachment on high speed, until thick and creamy. Stir in the ground almonds and tapioca starch, blending in well.

5. Fold one-third of the whipped whites into the batter and then, once just incorporated, fold in the remaining two-thirds. Divide the batter evenly between the eight ramekins and bake for 25–30 minutes, until the cakes spring back when gently pressed. Turn the ramekins upside down to cool them for about 15 minutes if serving warm.

6. To serve, tap each cake out onto a plate. Serve warm, dusted with icing sugar and with a spoonful of warm Espresso Chocolate Sauce (page 284) on the side. The cakes can be prepared up to a day in advance, but should be removed from the ramekins after cooling, and stored, wrapped in plastic wrap, at room temperature.

When baking without wheat flour, the protein (gluten) present in wheat flour that lends structure to baked goods needs replacing. In this case, boiling maple syrup thickens it and cooks the egg whites when it is added, making the whipped whites stable and strong, so that the cake holds its fluffy texture.

• • • • • • • •

Tapioca starch is a common ingredient in gluten-free baking. It has a stronger binding power than cornstarch and is neutral in taste, so doesn't impact flavour in your treats.

Victoria Sponge

This English sponge cake layered with cream and fresh strawberries is a true classic.
It is best enjoyed the day it is assembled, so factor that into your planning.

Makes one 2-layer 9-inch (23 cm) cake
Serves 10 to 12 • Prep 40 minutes • Bake 40 minutes plus chilling

Sponge Cake

6 | 6	eggs, at room temperature
1 cup | 200 g	granulated sugar
1 tsp | 5 mL	finely grated lemon zest
1 Tbsp | 15 mL	fresh lemon juice
1 cup | 150 g	all-purpose flour
¼ tsp | 1 g	salt
2 Tbsp | 30 g	unsalted butter, melted
1 tsp | 5 mL	pure vanilla extract

Cream and Berries

1 ½ cups | 375 mL	whipping cream
½ cup | 125 g	cream cheese, at room temperature
⅓ cup | 70 g	granulated sugar
2 Tbsp | 30 mL	fresh lemon juice
½ tsp | 2 mL	lemon zest
1 tsp | 5 mL	pure vanilla extract or vanilla bean paste
3 cups | 750 mL	hulled and sliced fresh strawberries
⅓ cup | 80 mL	good-quality strawberry jam icing sugar, for dusting

1. Preheat the oven to 325°F (160°C). Line the bottom of a 9-inch (23 cm) springform pan with parchment paper, but do not grease the pan.

2. Whip the eggs and sugar using electric beaters or in a stand mixer fitted with the whip attachment on high speed until they are almost white in colour, have more than tripled in volume, and hold a ribbon when the beaters are lifted, about 5 minutes. While mixing on medium speed, add the lemon zest and juice.

3. Sift the flour and salt and, still mixing on medium speed, add this to the bowl. Spoon about 1 cup (250 mL) of the batter into a bowl, and stir in the melted butter and vanilla. Add this all back to the main batter and stir until blended. Pour the batter into the prepared pan and bake for about 40 minutes, until the centre of the cake springs back when gently pressed. Cool the cake completely in the pan on a cooling rack.

4. For the cream, whip the cream using electric beaters or in a stand mixer fitted with the whip attachment on high speed until it holds a soft peak when the beaters are lifted. In a separate bowl, beat the cream cheese by hand to soften it, and beat in the sugar, lemon juice, zest, and vanilla. Fold in the whipped cream in two additions. Chill until ready to assemble.

5. When ready to assemble the cake, stir the berries with the jam to coat them. Run an offset spatula around the inside edge of the cake pan to loosen it, then remove it from the pan and peel off the parchment paper. Slice the cake in half horizontally. Spread half of the cream over the cake and top with half of the berries. Place the top of the cake over the berries, and top this with the remaining cream and berries, leaving an inch or two of the cake exposed around the outside edge. Dust this edge with icing sugar and chill until ready to serve. The cake can be assembled up to 4 hours in advance and refrigerated. The cake can be made (up to the end of step 3) up to a day in advance and stored, wrapped in plastic wrap, at room temperature.

A basic sponge cake recipe is an important foundation recipe to master because, just like a rich chocolate cake (page 114), it gives you the flexibility to play with the fillings and toppings of your choosing. Keep in mind that a light and airy sponge cake suits fillings and frostings of a similar light and airy texture—like the whipped cream used here, or the Fruit Mousse of the Fraisier Torte (page 148). Something dense like a fudge frosting would crush sponge cake and mismatch its delicate texture.

Adding softened cream cheese to the whipped cream filling helps stabilize it so that it doesn't shift or collapse. It also lends a hint of a cheesecake flavour to the dessert as a whole—a bonus perk!

• • • • • • • •

Local strawberries have such a brief season that they need to be celebrated! A cake like this makes them a star ingredient—just like you will be a star when you present this at the table.

Red Velvet Cake

To qualify as a red velvet cake, the cake's ingredients must include cocoa powder, buttermilk, white vinegar, and baking soda. The vibrant red colour is achieved with food colouring, but I also provide a natural variation using beets that results in more of a pink-hued cake.

Makes one 2-layer 8-inch (20 cm) square cake • Serves 10 to 12
Prep 50 minutes • Bake 35 minutes plus chilling

Cake

⅔ cup | 150 g	**unsalted butter, at room temperature**
2 cups | 400 g	**granulated sugar**
2 | 2	**eggs, at room temperature**
2 tsp | 10 mL	**pure vanilla extract**
2 ½ cups | 375 mL	**all-purpose flour**
¼ cup | 30 g	**regular cocoa powder (not Dutch process)**
1 tsp | 5 g	**baking soda**
½ tsp | 1.5 g	**baking powder**
¼ tsp | 1 g	**salt**
1 ½ cups | 375 mL	**buttermilk, at room temperature**
1 ½ Tbsp | 22 mL	**white vinegar**
1 tsp | 5 mL	**red food colouring paste (page 129)**

Cream Cheese Frosting

1 cup | 225 g	**unsalted butter, at room temperature**
1 ½ cups | 375 g	**cream cheese, at room temperature**
4 cups | 520 g	**icing sugar, sifted**
1 ½ tsp | 7 mL	**pure vanilla extract**

1. Preheat the oven to 350°F (180°C). Grease two 8-inch (20 cm) square pans and line them with parchment paper so that it comes up and over the sides.

2. Beat the butter using electric beaters or in a stand mixer fitted with the paddle attachment on medium-high speed until smooth. Add the sugar and beat until light and fluffy. Add the eggs one at a time, beating well after each addition, scraping the sides of the bowl if needed, and then beat in the vanilla.

3. In a separate bowl, sift the flour, cocoa powder, baking soda, baking powder, and salt. Add this alternately with the buttermilk, starting and ending with the flour. Stir the white vinegar and food colouring together and add this to the cake batter while you continue to beat on low speed. Mix until it's well combined. Scrape the batter into the prepared pans and spread to level it out.

4. Bake the cakes for about 35 minutes, or until a tester inserted in the centre of the cakes comes out clean. Cool the cakes in their pans on a cooling rack for 20 minutes, then turn them out onto the rack to cool completely.

5. For the frosting, whip the butter using electric beaters or in a stand mixer fitted with the paddle attachment on high speed until fluffy, then beat in the cream cheese until well blended and smooth. Add the icing sugar in two additions, beating first on low speed and then increasing the speed. Beat in the vanilla.

6. To assemble the cake, place the first layer of cake on your platter or plate and spread a generous amount of frosting on top. Top this with the second cake layer and frost the top and then the sides. Use your spatula to create any swirls or patterns you wish, then chill for at least 2 hours before slicing to serve. The cake will keep, refrigerated, for up to 3 days.

For an alternative to red food colouring paste, replace ¼ cup (60 mL) of the buttermilk
with ⅓ cup (25 g) of finely grated raw beets. Stir the beets in with the buttermilk and
follow the recipe as above. This version will have more of a muted pink tone than a
vibrant red, but the taste and texture of the cake will be the same.

· · · · · · · ·

This recipe can also be baked into 18 cupcakes.
Bake them for about 20 minutes at 350°F (180°C).

Carrot Cake with Cream Cheese Frosting

Carrot cake has become increasingly popular for birthday cakes and wedding cakes, often surpassing the big three: chocolate, vanilla, and lemon. With its moist texture, hint of spice, and, of course, rich cream cheese frosting, I can understand why.

Makes one 2-layer 9-inch (23 cm) cake
Serves 12 to 16 • Prep 45 minutes • Bake/Cook 30 minutes plus chilling

Cake

¾ cup | 180 mL	vegetable oil
3 | 3	eggs
1 cup | 200 g	packed light brown sugar
½ cup | 100 g	granulated sugar
1 tsp | 5 mL	pure vanilla extract
2 cups | 300 g	all-purpose flour
2 tsp | 6 g	baking powder
½ tsp | 2 g	baking soda
½ tsp | 2 g	salt
1 tsp | 3 g	ground cinnamon
½ tsp | 2 g	ground allspice
¼ tsp | 1 g	ground cloves
2 cups | 150 g	loosely packed, finely grated carrot
¾ cup | 100 g	lightly toasted walnut pieces or raisins (optional)
1 | 1	recipe Cream Cheese Frosting (page 128)
	lightly toasted walnut pieces, for garnish

1. Preheat the oven to 350°F (180°C). Grease two 9-inch (23 cm) round cake pans and line the bottoms with parchment paper.

2. For the cake, whisk the oil, eggs, both sugars, and vanilla by hand in a large bowl until well combined.

3. In a separate bowl, sift together the flour, baking powder, baking soda, salt, cinnamon, allspice, and cloves. Stir in the grated carrot and coat it with the flour (this will help extract the most colour). Add this to the wet mixture and stir until evenly blended (the batter will be wet). Stir in the walnut pieces or raisins, if using. Divide this between the two pans and bake the cakes for 25–30 minutes, until a tester inserted in the centre of the cake comes out clean. Cool the cakes for 30 minutes in their pans on a cooling rack, then turn them out onto the rack to cool completely, leaving the parchment on until cool.

4. Prepare the cream cheese frosting (page 128) to use at room temperature.

5. To assemble the cake, peel the parchment paper from the cake layers and place one layer on a plate or platter. Spread the top with a generous layer of frosting and top with the second cake. Frost the top and sides of the cakes, using a spatula to create swirls in the frosting. Sprinkle a few walnut pieces on the top of the cake as a garnish, or press some onto the sides of the cake. The cake will keep, refrigerated, for up to 3 days.

Most of the recipes flagged as Foundation in this book feature fundamental preparations you can use and adapt in other baking, while some others are just all-round favourites that are great for you to have in your repertoire for any occasion. A good carrot cake recipe definitely fits into that favourite category. I love carrot cake because it can be served as dessert after a nice dinner, it's a popular choice for birthday cake, or it's even a top choice as a wedding cake flavour.

A really good carrot cake is something you'll never regret mastering how to bake.

If using a box grater for your carrots, grate them finely (as opposed to using the coarse side of the grater, as is often called for in carrot cake recipes). By doing this, plus tossing the carrots with the flour, you'll get a cake with an even and bright orange hue to it.

• • • • • • • •

It is typical for vegetable cakes such as this to be made using vegetable oil, as opposed to butter. A neutral oil, such as canola, sunflower, or grapeseed, is best, so that it doesn't overpower the cake as an olive oil would. You could even use melted virgin coconut oil if you wish, in the same measure.

Tart Lemon Roulade

"Roulade" is the French term for a jelly roll or Swiss roll cake (page 116),
but in this recipe I kick the shape up a notch—it's heart-shaped. A simple and rich lemon
mascarpone mousse filling provides the finishing touch. You will need a jelly roll pan for this
recipe—a baking tray with at least a ½-inch (1 cm) lip to hold in the cake batter.

Makes one 10-inch (30 cm) roulade • Serves 10
Prep 50 minutes plus cooling • Bake 15 minutes plus chilling

Roulade

2 | 2	eggs
1 | 1	egg yolk
9 Tbsp | 135 g	granulated sugar
1 tsp | 5 mL	finely grated lemon zest
2 | 2	egg whites, at room temperature
⅛ tsp | 0.5 g	salt
⅔ cup | 90 g	cake and pastry flour
	icing sugar, for dusting

Lemon Mousse

1 ¼ cups | 310 mL	whipping cream
¼ cup | 60 g	granulated sugar
2 tsp | 10 mL	finely grated lemon zest
1 cup | 250 g	mascarpone cheese
¼ cup | 60 mL	fresh lemon juice

I use this lemon mascarpone filling for traditional cakes, too. It sets up nicely, is rich, and, since it doesn't require cooking like other cake fillings (pastry cream, for example), I can make it right before I'm ready to assemble my cake.

• • • • • • • •

It's important to leave the cake uncovered with the filling at each end. As you shape the roulade, the filling will shift and you'll need that extra cake to fold in to get a clearly defined heart shape.

1. Preheat the oven to 375°F (190°C). Line a 15- x 10-inch (38 x 25 cm) jelly roll pan with parchment paper, then grease and dust the parchment with flour, tapping out any excess.

2. For the cake, whisk the whole eggs, egg yolk, ¼ cup (60 g) of the sugar, and the lemon zest in a metal bowl placed over a saucepan of gently simmering water until it is just warmer than body temperature (test by dabbing a little on the inside of your wrist). Remove the bowl from the heat and whip the eggs using electric beaters or in a stand mixer fitted with the whip attachment on high speed until they have doubled in volume, about 4 minutes.

3. Whip the egg whites and salt in a separate, clean bowl using electric beaters or in a stand mixer fitted with the whip attachment on low speed until they are foamy. Increase the speed to high, gradually adding the remaining 5 Tbsp (75 g) of sugar as you whip. Continue to whip until the whites hold a medium peak when the beaters are lifted.

4. Sift the flour over the whipped whole egg mixture. Fold it in using a whisk, then fold in the whipped whites in two additions. Spread this mixture in the prepared pan, being sure that the batter is level. Bake the cake for about 10 minutes, until it springs back when gently pressed.

5. Let the cake cool in the pan for about 2 minutes on a cooling rack, then loosen the sides with a spatula. Sift a layer of icing sugar over the surface of the cake and cover it with a clean tea towel. Place a second pan (it can be any pan or even a cutting board of similar size to the jelly roll pan) over the towel and quickly invert the cake, removing the pan it was baked in. Peel off the parchment paper and dust the exposed surface with icing sugar. Roll the two short sides of the cake in toward the centre with the towel (you can rest the cake on one side to get it to stay in place better) and let it cool this way to set its "memory" so it won't crack once filled.

6. For the mousse, whip 1 cup (250 mL) of the whipping cream until it holds a soft peak.

7. Stir the remaining ¼ cup (60 mL) of cream and the sugar and lemon zest into the mascarpone cheese by hand, until the sugar has dissolved. Fold in the whipped cream and the lemon juice and chill until ready to assemble.

8. Carefully unroll the jelly roll cake and remove the tea towel. Spread the mousse over the cake, but leave 2 inches (5 cm) clear at both of the short ends. Roll both the short ends back toward the middle and press them gently to create a heart shape. You can then gently press from the centre of the cake down to create the point at the bottom of the heart. Wrap the roulade loosely in plastic wrap and chill it on its side until ready to serve. When ready to serve, dust with icing sugar and slice the roulade, plating it to show off the heart shape. The roulade will keep, refrigerated, for up to 2 days.

Molten Centre Chocolate Cakes

Everyone loves this cake, especially when that warm chocolate centre oozes out after the first cut with your fork. And the secret to a flowing centre EVERY time is right here!

Makes 4 individual cakes • Prep 15 minutes plus chilling • Bake/Cook 15 minutes

Chocolate Ganache

¼ cup | 60 mL	whipping cream
2 oz | 60 g	bittersweet couverture/baking chocolate, chopped

Molten Cakes

½ cup | 115 g	unsalted butter, cut into pieces
4 oz | 120 g	bittersweet couverture/baking chocolate, chopped
2 | 2	eggs, at room temperature
2 | 2	egg yolks, at room temperature
¼ cup | 60 g	granulated sugar
2 Tbsp | 15 g	cocoa powder
	icing sugar, for dusting (optional)

1. For the ganache, heat the cream until it just begins to simmer and then pour it over the chopped chocolate. Let it sit for a minute, then gently stir with a spatula, starting at the centre and widening the circles until the chocolate has fully melted and the ganache is smooth. Chill until firm, about 2 hours.

2. Preheat the oven to 425°F (220°C). Grease four 5-ounce (150 mL) ramekins, coat the insides with sugar, shaking out any excess, and place them on a baking tray.

3. For the cakes, melt the butter and chocolate in a metal bowl placed over a saucepan of gently simmering water, stirring until smooth. Remove from the heat.

4. Whip the eggs, egg yolks, and sugar using electric beaters or in a stand mixer fitted with the whip attachment on high speed until they have doubled in volume and hold a ribbon when the beaters are lifted, about 3 minutes. Fold in the melted chocolate (it can still be warm), then sift in the cocoa powder and fold it in (using the beaters or mixer on low speed). Divide this batter between the four ramekins and chill for 15 minutes.

5. Spoon the chilled ganache into four truffles (you can roll the truffles between your palms to shape them) and gently place one into the centre of each cake, pressing down into the batter slightly, but not to the bottom.

6. Bake the molten cakes for about 9 minutes, until the top of each cake has domed up a bit and has a dull finish. Let the cakes sit for at least 2 minutes. Lift each ramekin up (using a towel to protect your hands), run a spatula around the cake to loosen it, place a plate over top, invert, and lift off the ramekin. Garnish with a dusting of icing sugar and serve immediately.

This recipe is a perennial favourite—molten cake never goes out of fashion. Its method and style are truly original and can act as a source of inspiration for other recipes, like they did for the soft centre and warm exterior of my Warm Peanut Butter Cookie Cakes (page 136).

. . . .

It was from working as a restaurant pastry chef that I picked up this trick of dropping a truffle in the centre of the cake batter to guarantee the molten centre each time. When I'd get a rush of dessert orders in, it would inevitably happen that I would accidentally overbake a cake or two, and you can't know until you cut into it. Now you can benefit from the lesson I learned the hard way—and when you serve these to your guests, you won't be sweating as they take that first forkful!

You can make these ahead of time. Prepare the batter, fill the ramekins, and chill until you're ready to bake and serve. Simply add an additional 2 minutes to the baking time.

. . . .

Chocolate ganache is such a simple ratio: equal parts chocolate and whipping cream combine to create a fluid, decadent liquid when warm, and a dense, smooth, and rich substance when chilled. These two variations, and their various uses, make this a Foundation recipe that is valuable for any baker. When warmed, ganache can be used as a sauce when plating a dessert, or as part of a chocolate glaze, or even a soufflé; and when chilled, it is at the heart of chocolate truffles.

Warm Peanut Butter Cookie Cakes

The caramel portion of this recipe makes more than is needed for the gooey
soft centres of the peanut butter-caramel version of a molten centre chocolate cake (page 134).
Serve any extra caramel warmed up as a sauce on the side.

• • • • • • • •

The batter for these desserts needs to be frozen before baking,
so bear that in mind when you're planning your meal.

Makes 6 individual cakes • Prep 45 minutes plus freezing • Bake/Cook 20 minutes

Caramel

3 Tbsp | 45 mL	water
1 cup | 200 g	granulated sugar
1 Tbsp | 15 mL	white corn syrup
¼ cup | 60 mL	whipping cream
½ cup | 115 g	unsalted butter

Cakes

½ cup | 115 g	unsalted butter
½ cup | 100 g	granulated sugar
½ cup | 100 g	packed light brown sugar
⅔ cup | 165 g	smooth peanut butter
2 | 2	eggs, at room temperature
1 tsp | 5 mL	pure vanilla extract
1 cup | 150 g	all-purpose flour
1 tsp | 3 g	baking powder
¼ tsp | 1 g	baking soda
¼ tsp | 1 g	salt

1. For the caramel, bring the water, sugar, and corn syrup to a boil in a saucepan over high heat. Continue to boil, uncovered, occasionally brushing the sides of the saucepan with water, until the sugar turns a light amber colour. Remove the saucepan from the heat and carefully whisk in the cream and butter (watch out for the steam). Set the caramel aside to cool to room temperature, then chill until firm.

2. For the cakes, grease six 5-ounce (150 mL) ramekins and coat the insides with sugar, tapping out any excess.

3. Cream the butter with both sugars by hand until smooth and light. Beat in the peanut butter and then add the eggs one at a time, beating well after each addition. Beat in the vanilla.

4. In a separate bowl, sift the flour, baking powder, baking soda, and salt. Add this to the peanut butter batter and stir until evenly blended. Divide the batter evenly between the six prepared ramekins, holding back about ½ cup (125 mL) of the batter to spoon over the caramel filling. Make an impression in the centre of the batter in each dish and spoon in about 2 Tbsp (30 mL) of the chilled caramel. Top the caramel with the remaining batter, making sure that the caramel is completely covered. Completely wrap the dishes in plastic wrap and freeze until the batter is firm, at least 3 hours, or for up to 1 week.

5. To bake, preheat the oven to 400°F (200°C). Unwrap the ramekins, place them on a baking tray, and bake them from frozen for 20 minutes, until the top of the cakes are domed and an even golden brown. Let the cakes cool for just 5 minutes, then run a knife or spatula around the inside of each ramekin to loosen the cakes and tip them out onto a plate and serve immediately.

This dessert really is like a warm peanut butter cookie shell cuddling a soft centre of cakey batter and caramel sauce melded together. It smells heavenly as it bakes.

When filling your cakes with the caramel before baking, it's important that the caramel is completely covered by the batter. If the caramel is exposed, it will expand and push right up and out of the cake.

Boston Cream Pie

This dessert, which is actually a cake, inspired the doughnut of the same name that is now so popular. It is a simple vanilla cake filled with a vanilla custard and topped with a chocolate glaze.

Makes one 2-layer 9-inch (23 cm) cake • Serves 12
Prep 75 minutes plus cooling • Bake/Cook 45 minutes plus chilling

Cake

1 cup | 200 g	granulated sugar
¾ cup | 100 g	cake and pastry flour
½ cup | 75 g	all-purpose flour
1 ¼ tsp | 3.75 g	baking powder
¼ tsp | 1 g	salt
½ cup | 115 g	cool unsalted butter, cut into pieces
2 | 2	eggs
½ cup | 125 mL	milk
2 tsp | 10 mL	pure vanilla extract

Cream Filling

½ cup | 125 mL	whipping cream
½ cup | 125 mL	milk
½ | ½	vanilla bean (seeds only) (or 1 ½ tsp/7 mL vanilla bean paste)
3 | 3	egg yolks
3 Tbsp | 36 g	granulated sugar
1 ½ Tbsp | 11 g	cornstarch
2 Tbsp | 30 g	unsalted butter

Ganache Glaze

½ cup | 125 mL	whipping cream
4 oz | 120 g	bittersweet couverture/baking chocolate, chopped
1 Tbsp | 15 mL	vegetable oil
1 Tbsp | 15 mL	corn syrup

1. Preheat the oven to 325°F (160°C). Grease a 9-inch (23 cm) cake pan. Line the bottom of the pan with parchment paper and dust the sides of the pan with flour, tapping out any excess.

2. Sift the sugar, both flours, baking powder, and salt into a large bowl. Cut in the butter using electric beaters or in a stand mixer fitted with the paddle attachment on low speed until the flour has a rough, crumbly texture.

3. In a separate bowl, whisk together the eggs, milk, and vanilla. Pour this into the flour mixture and beat to combine on low speed then increase the speed to medium-high and beat until the batter is pale and thick, 3–5 minutes. Scrape the batter into the prepared pan and tap the pan on the counter to release any large air bubbles. Bake the cake for about 35 minutes, until a tester inserted in the centre of the cake comes out clean. Cool the cake in its pan on a cooling rack for 30 minutes, then turn it out onto the rack to cool completely.

4. While the cake is baking, prepare the filling. Heat the cream and milk in a small saucepan over medium heat with the vanilla bean seeds until the liquid just begins to simmer.

5. In a bowl, whisk the egg yolks with the sugar and cornstarch. Place the butter in a separate bowl, with a fine mesh sieve placed over it. Slowly pour the hot cream into the egg mixture while whisking, then return the entire mixture to the saucepan, constantly whisking over medium heat until it becomes glossy and thick, 2–3 minutes. Immediately pour it through

the sieve over the butter, then stir until the butter has melted. Place a piece of plastic wrap directly on the surface of the cream filling, cool to room temperature, and then chill until needed.

6. For the ganache glaze, bring the cream to just below a simmer over medium heat in a small saucepan and pour over the chopped chocolate. Gently stir until the chocolate has melted, then stir in the oil and corn syrup. Set aside to cool to room temperature before using.

7. To assemble, slice the cooled cake in half horizontally and place the bottom layer on a cake stand. Spread the chilled cream filling evenly over the cake layer and top with the other cake layer. Pour the cooled (but still fluid) ganache glaze over top and spread it so that it covers the top of the cake evenly, but not the sides. Chill the cake until ready to serve. The cake will keep, refrigerated, for up to 2 days.

This method for making the cake batter is called the "reverse method" since it is the reverse of a traditional cake recipe that starts by creaming butter and sugar, adding eggs, and then finishing with dry ingredients. I find this technique not only makes a gorgeous cake, but also uses fewer bowls—which means fewer dishes to wash!

• • • • • • • •

The seeds from the vanilla bean or bean paste add a lovely speckle visible within the filling. If you don't have either, you can use 1 ½ tsp/7 mL of vanilla extract instead.

• • • • • • • •

This Ganache Glaze is a Foundation recipe that can be used to top anything that needs a satiny, chocolate layer, like a doughnut, bundt cake, or a classic torte like my Opera Torte (page 150). It is the addition of the oil and corn syrup that gives this glaze its shine, prevents it from cracking as it sets, and means it slices easily.

Mini Chocolate Hazelnut Friands

Friands are distinguishable by their oval shape and typically contain ground nuts as a key element. A properly made friand will have a peak to it, which is another key characteristic of this particular petit four.

Makes 24 friands • Prep 30 minutes • Bake 20 minutes plus cooling

Friands

1 ½ cups	200 g	whole hazelnuts, toasted and peeled
1 ¼ cups	180 g	all-purpose flour
¼ cup	30 g	Dutch process cocoa powder
2 tsp	10 mL	instant espresso powder
¼ tsp	1 g	ground nutmeg
2 cups	260 g	icing sugar, sifted
¾ cup	175 g	unsalted butter, melted
6	6	egg whites, at room temperature

Ganache Glaze and Topping

4 oz	120 g	semisweet couverture/baking chocolate, chopped
1 Tbsp	15 g	unsalted butter
2 tsp	10 mL	corn syrup
1 ½ oz	45 g	white couverture/baking chocolate

These little cakes are a nice addition to a holiday cookie tin when you want to add variety, but need some that will keep, and in fact improve, over a few days.

• • • • • • • •

While the oval shape is traditional, using a standard mini muffin pan produces a nice, two-bite cake that is just right for a sweet treat.

1. Preheat the oven to 400°F (200°C). Grease a 24-cup mini friand pan or mini muffin pan.

2. For the friands, place the hazelnuts in a food processor with the flour, cocoa powder, espresso powder, and nutmeg and pulse until the nuts are finely ground. Place the sifted icing sugar in a large bowl and stir the nut mixture into it. Stir in the melted butter (the batter will be dense).

3. In a separate bowl, whisk the egg whites until they are foamy and then stir them into the batter. Use a small ice cream scoop to scoop the batter into the prepared pan. Bake for 15–20 minutes, until a tester inserted in the centre of a friand comes out clean. Immediately turn out the friands onto a cooling rack to cool completely.

4. For the ganache glaze, place the semisweet chocolate, butter, and corn syrup in a metal bowl resting over a saucepan of barely simmering water and stir gently until melted. Cool just enough so that the ganache clings to a spoon or spatula without running off. Dip the top of each friand into the glaze and set upright on a baking tray or platter to cool.

5. Melt the white chocolate in a metal bowl resting over a saucepan of barely simmering water, stirring gently until melted. Spoon the melted white chocolate into a little piping bag or use a fork to drizzle a pattern over each friand and let them set. The friands will keep for up to 5 days in an airtight container at room temperature (they actually taste better a day after they've been baked).

Mini Vanilla Cupcakes

These mini cupcakes rise beautifully, hold their shape,
and are absolutely light and lovely, perfect for any special occasion.
Each cupcake is decorated with a buttercream rose, so you can serve a garden of cupcakes.

Makes 36 cupcakes • Prep 75 minutes • Bake 18 minutes plus cooling

Cupcakes

½ cup | 115 g	unsalted butter, at room temperature
1 cup | 200 g	granulated sugar, divided
4 | 4	eggs, separated and at room temperature
2 tsp | 10 mL	vanilla bean paste or pure vanilla extract
1 cup | 100 g	coconut flour
⅓ cup | 45 g	tapioca starch
2 tsp | 6 g	baking powder (gluten-free, if necessary)
¼ tsp | 1 g	salt
½ cup | 125 mL	milk, at room temperature

Frosting

1 cup | 225 g	unsalted butter, at room temperature
4–8 | 500 g–cups | 1 kg	icing sugar, sifted
½ cup | 125 mL	milk
2 tsp | 10 mL	vanilla bean paste
	food colouring paste

1. Preheat the oven to 350°F (180°C). Line mini muffin pans with 36 paper liners.

2. Beat the butter and ¾ cup (150 g) of the sugar using electric beaters or in a stand mixer fitted with the paddle attachment at medium-high speed until fluffy. Add the egg yolks and vanilla and beat them in.

3. In a separate bowl, sift the coconut flour with the tapioca starch, baking powder, and salt. Add this to the butter mixture alternately with the milk, mixing well after each addition and starting and ending with the flour, and beating on high speed for 2 minutes to make the batter fluffy (there is no risk of overbeating when there is no gluten!).

4. Whip the egg whites in a separate, clean bowl using electric beaters or in a stand mixer fitted with the whip attachment on high speed until they are foamy, and then add the remaining ¼ cup (50 g) of sugar and whip until the whites hold a soft peak. Fold these into the batter in two additions. Use a small ice cream scoop to scoop the batter into the paper liners, filling them three-quarters full. Bake the cupcakes for 15–18 minutes, until they spring back when gently pressed. Cool the cupcakes in the muffin pan on a cooling rack before frosting.

5. For the frosting, beat the butter with 3 cups (390 g) of the icing sugar using electric beaters or in a stand mixer fitted with the paddle attachment on medium-high speed until fluffy. Add the milk and vanilla and mix slowly at first, scraping down the bowl often, until combined. Add the remaining icing sugar 1 cup (130 g) or so at a time, beating well until you have the ideal consistency for piping (the frosting should hold its shape, but not be too firm). The amount of icing sugar you add depends on the softness of your butter and the temperature of the room. Use the frosting at room temperature.

6. Divide the frosting into as many rose colours as you wish, with a separate bowl for tinting the frosting green for the leaves. For the leaves, use a small leaf tip; for the rose petals, use a large straight petal or curve petal tip. Fill the piping bags with the frostings.

7. To pipe a buttercream rose, start by piping a little mound in the centre of the cupcake (the bud). With the wide part of the piping tip resting on the cupcake at the bud, pipe a petal with a little lift up and then down again (remember, rose petals at the centre are smaller than on the outside). Repeat, overlapping the next petal a little over the first one and continue this circling outward until the rose covers the top of the cupcake. Pipe a few leaves around the outside and repeat. The cupcakes are best enjoyed at room temperature, but will keep, refrigerated, for up to 3 days.

To pipe a rosette, it's best to hold the cupcake in the air in one hand and pipe with the other (as opposed to piping while the cupcake rests on the counter). It does take a little practice, but I find using the image of a real rose helpful—you can see how the petals start small in the centre and become larger as you work out and the petals overlap each other. And remember: in nature, no two roses are identical.

· · · · · · · · ·

Professional bakers prefer paste colours to liquid because the colours are truer and easier to control, with many tones to choose from. Remember to start by adding just a little colour to your frosting with a toothpick and gradually add more as needed. Keep in mind that the colours will intensify as the cupcakes sit.

143

Key Lime Cheesecake

This decadent cheesecake melds the tartness of key lime pie with the creaminess of a rich cheesecake. A lime cheesecake layer is topped with a tangy lime curd and the dessert is topped with heaps of whipped cream and fresh blueberries, so it looks just like a stunning key lime pie. Use key limes—a small, sweet variety of lime from Florida—if you can find them, but regular limes will work just as well.

Makes one 9-inch (23 cm) cheesecake • Serves 12 to 16
Prep 90 minutes plus chilling • Bake/Cook 75 minutes plus chilling

Coconut Crust

1 ½ cups | 150 g	sweetened flaked coconut
¼ cup | 50 g	granulated sugar
¼ cup | 35 g	all-purpose flour
1 | 1	egg white, at room temperature

Cheesecake Base

3 cups | 750 g	cream cheese, at room temperature
10 oz | 300 mL	sweetened condensed milk
1 Tbsp | 15 mL	finely grated lime zest
2 tsp | 10 mL	pure vanilla extract
2 | 2	eggs, at room temperature
1 | 1	egg yolk, at room temperature
½ cup | 125 mL	fresh lime juice

Lime Curd

2 | 2	eggs
2 | 2	egg yolks
½ cup | 100 g	granulated sugar
1 Tbsp | 15 mL	finely grated lime zest
½ cup | 125 mL	fresh lime juice
½ cup | 115 g	unsalted butter, cut into pieces
¼ cup | 60 g	sour cream

Topping

1 cup | 250 mL	whipping cream
1 Tbsp | 4 g	instant skim milk powder
2 Tbsp | 12 g	granulated sugar
½ tsp | 2 mL	pure vanilla extract
½ cup | 125 mL	fresh blueberries, for garnish

1. Preheat the oven to 350°F (180°C). Lightly grease a 9-inch (23 cm) springform pan and place it on a baking tray.

2. For the crust, stir the coconut, sugar, and flour together. Whisk the egg white until it is frothy and then stir it into the coconut. Press this into the bottom of the prepared pan (if you are finding it sticky, wet your fingers with water before pressing). Bake the crust for about 18 minutes, until lightly browned around the edges. Cool completely before filling.

3. For the cheesecake base, reduce the oven temperature to 300°F (150°C). Beat the cream cheese using electric beaters or in a stand mixer fitted with the paddle attachment on medium-high speed until light and fluffy. Beat in the condensed milk, scraping the sides and bottom of the bowl well. Beat in the zest and vanilla. On a lower speed, beat in each egg and the yolk one at a time and scrape the bowl after each addition. Still on low speed, beat in the lime juice. Pour this over the cooled crust and bake for about 40 minutes, until the outside of the cheesecake is set but the centre still has a little jiggle to it. Prepare the lime curd while the cheesecake cools.

4. For the lime curd, whisk the whole eggs, egg yolks, sugar, and lime zest and juice in a metal bowl. Whisk in the butter and sour cream and place the bowl over a saucepan of gently simmering water, whisking often, until the lime curd has thickened, about 10 minutes. Strain the curd through a fine mesh sieve and spread it gently over the cheesecake. Once fully cooled to room temperature, chill the cheesecake, uncovered, for at least 6 hours.

5. For the topping, whip the cream and skim milk powder to a soft peak. Stir in the sugar and vanilla and spread the topping over the cheesecake, leaving a 2-inch (5 cm) border of lime curd visible around the outside. Top the cream with the blueberries and chill until ready to serve. The cheesecake will keep, refrigerated, for up to 3 days.

This decadent cheesecake may be made up of a number of steps, but the result is an impressively showy and complex dessert, worthy of a special occasion. The cheesecake batter uses condensed milk, a rich and sweet ingredient typical of a classic key lime pie.

• • • • • • • •

You will see this in other places in this book but it's worth repeating: adding instant skim milk powder is the secret to making a whipped cream that stays whipped and holds its shape even when spooned or sliced hours and hours after whipping.

Classic Vanilla Birthday Cake
with Caramel Pastry Cream

*Someone special deserves this cake. (You?) Just like a bakeshop cake,
this combination of delicate cake, creamy filling, and buttercream icing will
make anyone thrilled, no matter how many candles they may have to blow out!*

Makes one 2-layer 8-inch (20 cm) cake
Serves 10 to 12 • Prep 90 minutes • Bake/Cook 1 hour plus chilling

Vanilla Cake

¾ cup	175 g	unsalted butter, at room temperature
1 ⅓ cups	270 g	granulated sugar
3	3	eggs, at room temperature
2 tsp	10 mL	pure vanilla extract
2 ½ cups	325 g	cake and pastry flour
1 ½ tsp	4.5 g	baking powder
½ tsp	2 g	baking soda
¼ tsp	1 g	salt
1 cup	250 mL	buttermilk, at room temperature

Caramel Pastry Cream

3 Tbsp	45 mL	water
1 cup	200 g	granulated sugar
1 Tbsp	15 mL	white corn syrup
1 cup	250 mL	whipping cream
1	1	recipe Pastry Cream, chilled (page 86)

Basic Buttercream

¾ cup	175 g	unsalted butter, at room temperature
4–6 cups	520–780 g	icing sugar, sifted
6 Tbsp	90 mL	milk
1 ½ tsp	7 mL	pure vanilla extract

1. Preheat the oven to 350°F (180°C). Grease two 8-inch (20 cm) round cake pans. Line the bottom of each pan with parchment paper and then flour the sides of the pans, tapping out any excess.

2. For the cake, beat the butter and sugar using electric beaters or in a stand mixer fitted with the paddle attachment on medium-high speed until fluffy. Add the eggs one at a time, beating well after each addition. Stir in the vanilla.

3. In a separate bowl, sift together the flour, baking powder, baking soda, and salt. Add this alternately with the buttermilk, starting and ending with the flour and mixing well after each addition. Divide the batter evenly between the two pans.

4. Bake the cakes for 25–35 minutes, or until a tester inserted in the centre of the cakes comes out clean. Cool the cakes in their pans on a cooling rack for 20 minutes, then carefully turn them out onto the rack to cool completely. Remove the parchment paper.

5. For the caramel pastry cream, bring the water, sugar, and corn syrup to a full boil in a medium saucepan over high heat. Boil, uncovered and without stirring, occasionally brushing the sides of the saucepan with water, until the mixture is a light amber colour. Remove from the heat and carefully whisk in the cream (it will immediately steam) until smooth, then allow this to cool to room temperature. Whisk ⅓ cup (80 mL) of the caramel sauce into the chilled pastry cream and chill until ready to assemble. Reserve the rest of the caramel sauce.

6. For the buttercream, beat the butter using electric beaters or in a stand mixer fitted with the paddle attachment on medium-high speed until fluffy. Add 2 cups (260 g) of the icing sugar and beat on low speed to incorporate. Increase the speed to high and continue beating until fluffy. Add the milk and vanilla and beat on medium speed until incorporated (but don't worry if the mixture doesn't seem smooth at this point). Add another 2 cups (260 g) of icing sugar and beat, starting on low speed and increasing to high until a fluffy and spreadable consistency is achieved, adding a further 2 cups (260 g) if necessary (the softness of your butter will determine if you have to make this adjustment).

7. To assemble the cake, place one cake layer on a plate or platter. Fill a piping bag fitted with a large plain tip with about 1 cup (250 mL) of frosting and pipe a ring around the outside of the cake. Scrape half of the caramel pastry cream into the centre of the cake layer and spread it level. Top this with the second cake layer, spread a thin coating of frosting over the top and sides of the cake, and chill for 20 minutes (this is the crumb coat). Now completely coat the top and sides of the cake with frosting and level it smooth. Using a pastry bag fitted with a piping tip of your choice, pipe a design with the frosting on the outside of the top of the cake. Stir the reserved caramel sauce into the remaining half of the caramel pastry cream and spread this on the top of the cake. Chill until ready to serve. The cake can be assembled up to a day in advance and stored, uncovered, in the fridge.

The texture of this vanilla cake is rich and moist and very different from the lighter, fluffier sponge cake of my Victoria Sponge (page 126). This cake suits fillings and frostings that are denser or have more structure, like the caramel pastry cream and buttercream frosting included here.

Pastry cream makes a soft and lovely filling for a cake. It can also hold fruit if you wish to add some (sliced banana or berries are ideal).

•   •   •   •   •   •   •

This Basic Buttercream recipe makes a great standard buttercream that is easy to make and perfect for cupcakes—it is sweet and fluffy and holds its shape when chilled. It is less suited to detailed piping, like on a wedding cake for example, which better suits Italian Buttercream (page 150).

•   •   •   •   •   •   •

Piping a ring of buttercream around the outside edge of each cake layer as you stack is for more than just aesthetics. It holds the pastry cream inside the cake and keeps the layers level and even. No leaks or lopsided cakes here!

Fraisier Torte

This is more of a French spin on classic strawberry shortcake—that classic summertime combination of cake, cream, and fruit. Here, a single sponge cake layer is topped with a strawberry mousse. Strawberry halves line the outside of the cake. I love the fresh taste of this torte. It looks elegant and refined, and it really captures the freshness of strawberries picked at their peak. I reserve this torte for June, when strawberries are at their best where I live.

Makes one 9-inch (23 cm) cake • Serves 10 to 12
Prep 90 minutes • Cook 15 minutes plus chilling

1 | 1	recipe Victoria Sponge (page 126), cooled to room temperature

Fruit Mousse

2 | 2	egg whites, at room temperature
2 Tbsp | 10.5 g	unflavoured gelatin powder
¾ cup | 180 mL	cold water, divided
⅓ cup | 70 g	granulated sugar
2 cups | 500 mL	puréed and strained fresh strawberries (about 4 cups/1 L sliced)
1 ½ cups | 375 mL	whipping cream
2 tsp | 10 mL	pure vanilla extract
2 cups | 500 mL	whole, hulled strawberries

1. Whip the egg whites using electric beaters or in a stand mixer fitted with the whip attachment on high speed just until past the foamy stage (before it reaches a soft peak) and set aside.

2. Sprinkle the gelatin powder over ½ cup (125 mL) of the water, stir, and set aside. Bring the sugar and the remaining water to a boil in a saucepan over high heat and boil without stirring until it reaches 240°F (115°C) on a candy thermometer.

3. Start whipping the egg whites again, now on medium speed, and pour the sugar slowly and carefully down the side of the bowl. Once it has all been added, increase the speed to high, whipping for 30 seconds to a minute, just until the whites hold a soft peak but are still hot. Beat in the gelatin on high speed until it has dissolved into the whites, then continue to beat until the mixture cools to room temperature. Whisk in the puréed strawberries by hand.

4. In a separate bowl, whip the cream until it holds a soft peak and then stir in the vanilla. Fold this into the strawberry mixture in two additions, using a whisk.

5. To assemble the cake, run an offset spatula around the inside edge of the sponge cake pan and remove the cake, peeling away the parchment paper. Wash and dry the pan, reassemble it, and place the cake layer back in the bottom of the pan. Cut the hulled strawberries in half and place them on the cake so that the flat side of each berry is pressed up against the ring of the pan and they are very close together. Pour the mousse over the cake and berries and chill until set, at least 4 hours. Top the cake with any remaining strawberry halves right before serving. The cake can be made up to a day in advance and refrigerated, uncovered.

Mousses are delicious as desserts on their own or as a part of a torte. Fruit mousses are prepared differently than chocolate mousses, so this Fruit Mousse technique is a good foundation to learn. Once you become comfortable with it you can replace the strawberry purée with other fruit purées, such as raspberry or mango. To serve the Fruit Mousse as a dessert on its own, follow the method and then pour the mousse into glasses. Chill for at least 2 hours, and top with fresh strawberries right before serving.

• • • • • • • •

Take the time to sort through your strawberries before assembling this cake. Pick uniformly sized berries to use around the outside of the cake and use the rest for the purée for the mousse.

Opera Torte

*Opera torte is a classic torte created in Paris, made of thin layers of sponge
cake with a coffee buttercream and chocolate ganache. Traditionally it is not presented
as a whole cake, but is cut into individual rectangle portions before being displayed or served.
It is perfect with a cup of strong coffee.*

Serves 6 • Prep 2 hours • Bake/Cook 35 minutes plus chilling

Cake

2 | 2	eggs, separated and at room temperature
1 | 1	egg, at room temperature
¼ cup + 2 Tbsp | 75 g	granulated sugar, divided
⅔ cup | 80 g	ground almonds
6 Tbsp | 45 g	cake and pastry flour, sifted

Ganache Layer and Glaze

1 cup | 250 mL	whipping cream
8 oz | 240 g	bittersweet couverture/baking chocolate, chopped
2 oz | 60 g	chocolate chips
2 Tbsp | 30 mL	vegetable oil

Italian Buttercream

2 | 2	egg whites, at room temperature
½ cup + 2 Tbsp | 125 g	granulated sugar, divided
1 cup | 225 g	unsalted butter, at room temperature
1 Tbsp | 15 mL	coffee extract (or 1 Tbsp/15 mL very strongly brewed espresso, cooled)
1 tsp | 5 mL	pure vanilla extract

Coffee Syrup and Assembly

½ cup | 125 mL	hot coffee
3 Tbsp | 36 g	granulated sugar
1 ½ oz | 45 g	chocolate chips, melted
6 | 6	chocolate-covered coffee beans

1. Preheat the oven to 400°F (200°C). Line an 11- x 17-inch (28 x 43 cm) sheet pan with parchment paper.

2. For the cake, whip the egg yolks and the whole egg with ¼ cup (50 g) of the sugar using electric beaters or in a stand mixer fitted with a whip attachment on high speed until it is thick and pale and holds a ribbon when the beaters are lifted. In a separate bowl, stir the ground almonds and flour together.

3. In another bowl, whip the egg whites on high speed until foamy, then slowly add the remaining 2 Tbsp (25 g) of sugar, whipping until they hold a soft peak when the beaters are lifted. Fold the whipped whites into the yolks in two additions, then fold in the almond mixture. Spread this evenly over the prepared sheet pan, ensuring that the batter is as level as possible (the batter will only make a thin layer). Bake the cake for about 8 minutes, until golden brown, and allow to cool in the pan. Once cooled, the cake might dry out a bit—that is expected and just fine.

4. For the ganache, heat the cream until it just begins to simmer and then pour it over the chopped chocolate. Let this sit for a minute, then gently stir with a spatula, starting at the centre and widening the circles until the chocolate has fully melted and the ganache is smooth. Set aside to cool to room temperature.

5. For the Italian Buttercream, whip the egg whites with the 2 Tbsp (25 g) of sugar on high speed until just past foamy. Place the remaining ½ cup (100 g) of sugar in a small saucepan with 2 Tbsp (30 mL) of water and bring to a full boil over high heat, boiling until the sugar hits 240°F (115°C) on a candy thermometer. With the mixer on medium speed, carefully add the hot sugar to the whipped whites by pouring it down the side of the bowl (this helps to avoid splashing), then increase the speed and whip until the whites have cooled to room temperature, about 4 minutes. While whipping, add the butter a few pieces at a time until combined. If, while adding the butter, it appears that the buttercream is not fluffy, or seems curdled, do not worry—simply keep adding the butter, continue to beat, and it will come together. There is no risk of overbeating. Add the coffee extract and the vanilla and mix well. Use this at room temperature.

6. For the coffee syrup, stir the coffee and sugar together until the sugar dissolves.

7. For the assembly, remove the sheet of cake and cut it into three rectangles (about 6 x 11 inches/ 15 cm x 28 cm). Brush the bottom of one of the layers with the melted chocolate chips and let the chocolate set until firm (or chill for 3 minutes). Place this layer chocolate-side down on a flat cake board or platter. Brush it with coffee syrup, then spread half of the buttercream on top. Top this with a second cake layer, brush that with syrup, and then spread two-thirds of the cooled (but still spreadable) ganache over top. Place the final cake layer over the ganache, brush it with the remaining syrup, and spread the remaining half of the buttercream over top (or you can save about ¼ cup/60 mL for a garnish).

8. For the ganache glaze, re-warm the remaining ganache, add the chocolate chips and vegetable oil, and stir until smooth. Spread this over the top of the cake (but not the sides) and chill until set, about 2 hours.

9. Before serving, trim away the sides of the cake to reveal clean layers, then slice it into six rectangular portions (a hot, dry knife makes this easy). If you wish, pipe a little coffee buttercream on top of each and place a chocolate-covered coffee bean on top.

Don't be surprised when you see how the cake spreads and bakes into a very thin layer. This style of batter is meant to be thin to keep the taste focus on the other elements of the finished product: coffee buttercream and chocolate ganache in this case.

. . . .

The classic decoration to finish a slice of Opera Torte is the word "Opera" written in chocolate on top. This makes sense in a patisserie setting, so customers can easily distinguish it from other cakes on display, but for a home baker a simple accent of buttercream and a chocolate-covered coffee bean looks elegant and also gives you a hint about what to expect at first bite.

. . . .

Italian Buttercream, the buttercream used in this recipe, is a Foundation recipe. Its base is Italian meringue, made from cooking sugar and adding it to whipping egg whites, which builds a stable base for a strong buttercream. It is this stability that makes it ideal for smooth spreading and piping, and perfect for wedding cakes. The coffee included in this version makes it great for frosting a regular chocolate cake; take out the coffee and you've got a wonderful and versatile vanilla Italian Buttercream.

Elegant Raspberry Lemon Torte

This style of cake is often called a "charlotte," with a shared feature of cake and mousse completely encircled by a layer of ladyfingers. In this recipe, I use my Ladyfinger biscuit batter (page 54) to make the cake base that holds the tart and creamy lemon mousse filling.

Makes one 9-inch (23 cm) torte • Serves 12 to 16
Prep 2 hours • Bake/Cook 15 minutes plus chilling

1 | 1	recipe Ladyfinger batter (page 54)
½ cup | 125 mL	fresh lemon juice
1 cup | 200 g	granulated sugar, divided
4 | 4	egg yolks
½ cup | 115 g	unsalted butter, at room temperature
1 Tbsp | 15 mL	finely grated lemon zest
1 ½ cups | 375 mL	whipping cream
2 cups | 500 mL	fresh raspberries

1. Preheat the oven to 400°F (200°C). Line two baking trays with parchment paper. Trace an 8-inch (20 cm) circle on one sheet of parchment and flip it over so the ink is on the bottom.

2. Fill a piping bag fitted with a medium plain tip with the ladyfinger batter. Pipe a spiral of batter, following the circle and then spiralling inward to fill the circle. On the second baking tray, pipe 18 to 22 ladyfingers about 3 inches (7.5 cm) long. Bake for about 8 minutes (the circle of batter will take about 10 minutes) and allow the ladyfingers and base to cool on the tray before lifting them off.

3. Bring the lemon juice and ½ cup (100 g) of the sugar to a simmer in a saucepan over medium heat, stirring occasionally until the sugar has fully dissolved. In a bowl, whisk the egg yolks with the remaining ½ cup (100 g) of sugar. Slowly pour the lemon syrup into the eggs while whisking and then return the entire mixture to the saucepan. Whisk this mixture over medium heat until it just begins to bubble, about 2 minutes, then remove it from the heat and use electric beaters or a stand mixer fitted with the whip attachment to whip it until cool. Add the butter and zest and beat in until smooth.

4. Whip the cream to a soft peak and fold it into the lemon mixture in two additions.

5. To assemble the torte, place the disc of ladyfinger cake in the bottom of an ungreased 9-inch (23 cm) springform pan. Trim the bottom of the ladyfingers so they can stand upright around the inside edge of the pan and are the same height as the pan (2 inches/ 5 cm). Arrange these in the pan. Spread a 1-inch (2.5 cm) layer of mousse over the cake and arrange half of the raspberries over top. Spread the remaining mousse over the berries and use an offset spatula to ensure the mousse is level. Chill the torte for at least 4 hours.

6. To serve, remove the ring from the pan and slide the torte onto a serving platter. Arrange the remaining 1 cup (250 mL) of raspberries on top of the torte and chill until ready to serve. The torte can be prepared and assembled up to a day before serving.

I like that this lemon mousse doesn't need gelatin to set.
It's rich and creamy and not at all heavy. The acidity of the lemon juice thickens
the cream as the cake chills, giving it a perfect set so that it slices easily but holds its shape.

• • • • • • •

This is one of my favourite tortes. If you are making a cake for my birthday,
now you know which one to make for me!

Fondant-Covered Heart Cake

*You can make a grand, heart-shaped cake for a large group,
even if you don't have a heart-shaped cake pan—a square pan and a round pan,
both 8 inches (20 cm), are all that you need. Covered in rolling fondant, this cake
looks smooth and seamless, and can be decorated according to your whims.*

**Makes one large heart-shaped cake • Serves 24 to 30
Prep 2 hours 30 minutes • Bake 55 minutes plus chilling**

Cake

1 | 1	**double recipe Classic Lemon Pound Cake (page 112)**

Frosting

1 | 1	**recipe Basic Buttercream (page 146)**
	pink food colouring paste (page 155)

Assembly

2 lb | 900 g	**Rolling Fondant (page 163 or store-bought)**
	pink food colouring paste (page 155)
	icing sugar, for rolling
	fresh or Fondant Flowers (page 294) for garnish (optional)

1. Preheat the oven to 325°F (160°C). Grease an 8-inch (20 cm) square pan and an 8-inch (20 cm) round pan. Line the bottom of each pan with parchment paper, then grease the parchment and dust the pans with flour, tapping out any excess.

2. Spread the batter in the two pans so they are both level and the batter is the same height in each. Tap the pans to allow any air bubbles to escape. Bake the cakes for about 55 minutes, until a tester inserted in the centre of the cake comes out clean. Allow the cakes to cool for 20 minutes in the pan on a cooling rack, then turn them out onto the rack to cool completely.

3. For the frosting, prepare as per the recipe and add a little colouring paste until you achieve a light pink colour.

4. To assemble, cut each of the cakes in half horizontally to make two thin layers for each one. Spread a layer of buttercream on the bottom half and top with its remaining half. Place the square cake on a cake board in a diamond position (a point at the bottom). Cut the round cake into two evenly sized semicircles and place each one against the top two sides of the square (or diamond, depending on how you look at it), creating a heart shape. Trim the top of the cake, if necessary, to make it level. Cover the top and sides of the cake with the remaining buttercream and chill for 30 minutes, or up to 6 hours.

5. For the fondant, add a touch of pink colouring paste to the rolling fondant and knead it in well. Roll out the fondant (using icing sugar to keep it from sticking) into a large circle that measures just wider than the widest point of the heart, twice the height of the sides, and just under ¼ inch (0.5 cm) thick. Use a rolling pin to roll up the fondant and lift it over to the heart, unrolling it over the cake to cover it. Massage the fondant gently, working out any air pockets and pressing against the buttercream. Trim the fondant at the base of the cake, and decorate with fresh or fondant flowers (if using). The cake should not be refrigerated once it's covered with the fondant. It will keep, uncovered, for up to 1 day (the fondant seals in all of the moisture, keeping the cake fresh).

The double pound cake recipe makes a large batch of batter. If you have a small mixer, it's best to divide the recipe in half and make it twice, once for each pan.

· · · · · · · ·

You have the option of buying prepared rolling fondant, or I have a great recipe for homemade rolling fondant on page 163. You'll have to double the recipe to have enough to cover the cake, plus extra for any décor.

Food colouring pastes give you a richer colour than liquid colourings, and they come in a wide range of colours. Add just a little at a time, using a toothpick, and mix in well before adding more. The colour will intensify as the fondant or frosting sits, so restraint is a good idea.

· · · · · · · ·

Another food colouring tip for you: Add a few drops of glycerine (found at stores that carry cake supplies and food colouring pastes) if your cake is going to sit out on display or be exposed to sunlight. The colour will fade when exposed to sunlight, but glycerine will keep it true (and keeps the fondant nice and flexible, too, as you're rolling it—a bonus feature!).

Black Forest Roulade

This flourless dessert has all the textbook characteristics of a Black Forest Torte: chocolate cake, whipped cream, and kirsch-soaked cherries.

Makes one 10-inch (25 cm) roulade
Serves 12 to 16 • Prep 75 minutes • Bake/Cook 1 hour plus chilling

Flourless Jelly Roll

6 | 6	eggs, separated and at room temperature
¾ cup | 150 g	granulated sugar
½ cup | 60 g	Dutch process cocoa powder
⅛ tsp | 0.5 g	salt
	icing sugar, for dusting

Kirsch Cherries

1 cup | 250 mL	fresh, jarred, or frozen and thawed, pitted tart cherries
2 Tbsp | 25 g	granulated sugar
1 Tbsp | 15 mL	kirsch

Chocolate Cream

1 cup | 250 mL	whipping cream
2 oz | 60 g	bittersweet couverture/baking chocolate, chopped

Assembly

1 ¼ cups | 310 mL	whipping cream
1 Tbsp +1 tsp | 5 g	instant skim milk powder
2 Tbsp | 25 g	granulated sugar
	block of dark chocolate, for grating

1. Preheat the oven to 350°F (180°C). Line a 15- x 10-inch (38 x 25 cm) jelly roll pan with parchment paper.

2. Whisk the egg yolks and sugar by hand until lighter in colour, but not holding any air. Sift the cocoa powder over the yolks and whisk in.

3. Whip the egg whites and salt using electric beaters or in a stand mixer fitted with the whip attachment on high speed until they hold a medium peak when the beaters are lifted. Fold one-third of the whites into the yolk mixture using a whisk and then fold in the remaining two-thirds until evenly incorporated. Spread the batter evenly into the prepared pan. Bake the cake for 25 minutes until it has an even matte surface to it (the cake will rise up while baking and then fall once it is removed from the oven). Let it cool completely in the pan on a cooling rack.

4. For the cherries, simmer the cherries in a saucepan over medium heat for about 15 minutes or until the juices are reduced by half, then add the sugar and simmer for 5 minutes more. Remove the saucepan from the heat and stir in the kirsch. Cool and then chill the cherries until ready to assemble.

5. For the chocolate cream, bring the cream just to a simmer in a saucepan over medium heat. Place the chocolate in a bowl and pour the cream over it. Let this sit for 1 minute, then gently whisk until the chocolate has melted into the cream. Cool to room temperature, then refrigerate to chill completely.

6. Once chilled, whip the chocolate cream on medium speed until it holds a medium peak.

7. To assemble, whip the cream and skim milk powder on high speed until the cream holds a medium peak, then stir in the sugar.

8. Run a spatula around the outside edge of the cooled cake and turn it out onto a work surface dusted with icing sugar. Peel away the parchment paper and spread the whipped chocolate cream over the cake. Use a slotted spoon to distribute the cherries over the chocolate cream. Roll up the cake from the short side and carefully lift it onto your serving platter so that the seam is at the bottom. Spread the whipped cream over the roulade to completely cover it and use a vegetable peeler to grate the block of dark chocolate into curls to sprinkle on top. Chill until ready to serve. The roulade can be made up to 8 hours before serving.

This is the fanciest of the three jelly roll cakes featured in this chapter, but while it is elaborate, it is not any more difficult than the others. Unlike the other jelly roll cakes, which need to be rolled up while warm to set their spiral shape, this cake can cool in the pan before shaping (a perk of baking without gluten).

. . . .

I've nicknamed this chocolate filling my "cheater mousse." It is simply a ganache with a higher proportion of whipping cream so that, once chilled, it whips up just like whipped cream, but with a richness that reminds you more of milk chocolate than dark.

Rich Chocolate Mousse Cake

This chocolate mousse cake is a patisserie-style glazed mousse torte. It does take some time to make, assemble, and set, though, so start preparing it at least a day ahead of when you intend to serve it. Also, note that only one cake layer is needed for this recipe, but it is easiest to make the cake recipe in its full measure and freeze the second cake for a later use.

Makes one 9-inch (23 cm) cake • Serves 12 to 16
Prep 2 hours 30 minutes • Bake/Cook 1 hour plus freezing and chilling

Cake

½ cup	125 mL	boiling water
2 oz	60 g	unsweetened chocolate, chopped
¼ cup	60 g	unsalted butter, cut into pieces
1	1	egg, at room temperature
½ cup	100 g	granulated sugar
1 tsp	5 mL	pure vanilla extract
1 ¼ cups	180 g	all-purpose flour
1 tsp	3 g	baking powder
¾ tsp	4 g	baking soda
¼ tsp	1 g	salt
½ cup	125 mL	hot, strongly brewed coffee

Mousse

3 cups	750 mL	whipping cream, divided
12 oz	360 g	semisweet couverture/baking chocolate, chopped
3	3	egg yolks, at room temperature
½ cup	100 g	granulated sugar
⅓ cup	80 mL	water

Chocolate Glaze

½ cup	125 mL	water
1 cup	200 g	granulated sugar
½ cup	125 mL	whipping cream
½ cup	60 g	Dutch process cocoa powder, sifted
1 ½ Tbsp	8 g	unflavoured gelatin powder
¼ cup	60 mL	cold water

1. Preheat the oven to 325°F (160°C). Grease two 8-inch (20 cm) round cake pans, line the bottoms with parchment paper, and then lightly dust the sides of the pan with flour, tapping out any excess.

2. For the cake, whisk the boiling water, chocolate, and butter together in a large bowl until melted (the mixture will be visibly grainy) and set aside.

3. Whip the egg, sugar, and vanilla using electric beaters or in a stand mixer fitted with the whip attachment on high speed until the mixture doubles in volume (about 2 minutes on high speed) and then whisk in the warm chocolate mixture by hand.

4. Sift the flour, baking powder, baking soda, and salt over the batter and fold them in. Stir in the hot coffee (this will make the batter very fluid). Divide the batter evenly between the two pans.

5. Bake the cakes for about 25 minutes, until a tester inserted in the centre of the cake comes out clean. Allow the cakes to cool completely in the pans.

6. Line the bottom of a 9-inch (23 cm) springform pan with parchment paper. Do not grease the pan.

7. For the mousse, whip 1 ½ cups (375 mL) of the whipping cream until it holds a medium peak when the beaters are lifted. Chill until needed.

Continued . . .

8. Heat the remaining 1 ½ cups (375 mL) of cream over medium heat to just below a simmer and then pour it over the chopped semisweet chocolate. Let this ganache sit for 1 minute, then gently stir until incorporated. Set aside.

9. Whip the egg yolks using electric beaters or in a stand mixer fitted with the whip attachment on high speed until they turn a little pale, about 1 minute (they will not have increased in volume like egg whites would). Place the sugar and water in a small saucepan over high heat and boil (occasionally brushing the sides of the saucepan with water) until it reaches 250°F (120°C) on a candy thermometer. Start whipping the egg yolks again, now on medium speed, and carefully pour the hot sugar down the side of the bowl to avoid splashing, increase the mixer speed to high, and whip until the mixture has doubled in volume and cooled to about 104°F (40°C).

10. Measure the temperature of the ganache to ensure it is close to 104°F (40°C) as well and then fold it into the whipped yolks. Let this cool for 15 minutes, or until just above room temperature, then fold in the chilled whipped cream in two additions.

11. Pour half of the mousse into the lined springform pan. Slice through one of the cake layers to make two halves and place one over the mousse, as centred as possible. Pour the remaining mousse over the cake layer and gently place the other half of the cake layer on top, pressing gently just so the mousse covers the sides of the cake, but not so that it sinks in. Wrap the pan in plastic wrap and freeze the cake to set it, at least 4 hours, or overnight.

• • • • • • • •

Once you've mastered this cake, you'll deserve pastry chef certification. There are real pastry chef techniques involved all the way from the mousse and glaze methods to the assembly.

Freezing the mousse cake means:

1. It can be made days or even weeks ahead.
2. The mousse won't melt when you use the hair dryer to loosen the pan from the cake.
3. The glaze will go on and adhere quickly and evenly.

12. While the cake is setting, prepare the glaze. Bring the ½ cup (125 mL) water, sugar, and cream to a boil in a medium saucepan over medium-high heat. Once it is boiling, whisk in the cocoa powder and simmer (reducing the heat if necessary) for 4 minutes, stirring often (the consistency will not change). Remove from the heat. Soften the gelatin in the ¼ cup (60 mL) of cold water and then whisk this into the hot cocoa mixture until dissolved. Cool the glaze to room temperature and then chill completely, at least 3 hours.

13. To finish the cake, remove it from the freezer and invert the pan onto a cooling rack placed over a parchment-lined baking tray. Use a hair dryer on a low, hot setting to gently warm the pan so that the cake releases from the pan, the sides first and then the top. Warm the chilled glaze in a saucepan over medium-low heat, whisking occasionally until just melted and smooth. Pour this over the torte, spreading it gently with a spatula to ensure that it covers the top and sides of the torte evenly. Chill the cake for at least 30 minutes, then lift it onto your presentation plate, and store chilled until ready to serve. The cake will keep, refrigerated, for up to 4 days.

* * * * * * * *

Using a hair dryer to warm the metal pan makes the mousse cake come out easier and with smooth sides, so that the chocolate glaze goes on smoothly and sets with a mirror-like finish.

This glaze is also called a "mirror" glaze because of its glossy finish, even once set. I find it better to chill this glaze and then reheat it before using. You can then slowly heat it to the perfect pouring consistency.

Working with Fondant

There are two important foundation recipes included here: Rolling Fondant and Fondant Glaze. Both are particularly valuable if you are focusing on developing your cake decorating skills. The rolling fondant step is a key element in glazed petits fours. It creates a smooth top to the little cakes, so that when the glaze is poured over top, it runs over smoothly and makes each petit four look precise and perfect. Rolling fondant can be purchased in pre-made form at cake and specialty craft stores but it can be costly, and sometimes contains artificial ingredients used to flavour it and to give it its pliable, smooth structure. Making your own adds another layer to your cake baking projects, but it is relatively simple and economical. The agar agar powder it contains is a vegetable-based (seaweed, to be precise) thickener that keeps the fondant smooth and pliable. It can be found at health food stores or Asian groceries.

Fondant glaze is not available for purchase by home cooks (although commercial bakeries can access it). Its distinct fluidity and unique set definitely make it a recipe to have in your baker's tool kit.

• • • • • • • •

A candy thermometer is your best friend for the glazing step here. Give yourself plenty of time and heat the fondant glaze slowly, stopping between 105°F and 109°F (41–43°C). Within this temperature range, the glaze will flow evenly but not be too runny or too thick, and will set with a satin lustre. If it gets too hot, let the glaze cool to below 100°F (38°C) before heating again.

Take time when glazing to make sure the glaze covers each petit four fully on the first dip or pour. The glaze sets up very quickly, so a second pour will show its drips. Any glaze that collects under the cooling rack as you work can be scraped up and re-melted to be used again.

• • • • • • • •

Let the petits fours sit on the cooling rack for at least 1 hour after glazing. Then you can lift them off with a spatula, trimming away any rough edges at the bottom, before placing them in a paper liner, which is the traditional way to serve them.

Fondant-Glazed Petits Fours

*These are the classic glazed little cakes that make you feel like you're
8 years old when you eat them—so dainty and pretty.*

• • • • • • • •

*This cake recipe is ideally suited to petits fours that are covered with a poured fondant glaze—
the cake cuts into clean shapes with no crumbs to create rough edges or fall into the fondant.*

Makes 24 petits fours • Prep 2 hours 30 minutes • Bake/Cook 40 minutes plus freezing

Cake

7 oz | 200 g	Homemade Marzipan (page 295) or store-bought
¾ cup | 180 g	unsalted butter, at room temperature
¾ cup | 150 g	granulated sugar
4 | 4	eggs, at room temperature
¾ cup | 100 g	cake and pastry flour, sifted
½ cup | 125 mL	raspberry jam

Rolling Fondant

⅓ cup | 80 mL	cool water
1 Tbsp + ¼ tsp | 8 g	agar agar powder
½ cup | 125 mL	white corn syrup
2 Tbsp | 30 g	vegetable shortening
1 Tbsp | 15 mL	glycerine
4 ½– 6 cups | 585–780 g	icing sugar, sifted clear pure vanilla or almond extract

Fondant Glaze

8 cups | 1040 g	icing sugar, sifted
⅔ cup | 160 mL	hot water
¼ cup | 60 mL	white corn syrup
1 tsp | 5 mL	glycerine clear vanilla or almond extract food colouring paste dragées or Fondant Flowers (page 294) or other shapes, for décor

1. Preheat the oven to 375°F (190°C). Line a 15- x 10-inch (38 x 25 cm) baking pan with parchment paper.

2. For the cake, use a box grater to grate the marzipan into pieces (this will make it easier to blend into the cake batter). Beat the butter, sugar, and grated marzipan using electric beaters or in a stand mixer fitted with the paddle attachment on medium-high speed until light and fluffy. Add the eggs one at a time, mixing well after each addition. Add the flour and mix until well combined. Spread the batter into the prepared baking pan, level it off, and bake for 20–25 minutes, until the cake is a rich golden brown. Cool the cake completely in the pan on a cooling rack.

Continued . . .

3. For the rolling fondant, place the water in a small saucepan, sprinkle the agar agar powder over top, and then stir it in. Let this sit for 5 minutes and then heat on medium-low, stirring gently until the agar agar melts in (but the liquid won't turn clear at this point). Remove the saucepan from the heat, add the corn syrup, shortening, and glycerine, and stir until the shortening has melted (now the liquid will be clear).

4. Place 4 ½ cups (585 g) of the sifted icing sugar in a large bowl and pour in the liquid. Stir the mixture until it becomes too difficult to stir any more, adding more sifted icing sugar as needed, until the fondant comes together. Turn the fondant onto a surface dusted with icing sugar and knead it until it is smooth, adding a few drops of the vanilla or almond extract to taste. Wrap the fondant tightly in plastic wrap (or a resealable bag or airtight container) until you are ready to use it.

5. To ready the cake for dipping, run a knife around the inside edge of the baking tray to loosen the cake and turn it out onto a cutting board. Peel away the parchment and cut the cake in half vertically. Stir the raspberry jam to soften it and spread all but 2 Tbsp (30 mL) of it on one half of the cake. Top it with the second half. Spread the remaining 2 Tbsp (30 mL) of jam in a sheer layer on top of the cake.

6. On a work surface dusted with icing sugar, cut the rolling fondant in half and roll it to just under ¼ inch (0.5 cm) thick in a rectangle the same size as the cake. Place it on top of the cake and trim away the edges (it should only cover the top and not hang down the sides). Wrap the cake and freeze it for at least 1 hour or until you are ready to cover it with the pouring fondant (it can be frozen for up to 1 month).

7. Unwrap the cake and place it on a cutting board. Using a 1 ½-inch (4 cm) round or square cookie cutter (round petits fours are easier to coat than square) cut out individual cakes and place them on a cooling rack set over a clean baking tray.

8. For the pouring fondant, place the sifted icing sugar in a large metal bowl. Have ready a saucepan containing 1 inch (2.5 cm) of barely simmering water set over low heat. In a separate bowl, whisk together the ⅔ cup (160 mL) hot water, corn syrup, and glycerine and add this to the icing sugar, stirring until fluid. Check the temperature with an instant read thermometer. If it is less than 105–109°F (41–43°C), place the fondant on the water bath and whisk until it reaches this temperature range. Do not let it get warmer than 109°F (43°C) or the finish of the fondant will be matte and possibly grainy. If the fondant is too thick at the desired temperature, you can add a little tepid water, but just a few droplets at a time and make sure you fully whisk it in. If the fondant cools too much while pouring, reheat it to within the desired temperature range.

9. You will want to whisk the fondant in the bowl often to keep it from setting. You have two options for coating the petits fours:

   a) *Pouring*—using a ladle, pour the fondant over each little cake, one at a time, checking that all sides are completely covered. Any excess will run off the petits fours and onto the baking tray. You can scrape this back into the bowl and re-melt it to use a second time.

   b) *Dipping*—using large tweezers or truffle forks, immerse the little cake upside down in the fondant and carefully lift it up, ensuring that all sides are covered (you can't double-dip) and the bottom is exposed. Carefully turn the cake upright and place it on the cooling rack to set.

10. If decorating the petits fours with dragées, set them on top very soon after applying the fondant and before it fully sets. Fondant shapes (flowers, hearts of any colours) can be attached with a little brush of water or Royal Icing (page 294). To serve, place the petits fours in paper liners and store in an airtight container for up to 3 days. Do not refrigerate.

Other Pastries

Don't let the word "other" in this chapter title fool you. Some baked goods don't necessarily fall into a neat little box you can label, such as "cakes" or "pies," but they can be just as fulfilling to make and to eat. These recipes don't make up some hodgepodge collection, like the last few crumbs in the bottom of a cookie tin. I've chosen them carefully so they focus more on particular techniques, like mastering puff pastry or Danish dough from scratch, or making choux paste. These staples of a professional baker's kitchen can seem daunting in a home kitchen or to a novice baker, but my guidance will have you working your way through this chapter, one step at a time. I'll take you from rustic and simple Strawberry Shortcake right through to La Grande Maman of desserts: Croquembouche.

Simple

Scrumptious

Sensational

Puff Pastry Dough

This technique is based on the classic French method of making puff pastry but is assembled inverted, or "inside out." Where a traditional puff pastry is made by wrapping a block of butter (beurrage) in a flour/water dough (détrempe) and then folded, this recipe does the reverse and folds the dough with the butter. It is no more challenging than the traditional way, but it does result in a remarkably flaky and tender puff pastry that rises evenly and rolls out easily.

Makes about 3 lb (1.4 kg) of dough • Prep 2 hours plus chilling

Détrempe

4 cups | 600 g	all-purpose flour
1 cup | 250 mL	cool water
9 Tbsp | 130 g	unsalted butter, at room temperature
1 Tbsp | 12 g	granulated sugar
2 tsp | 10 g	salt
1 Tbsp | 15 mL	lemon juice or white vinegar

Beurrage

3 cups | 675 g	unsalted butter, at room temperature
1 cup | 150 g	all-purpose flour

The détrempe (the base of this dough) is best made using electric beaters or in a stand mixer fitted with the hook attachment. If you want to make it by hand, you will have to first mix the ingredients in a bowl and then turn them out onto a work surface to knead for at least 6 minutes to develop a smooth, elastic feel.

• • • • • • • •

Puff pastry, croissant dough, and Danish dough all fall into the family of laminated doughs—doughs which consist of multiple thin layers of flour dough divided by layers of butter. This thin layering is achieved by rolling and folding a lamination layer of butter (the beurrage) into the dough; as you keep rolling and folding the dough, that butter layer intersperses throughout the layers of flour dough. Then, as the pastry bakes, the many thin layers of butter melt and generate steam, pushing up the flour layers around them, and creating that distinctive flakiness you're aiming for.

1. For the détrempe, blend all of the ingredients together in a stand mixer fitted with the dough hook on low speed. Increase the speed one level and mix for 4 minutes until the dough is smooth and springs back when pressed with your finger. Shape it into an 8-inch (20 cm) square, wrap in plastic wrap, and chill for at least 30 minutes, or up to 2 hours.

2. For the beurrage, beat the butter with the flour using electric beaters or in a stand mixer fitted with a paddle attachment on medium speed until smooth. Line an 8-inch (20 cm) square pan with plastic wrap and scrape the mixture into the pan, spreading to level it. Cover and chill this until it is the same consistency as the détrempe, 30–90 minutes (use your fingers to gently press both—once the resistance of each feels the same, it's time to roll!). If the beurrage sets firmly or you're making it ahead, let it warm up to just cooler than room temperature before using.

3. For the lamination stage, remove the beurrage from the pan onto a well-floured work surface. Dust a heavy rolling pin with flour and roll the beurrage into a rectangle about 16 x 9 inches (40 x 23 cm). Lift the beurrage occasionally to ensure it isn't sticking to the work surface (after the first folding,

it doesn't stick at all). Place the détrempe in the centre of the beurrage and fold the beurrage over to completely envelop the détrempe. Roll the dough out to a rectangle measuring 20 x 10 inches (50 x 25 cm), flouring the dough and work surface as needed. Fold it into thirds, dusting off any excess flour with a pastry brush before folding. Rotate the dough 90 degrees and roll it out again to a 20- x 10-inch (50 x 25 cm) rectangle, brushing off the flour and folding into thirds again. Wrap the dough, label it #1 (for first fold), and chill for a minimum of 2 hours, or up to 1 day.

4. For the second fold, roll the dough again into a 20- x 10-inch (50 x 25 cm) rectangle, brush off excess flour, and fold into thirds again. Rotate it 90 degrees, roll and fold again, and then wrap and label it #2. Chill for a minimum of 2 hours, or up to a day.

5. For the final fold, roll and fold the dough into thirds for the final time (just once this time). The dough is now complete, but must be wrapped and chilled for a minimum of 2 hours before using. The puff pastry dough will keep, refrigerated, for up to 4 days, or can be portioned and frozen for up to 3 months, in an airtight container or wrapped in plastic wrap. Thaw in the fridge before using.

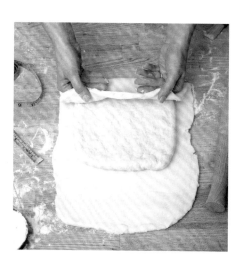  

Danish Pastry Dough

Danish pastry is in the same family of doughs as croissants and puff pastry. A lightly sweetened yeast dough, it has butter folded in, creating a pastry base for a rich morning treat.

Makes 1 lb (½ kg) dough (enough for 24 individual Danishes) • Prep 2 hours plus chilling

Sponge

1 ½ cups | 375 mL	warm water (115°F/46°C)
1 Tbsp | 10 g	instant dry yeast
1 cup | 150 g	all-purpose flour

Dough

1 ½ cups | 225 g	all-purpose flour
1 ¼ cups | 140 g	cake and pastry flour
¼ cup | 50 g	granulated sugar
1 tsp | 5 g	salt
1 ¼ cups | 285 g	cold unsalted butter, cut into pieces

I consider Danish pastry dough a foundation recipe as it is the base for many styles of breakfast pastries. Like puff pastry, it is a lamination dough, but it has the addition of yeast, which makes it lighter and airier. Croissant dough also contains yeast but is more butter-rich than Danish pastry dough.

• • • • • • • •

This version of Danish pastry dough is based more on the European Danish dough, which is a little flakier but also less sweet and less soft than the North American version.

• • • • • • • •

Danish dough is rather involved to make but, because of its soft texture, it's a little quicker and more forgiving than puff pastry dough, which really has to set in between its rollings and foldings.

1. For the sponge, mix the water, yeast, and flour together by hand in a large mixing bowl, or in a stand mixer fitted with the dough hook on low speed until blended. Let this stand for 5 minutes.

2. For the dough, add the all-purpose and cake and pastry flours to the sponge, along with the sugar, salt, and ¼ cup (60 g) of the butter. Mix using electric beaters (with the hook attachments) or in a stand mixer fitted with the dough hook attachment on low speed, until the flour is blended in. Increase the speed by one level and mix, adding the remaining 1 cup (225 g) of butter pieces, a little at a time, until the dough feels elastic but most of the butter pieces are still visible, about 2 minutes. Cover the bowl and allow this dough to rise for 30 minutes, then chill for at least 2 hours.

3. On a lightly floured surface, turn the dough out and dust with a little flour. Roll the dough out to a rectangle about 18 inches (45 cm) long and 10 inches (25 cm) wide. Bring the two short ends of the dough to meet in the centre, then fold the dough in half at the point where they meet (this is called the book fold). Chill the dough, covered, for just 1 hour.

4. Bring the dough out of the fridge and roll it again, this time into a rectangle measuring 18 x 10 inches (45 x 25 cm), turn the dough over, and fold it into thirds. Cover and chill for 1 hour. Repeat this step, then cover and chill the dough for at least 4 hours, or overnight before using. The dough can be frozen, well wrapped in plastic wrap, for up to 3 months. You can shape the Danishes before freezing or simply freeze the dough in portions.

Basic Choux Paste

This recipe is used to make Profiteroles and Éclairs (page 186), Gâteau St. Honoré (page 196), and also the cruller recipe (page 179). Unlike other pastry dough, choux paste is made by cooking the ingredients together and working with the dough while it is still warm. It seems to defy gravity when it bakes, cooking into light-as-air hollow shells that are waiting to be filled with cream.

Makes about 3 cups (750 mL) dough • Prep 20 minutes • Cook 5 minutes

¾ cup | 180 mL	milk
¾ cup | 180 mL	water
10 Tbsp | 145 g	unsalted butter
2 tsp | 8 g	granulated sugar
½ tsp | 2 g	salt
1 ⅔ cups | 340 g	all-purpose flour, sifted
5 | 5	eggs, at room temperature

Choux Paste is a base recipe for many desserts and offers a refreshing contrast to butter-rich pastries that are rolled to line pie or tart shells. It also has a different set of techniques that are important to master in order make you a better baker.

• • • • • • • •

When you start adding the eggs to the warm flour paste, don't be surprised how long it takes to work in the first egg smoothly—it's just the nature of this dough. Once the first egg is blended in, the remaining eggs work in far more easily.

• • • • • • • •

Use the dough while it is still warm and soft, as it is perfect to be piped and then baked or fried.

1. Bring the milk, water, butter, sugar, and salt up to a full simmer in a large saucepan over medium-high heat. Once a simmer is reached, reduce the heat to low and stir in the flour with a wooden spoon, stirring vigorously until the dough cleans the sides of the saucepan (no longer sticks). Scrape this mixture into a large bowl and use electric beaters or a stand mixer fitted with the paddle attachment to beat it on medium speed for a minute or two to cool it a little.

2. Break two of the eggs into a small dish and whisk just to blend them a little. Add these to the flour mixture and beat on medium speed until blended. Add the remaining three eggs one at a time, mixing well after each addition. Work with this pastry while it is still warm.

Caramel Apple Jalousie

I like the simplicity of this easy French dessert and I also like that it's not overly sweet. I would even suggest that this would make a fancy addition to a special breakfast or brunch. The layers of flaky puff pastry, wrapped around a warm and sweet apple filling, remind me of strudel when I eat it.

Makes one 10-inch (25 cm) dessert • Serves 6 to 8 • Prep 20 minutes • Bake 35 minutes

2 | 2	peeled and thinly sliced apples (Granny Smith work well)
¼ cup | 50 g	packed light brown sugar
¼ tsp | 1 g	ground cinnamon
⅓ cup | 65 g	Skor or other toffee bits
½ lb | 250 g	Puff Pastry Dough (page 170) or 1 sheet frozen store-bought butter puff pastry, thawed in the fridge
1 | 1	egg, whisked with 2 Tbsp (30 g) of water, for brushing
	turbinado sugar, for sprinkling

1. Preheat the oven to 400°F (200°C). Line a baking tray with parchment paper.

2. Toss the apples with the brown sugar, cinnamon, and Skor bits in a large bowl and set aside.

3. Place the cold puff pastry sheet on a lightly floured work surface and roll it into a 10-inch (25 cm) square. Cut a rectangle measuring 10 x 4 inches (25 x 10 cm), place it on the prepared baking tray, and brush it with egg wash. This is the jalousie base. Cut a second rectangle measuring 10 x 4 ½ inches (25 x 12 cm) and return it to the fridge to keep cold. Cut the remaining pastry dough into ½-inch (1 cm) strips. Layer the strips on top of the outside edges of the first piece of pastry to add height to the sides of the pastry, trimming to fit the pastry base and brushing with egg wash (this creates a frame to hold in the apple filling). Spoon the apples into the centre of this.

4. Pull the top portion of the pastry from the fridge and make small slits along the breadth of the pastry at ½-inch (1 cm) intervals, extending to ½-inch (1 cm) from the edge of the pastry. Place this over the apples, brush with egg wash, and sprinkle with turbinado sugar. Bake the jalousie for 10 minutes at 400°F (200°C) and then reduce the oven temperature to 375°F (190°C) and bake for an additional 20–25 minutes, until it is a rich golden brown. Serve the jalousie warm or at room temperature. The jalousie can be baked a day ahead, refrigerated, then warmed in the oven at 325°F (160°C) for 15 minutes.

Classic Farmhouse Strawberry Shortcake

This is a traditional North American shortcake—cake-like biscuit filled simply with whipped cream and fresh, ripe strawberries. Other shortcakes may use a sponge cake base with the cream and fruit. So long as you have the combination of cake, cream, and strawberries, it's a shortcake.

Makes 8 shortcake desserts • Prep 25 minutes • Bake/Cook 20 minutes

Shortcakes

2 cups | 300 g	all-purpose flour
¼ cup | 50 g	granulated sugar
1 Tbsp | 9 g	baking powder
1 tsp | 5 mL	finely grated lemon zest
½ tsp | 2 g	baking soda
¼ tsp | 1 g	salt
¼ cup | 60 g	cool unsalted butter, cut into pieces
⅔ cup | 160 mL	buttermilk
1 | 1	egg, whisked with 2 Tbsp (30 mL) water, for brushing

Filling

1 cup | 250 mL	whipping cream
2 Tbsp | 12 g	granulated sugar
½ tsp | 2 mL	pure vanilla extract
2 cups | 500 mL	sliced fresh strawberries
	icing sugar, for dusting

1. Preheat the oven to 375°F (180°C). Line a baking tray with parchment paper.

2. For the shortcakes, in a large bowl, stir the flour, sugar, baking powder, lemon zest, baking soda, and salt to combine. Cut in the butter until the mixture is coarsely crumbly in texture (but it won't look dramatically different). Stir in the buttermilk just until the dough comes together.

3. Turn the dough out onto a lightly floured work surface. Flatten and fold the dough over itself repeatedly, working in any dry flour mixture as you fold, until it all comes together (this will produce a flaky shortcake). Shape the dough into a rectangle that measures about 10 x 6 inches (25 x 15 cm) and ½ inch (1 cm) thick. Cut the dough into eight equally sized rectangles and place these 2 inches (5 cm) apart on the prepared baking tray. Brush the tops of the shortcakes with the egg wash and bake for 18–20 minutes, until the tops are an even golden brown. Cool the shortcakes to room temperature on the pan on a cooling rack.

4. For the filling, whip the cream to soft peaks, then whip in the sugar and vanilla. To assemble the shortcakes, split one in half horizontally. Place the bottom half on a plate and dollop a little whipped cream on it. Spoon the strawberries over top, then gently rest the top of the shortcake on the fruit. Dust the shortcake with icing sugar and serve immediately. The shortcakes are best served the day they are baked, but the dough can be portioned and frozen (wrapped in plastic wrap, together or individually) and thawed in the fridge before baking.

I live in Ontario, where June is strawberry season, and this strawberry shortcake is delightful when they are in season. The combination of this particular shortcake—which is almost biscuit-like and similar to a scone—with the whipped cream and fresh, ripe berries is so simple, and simply heavenly.

Crullers

These ruffly, eggy versions of doughnuts are a real treat.

Makes about 24 crullers • Prep 15 minutes • Cook 40 minutes

1 | 1   **recipe Basic Choux Paste (page 173)**

vegetable oil, for frying

icing sugar, for dusting

I pipe the crullers onto little squares of parchment so that they are easier (and safer) to lift and drop into the oil. It is possible to pipe the crullers right into the oil, carefully, but be sure to use a fabric piping bag. If hot oil droplets spit onto a plastic piping bag, they could cause a leak.

• • • • • • • •

If you are cooking your crullers in a saucepan as opposed to a fryer, keep your thermometer in the oil to monitor the temperature. You may have to adjust your heat settings to keep the oil at an even temperature (dropping in the crullers will lower the temperature of the oil).

1. Fill a large, deep, heavy-bottomed saucepan with about 2 inches (5 cm) of oil. The oil should come up to only a third the height of the saucepan. Heat this to 350°F (180°C) (use a candy/fryer thermometer) or use a tabletop fryer and follow the manufacturer's instructions. While the oil is heating, cut a few 3-inch (7.5 cm) squares of parchment paper and lightly grease them with oil or butter.

2. Fill a piping bag fitted with a large star tip with the choux paste (you may have to do this in batches). Pipe 3-inch (7.5 cm) circles of choux paste on the parchment paper and then gently slide them off the parchment into the oil, trying not to splash. You can also flip the piped crullers onto a slotted spoon and lower them into the oil. The dough will expand in the oil so do this in batches, leaving about 2 inches (5 cm) between each.

3. Cook the crullers for about 5 minutes, turning them halfway through cooking. Lift them out with a slotted spoon or straining spoon and place them on a paper towel–lined plate to cool. When almost cool, dust with icing sugar and serve immediately.

Apricot Almond Vol-au-Vents

A vol-au-vent is really like a tall tart shell made of puff pastry.
For this dessert, I make a frangipane filling and top it with an apricot baked right
in the centre. These tarts, and the two tart recipes that follow, will get you
feeling comfortable about rolling and shaping puff pastry into different styles.

Makes 4 individual tarts • Prep 40 minutes • Bake/Cook 30 minutes

¼ cup | 30 g	**ground almonds**
2 Tbsp | 25 g	**granulated sugar**
1 | 1	**egg**
¼ tsp | 1 mL	**pure almond extract**
½ lb | 250 g	**Puff Pastry Dough (page 170) or 1 sheet frozen store-bought butter puff pastry, thawed in the fridge**
2 | 2	**large fresh apricots turbinado sugar, for sprinkling**

1. Preheat the oven to 375°F (190°C). Line a baking tray with parchment paper.

2. Stir the ground almonds and sugar together. In a small dish, whisk the egg, then measure out and add 2 Tbsp (30 mL) to the almond mixture, stirring to combine. Stir in the almond extract. Add 1 Tbsp (15 mL) of water to the remainder of the whisked egg and use this as an egg wash to brush the tarts.

3. On a lightly floured surface, roll out the puff pastry dough into a 12-inch (30 cm) square, about ¼ inch (0.5 cm) thick. Using a 3 ½-inch (9 cm) round cookie cutter, cut eight circles from the dough. Place four of them on the baking tray and brush with the egg wash. Use a 2 ½-inch (6 cm) cutter to cut a hole in the centre of the remaining four circles and place them on the pastry circles on the tray. Dock the centre of the pastry with a fork.

4. Spoon the almond paste into the centre of the four tarts. Split the apricots in half, remove the pits, and place an apricot half, flat side down, in each tart. Brush the tops of the apricots and pastry with the egg wash and sprinkle with turbinado sugar. Bake the tarts for 25–30 minutes, until the pastry is a rich golden brown. Cool the tarts to room temperature on the pan on a cooling rack before serving. The tarts can be baked up to 1 day in advance and chilled, but should be served at room temperature.

A vol-au-vent can also be baked without a filling to be used later on (and then filled with savoury filling options such as a creamy seafood or mushroom). To do this, follow steps 1–3, then bake at 375°F (190°C) for 20–25 minutes. You may find the centre of the vol-au-vent rises up but, because of the flaky layers, you can remove the centre disc to make more room for filling. These can be baked hours ahead and re-warmed in the oven at 325°F (160°C) for 10 minutes before serving.

S'mores Tarts

Playful and fun, these simple tarts are filled with a combination of graham crackers, marshmallows, and milk chocolate. What a treat!

Makes 4 individual tarts • Prep 25 minutes • Bake/Cook 27 minutes

½ lb | 250 g	**Puff Pastry Dough (page 170) or 1 sheet frozen store-bought butter puff pastry, thawed in the fridge**
2 cups | 500 mL	**mini marshmallows**
8 | 8	**graham crackers**
6 oz | 180 g	**milk chocolate bar, cut into chunks, or milk chocolate chips**
1 | 1	**egg, whisked with 2 Tbsp (30 mL) water, for brushing**

1. Preheat the oven to 375°F (190°C). Line a baking tray with parchment paper.

2. On a lightly floured surface, roll out the puff pastry dough to a 12-inch (30 cm) square, about ¼ inch (0.5 cm) thick. Trim the edges and then cut the dough into four equally sized squares and place them on the prepared tray.

3. Place 1 graham cracker in the centre of each pastry square and sprinkle each one neatly with one-eighth of the marshmallows and chocolate chunks or chips. Top with the remaining graham crackers. Fold the pastry to just come over the top of the filling (covering it by about 1 inch/2.5 cm on each side) and press down the corners and edges quite firmly to secure (the tart will open up a bit as it bakes).

4. Brush the puff pastry with the egg wash and bake for 15 minutes. Pull the tarts from the oven and top the centre of each one with the remaining marshmallows and chocolate. Return the tarts to the oven to bake for another 10–12 minutes, until the pastry is golden brown. Like campfire s'mores, these tarts are best served warm, but allow them to cool for 15 minutes before serving.

The technique for folding this style of tart is the simplest of the three Simple tarts in this chapter. The pastry puffs as it bakes, so it will push itself open a bit, but I find that the rustic look matches well with the campfire-style filling. It's not meant to be too fancy.

•   •   •   •   •   •   •   •

If you wish to prepare the tarts ahead of time, assemble the pastry to step 3 and then refrigerate, uncovered, on a baking tray. When ready to bake, follow step 4.

Salted Caramel Pear Tarts

Pears are one of my favourite fruits to work with in baking—they are delicate and sweet and their softness, once baked, contrasts with and highlights the tender, flaky puff pastry of this elegant tart. Salted caramel desserts sometimes sound as if they are going to be a big effort, but this one is really quite simple to make.

Makes 4 individual tarts • Prep 25 minutes plus chilling • Bake 25 minutes

½ lb | 250 g	**Puff Pastry Dough (page 170) or 1 sheet frozen store-bought butter puff pastry, thawed in the fridge**
1 | 1	**egg, whisked with 2 Tbsp (30 mL) water, for brushing**
2 | 2	**ripe Bartlett pears**
¼ cup | 50 g	**packed dark brown sugar**
¼ cup | 60 mL	**whipping cream**
	pinch coarse sea salt or fleur de sel

1. Preheat the oven to 375°F (190°C). Line a baking tray with parchment paper.

2. On a lightly floured surface, roll out the puff pastry dough into a 12-inch (30 cm square), about ¼ inch (0.5 cm) thick. Trim the edges and then cut the dough into four evenly sized squares and place them on the prepared baking tray. Using a paring knife, cut an "L" mark into two opposing corners, leaving about ½ inch (1 cm) between them. Follow the line of those corners, but keep ½ inch (1 cm) within the outer edge. Brush the surface of the puff pastry with the egg wash. Lift the cut corners of the pastry, cross them over each other (one over, one under) and lay them flat (now on opposite sides) so that the cut corners line up with their opposing base corners. Brush the edges of the pastry with the egg wash and prick the centre base of the tart shell with a fork. Chill the pastry while preparing the filling.

3. Peel, halve, and core the pears. Slice each pear half widthwise into ¼-inch (0.5 cm) slices and arrange them in the centre of each tart shell. Sprinkle the pear slices with the brown sugar, then drizzle the cream over top. Sprinkle the tarts with a little sea salt and bake for 20–25 minutes, until the pears are tender and the pastry is a rich golden brown. The tarts can be served warm or at room temperature, and are best enjoyed the day they are baked.

This crossover technique turns a simple square of puff pastry into a tart shell with an edge to hold in a filling, with no trim or waste. I also use this technique when making a savoury tomato basil tart—I use chopped tomatoes with fresh basil and a little garlic baked in the centre and top them with a crumbling of fresh goat cheese when the tart comes out of the oven.

Spiral Raisin Danishes

*This is a classic Danish style, and a good place to start
if you're making Danishes for the first time.*

Makes 12 Danishes • Prep 25 minutes plus resting • Bake 30 minutes

½	½	recipe Danish Pastry Dough (page 172)
2–3 Tbsp	30–45 g	butter, melted
		cinnamon sugar, for sprinkling
½ cup	70 g	raisins
1	1	egg, whisked with 2 Tbsp (30 mL) of water, for brushing
½ cup	125 mL	apricot jam or apple jelly

1. On a lightly floured surface, roll out the Danish dough into a 12-inch (30 cm) square. Brush the dough with melted butter and sprinkle generously with cinnamon sugar and then the raisins. Roll up the dough and cut it into 12 pieces. Line a baking tray with parchment paper and place the Danishes on the tray, tucking each end of the spiral underneath. Cover the Danishes with a tea towel and leave them to rise on the counter for 1 hour 30 minutes; they will almost double in size.

2. Preheat the oven to 375°F (190°C).

3. Brush the risen Danishes with the egg wash and bake for 25–30 minutes, until they are a rich golden brown. Allow to cool for 20 minutes on the baking tray on a cooling rack.

4. To glaze the Danishes, melt the apricot jam or jelly in a small saucepan over medium-low heat (if using apricot jam, strain out the fruit pieces before using). Brush the jam or jelly over each Danish, let set for 1 minute, and then serve. The Danishes should be enjoyed the day they are baked but they can be prepared a day ahead (see note).

The amount of cinnamon sugar you sprinkle over the pastry before you roll it up is up to you. If you like a very sweet pastry, sprinkle a generous amount. If you'd like just a hint, then a thin, even layer will do.

• • • • • • • •

It's traditional to glaze Danishes with a melted apricot jam. This adds the perfect hint of sweetness and shine, but also helps to keep the Danishes fresher for longer.

• • • • • • • •

If you are serving these for breakfast or brunch, you can do all of the assembly work the evening before and store the filled Danishes on the baking tray, covered with a tea towel, overnight. Pull them out of the fridge and let them rise up for 2 hours before brushing with egg wash and baking.

Cherry Danish Twists

This style of Danish is filled before it is baked so it suits a pre-cooked filling. When given a choice, I always reach for a cherry Danish, but other intense fruits work well, too, like blueberry or lemon.

Makes 12 Danishes • Prep 30 minutes plus resting • Bake 30 minutes

½ | ½	**recipe Danish Pastry Dough (page 172)**
½ cup | 125 g	**cherry jam**
1 cup | 250 mL	**pitted tart cherries (frozen and thawed, or jarred), well drained**
1 | 1	**egg, whisked with 2 Tbsp (30 mL) of water, for brushing**
½ cup | 125 mL	**apricot jam or apple jelly**

A prepared pie filling (cherry, blueberry, etc.) is commonly used in commercial bakeries, but I like the freshness and simplicity of fruit stirred with jam. To make blueberry Danishes, use fresh or frozen blueberries and blueberry jam in the same measure as the cherries and cherry jam.

1. On a lightly floured surface, roll out the dough into a 12-inch (30 cm) square, trim the edges, and cut it into twelve 1-inch (2.5 cm) strips. Twist each strip without stretching it too much and then shape each twist into a spiralled circle. Line a baking tray with parchment paper. Place each spiral on the tray and tuck the end of the spiral underneath each pastry. Cover the tray with a tea towel and leave the pastry to rise on the counter for 1 hour 30 minutes.

2. Preheat the oven to 375°F (190°C).

3. Stir the cherry jam and drained cherries together to make the filling. Brush each pastry with egg wash and then drop 1 Tbsp (15 mL) of the cherry filling into the centre of each Danish, using the back of your spoon to gently press down the dough in the centre to hold the filling in place. Bake the Danishes for about 30 minutes, until they are a rich golden brown. Allow the Danishes to cool for 20 minutes on the baking tray on a cooling rack.

4. To glaze the Danishes, melt the apricot jam or jelly in a small saucepan over medium-low heat (if using apricot jam, strain out the fruit pieces before using). Brush the jam or jelly over each Danish, let set for 1 minute, and then serve. The Danishes should be enjoyed the day they are baked but they can be prepared a day ahead (page 183).

Tropical Fruit Pinwheel Danishes

These Danishes are shaped and baked, and then the lemon curd and fresh tropical fruit are added afterwards, making them fresh-tasting and visually stunning.

Makes 12 Danishes • Prep 50 minutes plus chilling and resting • Bake/Cook 20 minutes

½ | ½	**recipe Danish Pastry Dough (page 172)**
¼ | ¼	**recipe Lemon Curd (page 206)**
1 | 1	**egg, whisked with 2 Tbsp (30 mL) water, for brushing**
1 ½ cups | 375 mL	**prepared fresh tropical fruits**
½ cup | 125 mL	**apricot jam or apple jelly**

1. On a lightly floured surface, roll out the Danish dough to a rectangle measuring 16 x 12 inches (40 x 30 cm) and trim the edges. Cut the pastry into twelve 4-inch (10 cm) squares. To make the pinwheel shape, cut a line through the dough from each corner toward the centre; the cut should be about 1 ½ inches (3.5 cm) long and go all the way through the dough. Bring one point from each corner into the centre and press in firmly where all four points meet right in the middle, so that it looks like a pinwheel. Line a baking tray with parchment paper and place the Danishes on the tray. Cover with a tea towel, and let the pastry rise for 1 hour 30 minutes.

2. Preheat the oven to 375°F (190°C).

3. Press down on the centres of the Danishes, where the points meet, so that they stay in place when baking. Brush them with egg wash and bake for about 20 minutes, until they are a nice golden brown. Allow the Danishes to cool completely on the tray on a cooling rack before adding the topping.

4. To assemble, dollop a small spoonful of lemon curd in the centre of each Danish. Arrange small pieces of tropical fruit on top of the curd. Heat the apricot jam or apple jelly until bubbling (strain the apricot jam if there are fruit pieces) and brush this over the fruit and pastry to secure the fruit in place and add shine. The Danishes should be enjoyed the day they are baked but they can be prepared a day ahead (page 183).

Profiteroles and Éclairs

Profiteroles, or cream puffs, are immensely satisfying and appealing. Éclairs are a larger, longer version of profiteroles. I have provided options here for either a chocolate or a vanilla glaze, and the choice of which to use is yours—both will bring out your inner princess!

Makes 36 profiteroles and 12 éclairs • Prep 45 minutes • Bake 25 minutes plus chilling

1 | 1	recipe Basic Choux Paste (page 173)
1 | 1	recipe Pastry Cream, chilled (page 86)

Vanilla Glaze

1 ½ cups | 195 g	icing sugar, sifted
3 Tbsp | 45 mL	milk
1 ½ Tbsp | 22 g	unsalted butter, melted

Chocolate Glaze

4 oz | 120 g	bittersweet couverture/baking chocolate, chopped
¼ cup | 60 g	unsalted butter
1 Tbsp | 15 mL	corn syrup

1. Preheat the oven to 400°F (200°C). Line two baking trays with parchment paper.

2. Fill a piping bag fitted with a large plain tip with the choux paste. Pipe 12 éclairs, each about 4 inches (10 cm) long and 1 ½ inches (3.5 cm) wide, onto the first baking tray and pipe 36 profiteroles, each about 1 ½ inches (3.5 cm) in diameter, onto the second tray (you may need two trays for the profiteroles). Wet your finger in cool water and tap down any points on the paste.

3. Bake the éclairs and profiteroles for 10 minutes, then reduce the heat to 375°F (190°C) and bake for about 15 more minutes (the éclairs may take a bit longer), until they are a rich golden brown colour and are very light in weight (don't bake these in a convection oven or they'll blow away). Allow the pastries to cool completely on the pan on a cooling rack before filling.

4. To fill, stir the pastry cream to soften it and fill a piping bag with a medium plain tip (or an éclair or doughnut tip, if you have one). Use a skewer to first poke a small hole in the end of each éclair and the side of each profiterole. Insert the piping bag tip into each pastry and fill with cream until you feel resistance. Chill until ready to glaze.

5. Prepare either the Vanilla Glaze or the Chocolate Glaze. For the vanilla, whisk the icing sugar and milk together until smooth, and then stir in the melted butter. For the chocolate, place the chocolate, butter, and corn syrup in a metal bowl and set it over a saucepan of barely simmering water, stirring until the chocolate has melted. Remove the bowl from the heat.

6. Dip the tops of the éclairs or profiteroles in the glaze and set them on a cooling rack to dry for an hour before serving or chilling to serve later. They should be enjoyed within a day of filling and glazing.

A doughnut tip is a piping tip that narrows to a long, angled tip so it can fit into the centre of a doughnut (or éclair) without creating too large of a hole. If you don't have one, a medium-sized plain tip will work well.

. . . .

When filling profiteroles, I always look for the weak spot to insert the piping tip. Some people fill the profiteroles at the bottom, but I find that if I fill from a weak spot (a point where the pastry seems thin, usually at a crease) then the cream stays in place and doesn't ooze out accidentally.

Another classic use for profiteroles is to fill them with ice cream and drizzle a warm chocolate sauce over top. Sinful and delicious!

. . . .

Unfilled éclairs and profiteroles can be made up to 1 day ahead of time and stored in an airtight container for up to 2 days, or frozen for up to 3 months and thawed before filling.

. . . .

Feel free to add a touch of food colouring of your choice to the Vanilla Glaze if you'd like to add flair.

Cabernet Poached Pear and Walnut Strudels

Red wine–poached pears are wrapped in phyllo pastry along with walnuts and baked up into flaky parcels. The poaching syrup becomes a gorgeous spiced glaze to serve with these individual desserts.

Makes 4 individual desserts • Prep 45 minutes • Bake/Cook 45 minutes

Pears

3 cups | 750 mL	Cabernet Sauvignon or Cabernet Franc wine
3 cups | 600 g	granulated sugar
2 | 2	cinnamon sticks
3 | 3	whole star anise
4 | 4	Bartlett pears, peeled, halved, and cored

Assembly

8 | 8	sheets phyllo pastry
⅓ cup | 75 g	unsalted butter, melted
½ cup | 75 g	lightly toasted walnut pieces
1 | 1	egg, whisked with 2 Tbsp (30 mL) water, for brushing
2 Tbsp | 25 g	granulated sugar
¼ tsp | 1 g	ground cinnamon

1. Bring the wine, sugar, cinnamon sticks, and star anise to a simmer in a medium saucepan over medium heat. Add the pears and then place a piece of parchment paper directly on the surface of the liquid and let the pears poach on medium heat (just a few bubbles gently rising to the surface) until they pierce easily with a fork. Let the pears cool in the liquid and then chill them in it until you are ready to assemble them.

2. Preheat the oven to 375°F (190°C). Line a baking tray with parchment paper.

3. On a clean work surface, lay out one sheet of phyllo pastry and brush it with a thin layer of melted butter. Place a second, third, and fourth sheet of phyllo over top, brushing each time with butter. Cut this stack of pastry sheets in half lengthwise.

4. Strain the pears and reserve the liquid if desired (see my note below). Arrange two pear halves side by side at the end of each of the first two phyllo rectangles and sprinkle with some walnut pieces. Tuck in the sides of the phyllo and then roll up the pastry. Place the pastry, seam side down, on the prepared baking tray. Repeat with the remaining four sheets of phyllo and the pears and walnuts. Brush the tops of each strudel with egg wash. Stir the 2 Tbsp (25 g) of sugar and cinnamon together and sprinkle over top.

5. Bake the strudels for about 20 minutes, until they are an even golden brown. Slice the strudels on an angle to plate them. The strudels can be served warm, at room temperature, or chilled. They can be assembled ahead of time and chilled until ready to bake.

When you first poach the pears in red wine, they may cook through but the red wine colour won't seep all the way through unless the pears sit in the liquid for a day or two. They can be used right away, but it's up to you how intense you want that red wine hue to be.

• • • • • • • •

If you like, the pear poaching liquid can be reserved and then reduced to create a glaze, perfect for churning into a sorbet if you have an ice cream maker.

Cheese pairs well with this combination of pear and walnut. Try adding a slice of brie or blue cheese to the inside of the strudels and serve them warm, or pass around a cheese board when serving these, and let your guests choose as they wish.

Chocolate Hazelnut Napoleon

*Also known as a mille feuille, this slice of puff pastry heaven matches a
thick chocolate hazelnut custard with flaky layers of baked puff pastry.*

Makes 6 individual napoleons • Prep 90 minutes • Bake/Cook 40 minutes plus chilling

Chocolate Hazelnut Pastry Cream

1 cup | 250 mL	evaporated milk
½ cup | 125 mL	milk
3 | 3	egg yolks
3 Tbsp | 22 g	cornstarch
5 oz | 150 g	bittersweet couverture/baking chocolate, chopped
2 Tbsp | 30 g	unsalted butter, at room temperature
2 Tbsp | 30 mL	hazelnut liqueur (optional)
1 tsp | 5 mL	pure vanilla extract
⅓ cup | 85 g	pure hazelnut butter, well stirred

Assembly

1 lb | 500 g	Puff Pastry Dough (page 170) or 2 sheets frozen store-bought puff pastry, thawed
	icing sugar, for dusting

*It may seem counterintuitive to weigh down
your sheets of pastry to bake them. Isn't the idea
to have the puff bake up flaky? That may be true,
but if left uncovered, the puff pastry would bake up
too flaky, and then crumble and collapse
between the layers of the pastry cream.*

• • • • • • • •

*When making elaborate recipes such
as this, linear measuring is important so that
everything lines up. I rely on my flexible, fabric
measuring tape for these tasks. It's an inexpensive
tool found at fabric stores or departments,
and can be easily washed if a little chocolate
pastry cream, for example, gets on it.*

1. For the pastry cream, heat the evaporated milk and milk in a medium saucepan over medium heat until just below a simmer. In a bowl, whisk the egg yolks and cornstarch together. Place the chocolate and butter in a separate bowl and place a sieve over top this bowl.

2. Pour the hot milk over the egg mixture, whisking constantly until it has all been added. Return this to the saucepan and whisk over medium heat until the custard thickens and turns glossy, about 3 minutes. Remove the saucepan from the heat and pour it through the sieve and over the chocolate and butter. Whisk this until the chocolate has melted and the custard is smooth. Whisk in the hazelnut liqueur (if using) and vanilla, then whisk in the hazelnut butter. Place a piece of plastic wrap directly on the surface of the custard, cool to room temperature, then chill until set, about 3 hours.

3. Preheat the oven to 400°F (200°C). Line a baking tray with parchment paper, and have a second baking tray of the same size on hand.

4. Cut the pastry dough into three equal pieces. If using store-bought sheets, measure and trim each piece to a rectangle measuring about 14 x 5 inches (35 x 12.5 cm) (you will have extra trim). If using homemade dough, on a lightly floured surface, roll out each piece to a rectangle measuring about 14 x 5 inches (35 x 12.5 cm). Alternatively, you can roll out each piece to about 8 x 4 inches (20 x 10 cm) and then finish rolling the dough through a pasta roller set to the widest setting (this makes for a pastry that bakes evenly and level). If necessary,

stack the three pieces of dough and trim the edges so that they are all the same size (they will be closer to 12 x 4 inches/30 x 10 cm once trimmed). Chill the dough for 15 minutes.

5. Place the three pieces of dough on the prepared baking tray, leaving an inch (2.5 cm) between them, and dock with a fork. Place a second sheet of parchment paper over the pastry and place the second baking tray on top. Bake the pastry for 10 minutes, then place a heavy weight on top of the top baking tray (a cast iron skillet, or even two bricks wrapped in foil, approximately 2 lb/1 kg) and bake for 10 minutes more. Remove the weights, the top baking tray, and parchment and bake for about 10 more minutes, until the pastry is a rich golden brown. Cool completely in the pan on a cooling rack before assembling.

6. To assemble, place one of the pastry pieces on a platter or flat board. Stir the pastry cream to soften it and spread half of it over the pastry. Top it with a second sheet of pastry and spread the remaining half of the pastry cream over top. Top this with the third piece of pastry and press it down ever so gently. Chill for 1 hour.

7. Dust the top of the napoleon generously with icing sugar. Using a sharp chef's knife, trim the edges of the pastry if needed, then cut the napoleon into six evenly sized portions. Refrigerate the napoleons, uncovered, until ready to serve. The napoleons can be prepared and fully assembled up to a day in advance, then loosely covered and refrigerated until ready to serve.

Filled Danish Braid

Dried fruits are at the centre of this braided loaf, making it an ideal recipe for a holiday brunch.

Serves 12 • Prep 45 minutes plus resting • Bake/Cook 30 minutes

Fruit Filling

½ cup | 75 g	raisins
½ cup | 70 g	dried cranberries
½ cup | 80 g	pitted dried prunes, cut in half
¼ cup | 60 g	diced candied citrus peel (orange or lemon)
	juice and zest of 1 orange
½ tsp | 2 g	ground cinnamon
½ tsp | 2 g	ground ginger

Cheese Filling

½ cup | 125 g	cream cheese, softened
2 Tbsp | 25 g	granulated sugar
1 | 1	egg yolk
¼ tsp | 1 mL	pure vanilla extract

Assembly

½ | ½	recipe Danish Pastry Dough (page 172)
1 | 1	egg, whisked with 2 Tbsp (30 mL) water, for brushing
1 | 1	egg white, at room temperature

Sugared Almonds

2 Tbsp | 25 g	granulated sugar
1 cup | 100 g	sliced almonds
½ cup | 60 g	icing sugar, sifted
1 Tbsp | 15 mL	milk

The sugared almonds are a versatile component of this recipe. While I sprinkle them on top of the baked braid to add crunch, they are also fantastic on top of a tart (like White Chocolate Cranberry Mousse Tart, page 100), a trifle, or even a bowl of ice cream with fruit. They can be stored in an airtight container for up to a month.

1. For the fruit filling, toss the raisins, cranberries, prunes, and candied citrus peel with the juice, zest, cinnamon, and ginger. Set aside, stirring occasionally.

2. For the cheese filling, beat the cream cheese with the sugar until smooth and then beat in the egg yolk and vanilla. Set aside.

3. To assemble, on a lightly floured surface, roll out the Danish pastry dough to a rectangle measuring 15 x 10 inches (36 x 25 cm). Lightly mark two parallel lines down the longer length of the pastry about 3 ½ inches (9 cm) in from each edge (use the back of a knife for this as you have to be careful not to cut through the pastry; these are guidelines only, not cuts). Use a pastry wheel to cut strips (1 ½ inches/3.5 cm wide) at a 45° angle, starting from the outer edge of the pastry and cutting inward to meet the guideline at the 3 ½ inches (9 cm) mark. You will fit 7–10 strips per side, and create a chevron pattern that does not meet in the middle. Spread the cheese filling down the middle of the pastry and top it with the fruits—drizzle any excess juice from the fruit bowl over the fruit. Trim away any excess pastry and fold over a bit of pastry at the top and bottom of the rectangle. Alternating strips from each side, fold the strips over the filling so that they reach the opposite side and create a braided look. Once you reach the end of the pastry, tuck the last two strips underneath. Line a baking tray with parchment paper and lift the braid carefully to the prepared tray. Cover with a tea towel, and let rise for 1 hour 30 minutes.

4. Preheat the oven to 375°F (190°C).

5. Brush the Danish braid with the egg wash and bake for about 30 minutes, until it is a rich golden brown. Cool the pastry completely on the baking tray on a cooling rack before glazing and topping with sugared almonds. Leave the oven on.

6. For the sugared almonds, line a baking tray with parchment paper. Whisk the egg white by hand until foamy and then whisk in the sugar until dissolved and the white is still foamy. Stir in the almonds to coat well and spread them on the prepared baking tray. Bake the almonds at 375°F (190°C) until browned, 12–15 minutes, then cool on the tray on a cooling rack before using (this will make more than you need for this recipe).

7. To decorate the Danish braid, whisk the icing sugar and milk together and drizzle this over the pastry. Lightly crumble the almonds over this glaze and let it set for 30 minutes before serving. The Danish braid is best enjoyed the day it is baked. It can be assembled, but not baked, 1 day ahead to help with timing if you're planning to have it in the morning.

Classic Cherry Strudel

*This is the authentic Viennese-style cherry strudel, where the dough is
stretched out as thinly as possible and rolled over its fruit filling.
To stretch out the strudel you need a clean (but not valuable) tablecloth.*

Makes 1 strudel • Serves 8 to 10 • Prep 90 minutes plus resting • Bake/Cook 1 hour

Cherry Filling

4 cups | 1 L	pitted tart cherries (these can be from frozen or jarred)
2 cups | 400 g	granulated sugar
2 | 2	cinnamon sticks
3 Tbsp | 22 g	cornstarch

Strudel Dough

1 ½ cups | 225 g	all-purpose flour
1 cup | 150 g	bread flour
¼ tsp | 1 g	salt
1 cup | 250 mL	warm water
3 Tbsp | 45 mL	vegetable oil
½ tsp | 2 mL	apple cider vinegar

Assembly

⅓ cup | 75 g	unsalted butter, melted
⅔ cup | 90 g	dry breadcrumbs
1 | 1	egg, whisked with 2 Tbsp (30 mL) water, for brushing
	icing sugar, for dusting

1. For the cherry filling, bring the cherries, sugar, and cinnamon sticks up to a simmer in a saucepan over medium-high heat and simmer for 10 minutes. Whisk the cornstarch in a small bowl with a little cold water and add this to the cherries, stirring until the juices have thickened and the cherries are glossy. Set aside to cool before using.

2. For the strudel dough, blend the all-purpose and bread flours with the salt in a stand mixer fitted with the paddle attachment. Add the water, oil, and vinegar and mix on low speed until the dough comes together and then increase the speed by one level and knead for 2–3 minutes (the dough will seem sticky but will be smooth and elastic). Turn the dough out onto a lightly floured work surface and continue to knead it until it has a smooth but elastic texture. Place the dough in a bowl, cover, and set aside to rest at room temperature for at least 1 hour.

3. To assemble, preheat the oven to 375°F (190°C). Line a baking tray with parchment paper.

4. Lay a clean tablecloth (about 40 inches/100 cm square) out over your work surface and dust it evenly with flour. Place the strudel dough in the middle of the tablecloth and use your hands or a dusted rolling pin to spread the dough out as far as you can. Now switch to only using your hands (keep them dusted with flour) and pull and stretch the dough from underneath, using the back of your hands, until it is almost transparent (it's all right if a hole pops up here or there).

  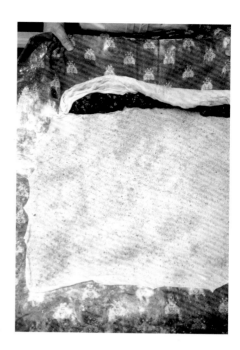

5. Once the dough is stretched as far as it can be, brush the entire surface gently with the melted butter (or spread it with your hand). Sprinkle the dough with breadcrumbs, then spoon the cool cherry filling over one end of the dough. Trim away the end pieces of dough to create clean edges and, using the tablecloth for leverage, lift and roll up the strudel dough loosely and quickly. Use the tablecloth to lift it onto the prepared baking tray (you can curve it, if it is bigger than the tray) and pinch the edges to ensure the strudel is sealed.

6. Brush the top with egg wash and bake for about 45 minutes, until it is a rich golden brown. Allow the strudel to cool for at least 20 minutes on the tray on a cooling rack before slicing. Dust each slice generously with icing sugar to serve. This strudel is best served the day it's baked, but can be stored, refrigerated, for up to 3 days.

Making strudel from scratch does take a little practice, since you really need to get to know the feel of your dough. Using the paddle attachment rather than the dough hook for step 2 ensures that the dough really gets pressed and stretched as it works around the bowl. The texture of strudel dough is different than bread dough, and we're also making a smaller volume, so the paddle is more effective.

• • • • • • • •

The dough takes extensive kneading to develop the glutens in it so that it can be stretched thinly without tearing (hence the call for bread flour in the recipe—it's got a higher gluten content), yet it takes a gentle and patient hand to stretch it out thinly and evenly.

• • • • • • • •

If the strudel dough starts springing back on you as you stretch it, just walk away for 5 minutes. This will give the dough a chance to relax so that when you go back to it, it'll stretch easily.

• • • • • • • •

You can make this dough ahead of time and chill it before stretching, but be sure to bring it fully up to room temperature before you start stretching.

Gâteau St. Honoré

This classic French torte is named after St. Honoré, the patron saint of pastry chefs. Not a cake-based confection, this torte has a puff pastry base, topped with pastry cream and whipped cream and surrounded by profiteroles dipped in caramelized sugar.

Makes one 9-inch (23 cm) torte • Serves 10 to 12 • Prep 90 minutes • Bake/Cook 1 hour plus chilling

½ lb | 250 g	**Puff Pastry Dough (page 170) or 1 sheet frozen store-bought butter puff pastry, thawed**
1 | 1	**recipe Pastry Cream (page 86), chilled**

Profiteroles

½ | ½	**recipe Basic Choux Paste (page 173), still warm**
3 Tbsp | 45 mL	**water**
1 cup | 200 g	**granulated sugar**
1 Tbsp | 15 mL	**white corn syrup**

Assembly

1 ½ cups | 375 mL	**whipping cream**
1 ½ Tbsp | 6 g	**instant skim milk powder**
3 Tbsp | 36 g	**granulated sugar**
1 tsp | 5 mL	**pure vanilla extract**
2 Tbsp | 30 mL	**raspberry purée**
1 cup | 125 mL	**fresh raspberries**

You may have picked up by the number of steps in this recipe that this is not a last-minute dessert. It also uses a wide array of professional baking techniques, so if you've accomplished this dessert, you deserve to feel good about it! And your friends and family will love you for it.

• • • • • • •

The caramel-dipped profiteroles, displayed with the discs of caramel on top, are meant to represent the halo on St. Honoré's head. How sweet!

1. Preheat the oven to 375°F (190°C). Line a baking tray with parchment paper.

2. Roll out the puff pastry and cut it into a 9-inch (23 cm) circle (or use the shell from a 9-inch/23 cm removable tart pan to cut a circle with a pretty fluted edge) and place this on the prepared baking tray. Dock the pastry with a fork and bake for 20–25 minutes until an even golden brown. Cool on the pan on a cooling rack.

3. For the profiteroles, preheat the oven to 400°F (200°C) and line two baking trays with parchment paper.

4. Fill a piping bag fitted with a large plain tip with the choux paste. Pipe 16–18 profiteroles, each about 1 ½ inches (3.5 cm) in diameter. Wet your finger in cool water and tap down any points on the batter.

5. Bake the profiteroles for 10 minutes, then reduce the oven temperature to 375°F (190°C) and continue to bake for about 15 more minutes, until they are a rich golden brown colour and feel very light. Allow the profiteroles to cool completely in the pan on a cooling rack before filling.

6. To fill, stir the pastry cream to soften it and fill a piping bag with a medium plain tip (or an éclair or doughnut tip, if you have one—page 187). Use a skewer to first poke a small hole in the side of each profiterole. Insert the piping bag and fill each one with cream until you feel resistance. Save any remaining pastry cream for the torte. Chill until ready to dip in caramelized sugar.

7. Bring the water, sugar, and corn syrup up to a boil in a small saucepan over high heat and continue to boil, uncovered and without stirring, and occasionally brushing the sides of the saucepan with water, until the sugar is a light amber colour. Ready a bowl of ice water and carefully set the bottom of the saucepan in the ice water to stop the sugar from cooking further.

8. Lightly grease a parchment-lined baking tray. Using tongs, carefully dip the tops of the profiteroles halfway into the caramelized sugar and place them, caramel side down, on the prepared baking tray to set. If the caramel in the saucepan begins to set before you have finished, you can reheat the caramel on low heat.

9. To assemble, whip the cream with the skim milk powder until it holds a soft peak and then stir in the sugar and vanilla. Divide the cream in half and stir the raspberry purée into one half. Fill two piping bags fitted with a large plain or star tip with one cream each.

10. Place the baked puff pastry disc on a serving plate. Spread the remaining pastry cream on the bottom, leaving ½ inch (1 cm) of space around the outside edge. Arrange the dipped profiteroles around the outside of the puff pastry with their flat, caramel-dipped tops facing up. Sprinkle the fresh raspberries over the pastry cream. Pipe alternating straight lines, circles, or other patterns with the two colours of whipped cream and chill until ready to serve. The St. Honoré is best served the day it is assembled, but the separate parts—pastry base, profiteroles, and pastry cream—can be prepared 1 day ahead.

Croquembouche

This grand tower of cream puffs is glued together with caramelized sugar.
A grand dessert for a special occasion, it needs to be assembled as close as
possible to the time when it is to be served, so do plan for this.

Makes 1 tower of 50–60 profiteroles • Prep 3 hours plus
choux paste and pastry cream • Bake/Cook 45 minutes

1 | 1	**double recipe Basic Choux Paste (page 173)**
1 | 1	**recipe Pastry Cream (page 86)**
9 Tbsp | 90 mL	**water**
3 cups | 600 g	**granulated sugar**
3 Tbsp | 45 mL	**white corn syrup or glucose**

1. Preheat the oven to 400°F (200°C). Line four baking trays with parchment paper.

2. Fill a piping bag fitted with a large plain tip with the choux paste. Pipe out profiteroles, each about 1 ½ inches (3.5 cm) in diameter. Wet your finger in cool water and tap down any points on the batter. It is all right for the piped profiteroles to sit out on the counter if you have to bake them in batches.

3. Bake the profiteroles for 10 minutes, then reduce the oven temperature to 375°F (190°C) and bake for about 15 more minutes, until they are a rich golden brown colour and feel very light. Allow the profiteroles to cool completely on the pans on a cooling rack before filling.

4. To fill, stir the pastry cream to soften it and fill a piping bag with a medium plain tip (or an éclair or doughnut tip, if you have one—page 187). Use a skewer to first poke a small hole in the side of each profiterole. Insert the piping bag and fill each one with cream until you feel resistance.

5. Cover a 12-inch (30 cm) Styrofoam cone with parchment paper (the cone can be found at any craft store) and place this on a parchment-lined baking tray.

Continued . . .

6. Bring the water, sugar, and corn syrup up to a boil in a small saucepan over high heat and continue to boil, uncovered and without stirring, and occasionally brushing the sides of the saucepan with water, until the sugar is a light amber colour. Ready a bowl of ice water and carefully set the bottom of the saucepan in the ice water to stop the sugar from cooking further.

7. Using tongs, carefully dip the bottoms of the profiteroles into the caramelized sugar and place them around the bottom of the cone with the caramel bottom facing the cone, and so that they touch each other and the base of the cone. Continue dipping and arranging the profiteroles, working upward until you have completely covered the cone. If the caramel in the saucepan begins to set before you have finished, you can reheat the caramel on low heat. If you wish, dip a fork in the caramel and carefully "spin" sugar around the outside. Let the sugar set for 1 hour, then carefully lift the croquembouche up, remove the cone and parchment, and place the croquembouche on a serving platter. Do not refrigerate.

You can make the separate components of a croquembouche well ahead of time—it's just the assembly of the tower that needs to happen within a few hours of when you plan to display and serve this grand dessert. In terms of a schedule, try this:

2 days ahead (or more): Make all the profiteroles. Freeze (if making more than 2 days ahead) or store at room temperature in resealable bags.

1 day ahead: Make the pastry cream and chill it. Prepare your Styrofoam base.

Day of: Thaw the profiteroles to room temperature. Fill the profiteroles. Caramelize the sugar and assemble the tower.

It's important to make sure your profiteroles are at room temperature before assembling the tower, which is why you don't want to fill them and store them chilled for too long. If the profiteroles are cold, condensation develops when they are dipped into the warm caramel, weakening your tower.

. . . .

When I was taught to build a croquembouche, I was shown how to assemble it free-form, with no support underneath, and tension would ensue on every occasion. Inevitably I would end up with a slightly crooked or uneven croquembouche, resembling something more from Dr. Seuss than a pastry shop window. Once I figured out that I could use a Styrofoam core, I totally relaxed, knowing that the tower would hold a perfectly straight shape. Now I really like building croquembouches!

Other
Desserts

Maybe this chapter should be called the "cravings" chapter. Sometimes you just need a particular taste or texture. Maybe it's a tart yet creamy lemon curd, or the crisp snap and melting away of a meringue. Perhaps you're craving a playful confection like marshmallows or a caramel apple, or you want to completely treat yourself to a cheesecake pop.

This diverse collection of recipes truly offers something for everyone. Some of these recipes are fundamental recipes that every passionate home baker should have in their repertoire, such as a Classic Vanilla Bean Crème Brûlée (page 211), and others are fanciful treats to suit a playful mood, like toasted Coconut Marshmallows (page 227), which still adhere to classic techniques.

For me, this chapter is like getting homework in your favourite class at school—it hardly feels like work.

Simple

Scrumptious

Sensational

Lemon Curd

*This classic tart lemon curd is soft and creamy. Spoon it into a tart shell,
ripple it into ice cream, use it as a filling for a cake, or fold it into whipped cream.*

Makes about 3 cups (750 mL) • Prep 15 minutes • Cook 10 minutes plus chilling

1 cup | 225 g	unsalted butter
1 ⅔ cups | 340 g	granulated sugar
2 Tbsp | 30 mL	finely grated lemon zest
4 | 4	eggs
1 cup | 250 mL	fresh lemon juice
1 tsp | 3 g	cornstarch

1. Melt the butter, sugar, and lemon zest in a saucepan over medium heat, stirring occasionally until the butter melts fully (the sugar will not dissolve at this point). Whisk the eggs, lemon juice, and cornstarch together and then whisk them into the saucepan. Continue to whisk the curd over medium heat until it thickens and just begins to bubble, about 8 minutes.

2. Pour it through a strainer and directly cover the surface of the curd with plastic wrap. Cool the curd to room temperature, then chill completely. The curd will keep, refrigerated, for up to 3 weeks.

I consider this Lemon Curd recipe a Foundation recipe because it has a unique method worth mastering, and it also has many uses in a pastry kitchen. It can be served alongside scones as part of high tea; used to fill little tart shells or as a sauce accompaniment; or used as below.

Lemon Curd Whip with Berries

*Lemon curd on its own has an intense sweet and tart contrast, so even
a little spoonful is fulfilling. To stretch lemon curd into a rich dessert portion,
I fold it into whipped cream and serve it with fresh berries.*

Serves 6 • Prep 10 minutes plus chilling

1 cup | 250 mL	chilled Lemon Curd (above)
¾ cup | 180 mL	whipping cream
1 ½ cups | 375 mL	mixed fresh berries

1. Whip the cream to soft peaks. Fold the curd into the whipped cream and layer it in glasses with the berries. This can be served immediately or chilled for up to 6 hours.

Caramel Apples

Caramel apples are a great treat to make with the kids, but keep in mind that the caramel will be very, very hot. If you're doing this with younger kids, it's best if an adult dips the apples and lets them cool a moment before the kids dip them into whatever dipping items they wish.

Serves 8 • Prep 20 minutes • Cook 5 minutes

8 | 8	red apples, at room temperature
8 | 8	lollipop sticks
¼ cup | 60 mL	water
2 cups | 400 g	granulated sugar
½ cup | 125 mL	white corn syrup
½ cup | 115 g	unsalted butter, cut into pieces
1 tsp | 5 mL	pure vanilla extract
	pinch salt
	dipping items: granola, toasted coconut, Reese's Pieces (or M&M's), salted peanuts, mini marshmallows, chocolate chips, crushed pretzels

Red apples are best for dipping into caramel because the skins of green apples may turn brown under the caramel layer, which sometimes shows through as looking bruised.

• • • • • • • •

When dipping the apples in the caramel, it's important that they are at room temperature and fully dried after washing. Any droplets of water could cause the caramel to melt and slide off.

• • • • • • • •

Brushing the inside of the saucepan as the sugar boils helps to prevent any sugar droplets from sticking to the saucepan and potentially crystallizing (which could spread through the rest of the sugar mass and cause a grainy caramel). The water does no damage to the sugar as it cooks—it simply evaporates as steam.

1. Line a baking tray with parchment paper. Have all your ingredients measured out and close at hand, with all your dipping items in separate small bowls.

2. Wash and dry the apples well. Insert a lollipop stick into the top of each apple, but be sure that it doesn't poke through to the bottom. Place the apples on the baking tray.

3. Place the water in the bottom of a medium saucepan and add the sugar and corn syrup. Bring the sugar up to a full boil over high heat without stirring, occasionally brushing down the sides of the saucepan with water and boiling until the sugar turns a light amber colour. Immediately remove the caramel from the heat and whisk in the butter (be careful of the steam). Once the mixture stops bubbling and the butter is completely whisked in, whisk in the vanilla and salt.

4. Dip an apple into the caramel (do take care, as it will still be very hot) and spin it slowly to let any drips run off and the caramel set a little. Dip the apples into the dipping items of your choice, or simply leave plain. Place the apple back on the baking tray to set and repeat with the other apples. If the caramel in the saucepan sets as you are dipping, warm it over low heat, stirring gently until melted again.

Crème Caramel

*Crème caramel is quite different in taste and texture from crème brûlée.
Because it is made using milk instead of cream, and with some whole eggs, the texture is lighter
and very refreshing. It sets firmer though, so it can be turned out onto a plate.*

Makes 4 individual desserts • Prep 20 minutes • Bake/Cook 35 minutes plus chilling

Custard

2 | 2	eggs
2 | 2	egg yolks
6 Tbsp | 75 g	granulated sugar
2 cups | 500 mL	2% milk
1 tsp | 5 mL	pure vanilla extract
	pinch salt

Caramel

3 Tbsp | 45 mL	water
½ cup | 100 g	granulated sugar
1 tsp | 5 mL	lemon juice

1. Preheat the oven to 300°F (150°C). Place four 5-ounce (150 mL) ramekins in a baking pan with sides just taller than the ramekins.

2. In a large mixing bowl, whisk the whole eggs and egg yolks with the sugar. Whisk gently while adding the milk, and then whisk in the vanilla and salt. Strain the mixture through a fine mesh sieve and let it sit while preparing the caramel, to let any bubbles dissipate.

3. Bring the water, sugar, and lemon juice up to a full boil over high heat without stirring, and continue to boil until the mixture turns an amber colour. While the sugar boils, occasionally brush the sides of the saucepan with water, to keep the sugar from crystallizing. Divide the caramel equally between the four ramekins. Let cool for a minute.

4. If there are still quite a few bubbles visible on the custard surface, use a spoon to lift them away. Slowly pour the custard mixture into the ramekins, and dab off any new bubbles with a paper towel. Pour boiling water into the baking pan so that it comes halfway up the sides of the ramekins. Cover the baking pan with aluminum foil (or a lid) and carefully take this to the oven. Bake for 30–35 minutes, until a tester inserted in the centre of the custard comes out clean. Immediately (but carefully) remove the ramekins from the water bath to cool on a cooling rack. Chill completely, uncovered, for at least 3 hours.

5. To serve, run an offset spatula around the inside edge of a ramekin. Place a dessert plate over the ramekin and invert both. Lift the ramekin off, leaving the custard on the plate with the caramel as a sauce. The crème caramels can be prepared up to a day in advance and stored, loosely covered, in the fridge.

Chilling the crème caramel completely is part of its appeal. Because it is silky and light (unlike a rich crème brûlée), it needs to be ice cold to be refreshing.

. . . .

Custards such as this one are cooked in a water bath for the gentle, even heat. If they are baked on just a baking tray, the eggs overcook on the outside before the middle has set.

Removing the ramekins from the water can be a bit tricky, since they are so hot. I use my canning jar tongs to remove the ramekins from the water bath without burning my fingers—they have a wide grip that is rubber coated, so the ramekins don't slip.

Classic Vanilla Bean Crème Brûlée

A well-made crème brûlée is a beautiful thing. Simple ingredients,
simply prepared, but ohhhh that magical result!

Makes 6 individual desserts • Prep 20 minutes • Bake/Cook 30 minutes plus chilling

2 ¾ cups | 680 mL	**whipping cream**
1 | 1	**vanilla bean or 1 Tbsp (15 mL) vanilla bean paste**
4 | 4	**egg yolks**
1 | 1	**egg**
¾ cup | 150 g	**granulated sugar, plus extra for the brûlée**

Crème brûlée is a Foundation recipe because its method includes making a rich custard, and then melting and caramelizing the sugar on top. It is a dessert that transcends trends: you will always find crème brûlée on restaurant dessert menus, and it is a great option to have in your back pocket when looking to impress guests at home.

• • • • • • • •

It's important to take the time to dab away any air bubbles at the surface of each crème brûlée dish after you've poured in the custard. Once cooked, the bubbles inhibit an even sugar layer from caramelizing on top of the dessert. Use a corner of paper towel to carefully do this.

• • • • • • • •

I find it easier to get an even brûlée when I sprinkle the sugar on in repeated, thin layers. If too much sugar is sprinkled on, then the top of it burns before the sugar underneath has liquefied. With a thin layer sprinkled over an already torched layer, the warmth immediately starts melting the sugar crystals, which also fall in between the liquid sugar droplets, ultimately becoming one even layer. Get your spoon ready!

1. Preheat the oven to 325°F (160°C). Place six 6-ounce (180 mL) ramekins in a large pan where the sides of the pan are higher than the ramekins.

2. Heat the cream in a saucepan on medium-low with the scraped seeds of the vanilla bean pod (and the pod, too, if you wish). If using vanilla bean paste, whisk it into the cream and heat. Heat the cream for about 5 minutes, watching carefully so that it doesn't boil over.

3. In a bowl, whisk the egg yolks, whole egg, and sugar together. Whisk in the hot cream slowly, whisking constantly (but not overly vigorously) until it has all been added. Strain into a bowl and then ladle or pour it into the ramekins. If any small bubbles appear on the surface of the custards, use the corner of a paper towel to dab them off (the bubbles, if left on, prevent the brûlée from browning easily and evenly).

4. Pour boiling water carefully into the baking pan so that it comes just past halfway up the ramekins and carefully take this to the oven. Bake the custards for about 30 minutes, until they are set around the edges but still have a little jiggle to them when gently moved. Let the custards cool for 10 minutes in the water bath, then remove them using a tea towel or oven mitt to cool completely on a cooling rack. Chill the custards, uncovered, for at least 3 hours and up to a day.

5. To serve, sprinkle each custard with a thin layer of sugar. Carefully ignite a kitchen butane torch and caramelize the sugar by moving the torch back and forth over the custard, about an inch or two away from it. Sprinkle another thin layer of sugar over the first layer and torch it, repeating another two times or until the desired caramel layer is achieved. Serve immediately.

Birds' Nests

These crispy, light meringue nests, also called common meringue,
are made using a French meringue method. Filled with a little whipped cream
and topped with berries, they are anything but common, though.

Makes 6 individual desserts • Prep 30 minutes • Bake 65 minutes

French Meringue

3 | 3	egg whites, at room temperature
¾ tsp | 4 g	cream of tartar
¾ cup | 150 g	granulated sugar

Assembly

¾ cup | 180 mL	whipping cream
2 Tbsp | 25 g	granulated sugar
½ tsp | 2 mL	pure vanilla extract
1 cup | 250 mL	mixed fresh berries

1. Preheat the oven to 300°F (150°C). Using a marker, trace six circles, each 2 ½ inches (6 cm) across and with at least 2 inches (5 cm) between them, on parchment paper. Flip the paper over onto a baking tray.

2. For the French Meringue, whip the egg whites and cream of tartar using electric beaters or in a stand mixer fitted with the whip attachment on low speed until the whites are foamy, then increase the speed to high and slowly pour in the sugar while whipping. Continue to whip the whites on high speed until they hold a stiff peak when the beaters are lifted.

3. Fill a piping bag fitted with a large star tip with the meringue and pipe circles within the lines drawn on the parchment, completely filling the circles. Pipe a ring or meringue on top of the outside edge, creating the "nest" effect, spiralling up to about 2 inches (5 cm) above the base.

4. Place the meringues in the oven and immediately reduce the temperature to 275°F (135°C). Bake the meringues for 45–65 minutes (this timing will be affected by the outdoor temperature and humidity—the meringues take longer if it is humid or warm outside). If you find that the meringues are starting to brown (start checking after 20 minutes), crack open the oven door and continue to bake. Cool the meringues completely to room temperature on the baking tray on a cooling rack, then gently lift to store in an airtight container for up to 1 day until ready to serve.

5. To assemble, whip the cream to soft peaks and stir in the sugar and vanilla. Place a bird's nest onto each plate, dollop the cream into the centre of the nest, and top with berries. Serve immediately.

French (or common) Meringue is the simplest of three meringue styles learned by pastry chefs, and is made simply by whipping egg whites with sugar at room temperature. The other types of meringue are Swiss (the whites and sugar are warmed together) and Italian (where the sugar is boiled and poured into the whipped whites, as in the Coconut Marshmallows, page 227). If you've never made meringue before, these nests are the best place to start.

• • • • • • • •

Making a meringue is the best way to get to know your oven. Meringues are very heat-sensitive, and you may notice that they start to brown in one spot in your oven (most ovens have a hot spot). If they all start to brown, it's a sign your oven is running hotter than the temperature you set. If you think this could happen, crack the oven door for 5 minutes at 15-minute intervals to cool the oven down.

Classic Dark Chocolate Mousse

Chocolate mousse can coax a smile and a hum of satisfaction out of even the most reticent dinner guest. Who can resist something that is so rich and luscious, but also as light as air?

Serves 6 to 8 • Prep 25 minutes • Cook 10 minutes plus chilling

7 oz | 210 g	bittersweet couverture/baking chocolate, chopped
2 Tbsp | 30 g	unsalted butter
1 cup | 250 mL	whipping cream
¼ cup | 60 mL	brewed espresso, cooled
3 Tbsp | 45 mL	brandy (optional)
3 | 3	egg whites, at room temperature
	pinch salt
3 Tbsp | 36 g	granulated sugar
	bittersweet chocolate shavings, for garnish

1. Melt the chocolate and butter in a metal bowl placed over a saucepan of barely simmering water, stirring gently until melted. Remove from the heat and allow to cool while you prepare the other mousse components.

2. Whip the cream using electric beaters or in a stand mixer fitted with the whip attachment on high speed until soft peaks form, then stir in the espresso and brandy (if using). Chill until ready to use.

3. In a clean bowl, whip the egg whites with the salt on high speed until foamy, then gradually add the sugar while continuing to whip the whites until they hold a soft peak when the beaters are lifted.

4. By now the chocolate should be cooled to just above room temperature. Fold the whipped cream quickly into the chocolate in two additions, then fold in the whites all at once (the mousse will be soft). Pour this into serving dishes and chill, uncovered, until set, about 3 hours. Top with chocolate shavings before serving. The mousse can be made a day ahead and refrigerated, loosely covered.

Chocolate mousse is an iconic dessert. Every pastry chef apprentice learns how to make it in their first year at school, which makes it a true Foundation recipe, and one that everyone should try their hand at. This particular recipe is for a textbook, rich, French-style mousse that gets poured into glasses to set, and epitomizes what we think of as a classic chocolate mousse. Other mousse methods are better suited for layering into cakes, like the one that is part of my Rich Chocolate Mousse Cake (page 159).

• • • • • • • •

Don't panic when you see that the chocolate mousse mixture seems fluid after you've folded in the egg whites. That's factored into the recipe (optional) and it allows you to easily pour the mixture into your serving glasses. It will set up beautifully and be light and airy.

Lemon Blueberry Trifles

These individual trifles look pretty displayed in juice or other glasses.
Depending on the diameter of the glass, you can adjust the depth of the coconut dacquoise layers,
which are nestled in between a lemon cream and fresh blueberries.

Makes 6 individual desserts • Prep 45 minutes • Bake 15 minutes

Coconut Dacquoise

3 | 3	egg whites, at room temperature
3 Tbsp | 36 g	granulated sugar
¾ cup | 100 g	icing sugar
¼ cup | 30 g	cake and pastry flour
⅔ cup | 60 g	unsweetened desiccated coconut

Lemon Cream and Assembly

1 cup | 250 mL	whipping cream
½ cup | 125 g	cream cheese, softened
¼ cup | 50 g	granulated sugar
1 ½ tsp | 7 mL	finely grated lemon zest
3 Tbsp | 45 mL	fresh lemon juice
1 tsp | 5 mL	pure vanilla extract
1 ½ cups | 375 mL	fresh blueberries
	toasted coconut (any type), for décor

1. Preheat the oven to 350°F (180°C). Line the bottom of a 13- x 9-inch (33 x 23 cm) baking pan with parchment paper.

2. Whip the egg whites with electric beaters, or in a stand mixer fitted with the whip attachment, on high speed until they are foamy and then add the granulated sugar, continuing to whip until the whites hold a medium peak when the beaters are lifted.

3. In a bowl, sift the icing sugar and flour together and then stir in the coconut. Add this all at once to the whipped whites and fold until blended (the whites will deflate as you fold). Spread this into the prepared pan and bake for about 15 minutes until lightly but evenly browned on top. Allow this dacquoise to cool completely before assembling the trifle (the dacquoise can even be baked a day ahead).

4. For the lemon cream, whip the cream until it holds soft peaks and set aside. Beat the cream cheese and sugar (by hand or with beaters) until smooth and add the lemon zest, lemon juice, and vanilla. Fold in the whipped cream.

5. Select individual glasses for the trifle. Use a round cookie cutter just smaller than the diameter of the glasses to cut out discs of dacquoise (two or three per glass—three if the glasses are tall and narrow). Fill a piping bag fitted with a large plain tip with the lemon cream.

6. To assemble the trifles, pipe a layer of lemon cream in the bottom of each glass. Sprinkle a few blueberries over the lemon cream, then top with a dacquoise disc. Top the disc with lemon cream, then berries, then a second dacquoise disc. Repeat this if you are using tall, narrow glasses. Finish with a final layer of the lemon cream, a few berries, and a sprinkling of toasted coconut. Chill the trifles until ready to serve. The trifles will keep for a day, refrigerated.

A dacquoise is a meringue-based sponge cake, using just egg whites in place of whole eggs.
The result is a cake that is crisp on the outside and soft in the centre.

Just because I've made these trifles as individual desserts doesn't mean you have to.
You can cut larger rounds of dacquoise and layer them with the cream and fruit in a larger bowl
if you wish—just make sure it's glass, so that you can see the pretty layers!

English Sticky Toffee Pudding

This warm, sweet, and delicate date cake is the perfect finish to a fall meal.

Makes 6 individual desserts • Prep 30 minutes • Bake 30 minutes

1 cup | 160 g	loosely packed, pitted, and chopped dates
¾ cup | 180 mL	hot English Breakfast or Orange Pekoe tea
½ tsp | 2 mL	pure vanilla extract
¾ tsp | 4 g	baking soda
6 Tbsp | 90 g	unsalted butter, at room temperature
¾ cup | 150 g	granulated sugar
2 | 2	eggs, at room temperature
1 ⅓ cups | 200 g	all-purpose flour
1 tsp | 3 g	baking powder

Savarins are baked in a particular ring-shaped pan, which should be available at most kitchen stores. I like to use the ring shape for my puddings and pour the toffee sauce into the hole in the centre. That way when you cut into the cake, the toffee sauce spills out from the centre invitingly.

• • • • • • • •

Dates are the singular flavour in a sticky toffee pudding, so while you might think cinnamon or other spices fit in here, the classic style lets simplicity reign (you can even skip the vanilla if you wish).

1. Preheat the oven to 350°F (180°C). Grease six 5-ounce (150 mL) ramekins or individual savarin rings and place them in a roasting pan with sides higher than the baking dishes.

2. Place the dates in a bowl and pour the hot tea over top. Let the mixture sit for a few minutes, then stir in the vanilla and then the baking soda.

3. In a separate bowl, beat the butter and sugar until blended, then add the eggs one at a time, beating well after each addition. Sift the flour and baking powder over the butter mixture and stir to blend. Add the still-warm date mixture and stir until evenly combined. Divide this evenly between the prepared dishes.

4. Pour boiling water around the dishes so that it comes halfway up their sides, and cover the entire pan with aluminum foil. Bake the puddings for about 30 minutes, until the pudding springs back when gently pressed. Carefully remove the ramekins from the roasting pan, let them cool for 10 minutes, then turn them out onto plates and serve warm with Toffee Sauce (page 284). The cakes can be prepared and baked in advance, refrigerated for up to 2 days, and then microwaved for just 10–15 seconds to re-warm.

Fresh Berry Crème Brûlée

This version of crème brûlée is smooth and creamy, as you would hope it would be, but it also has an airiness to it because the egg yolks are whipped. With each bite, the creaminess comes through then melts away so quickly that you need to instantly dive in for your next bite.

Makes 8 individual desserts • Prep 30 minutes plus chilling • Cook 10 minutes

1 cup | 250 mL	**fresh raspberries**
1 cup | 250 mL	**fresh blueberries**
3 cups | 750 mL	**whipping cream**
1 | 1	**vanilla bean or 1 Tbsp (15 mL) vanilla bean paste**
1 tsp | 5 mL	**finely grated lemon zest**
10 | 10	**egg yolks**
½ cup | 100 g	**granulated sugar, plus extra for the brûlée**
1 ½ Tbsp | 22 mL	**lemon juice**

1. Divide the raspberries and blueberries evenly between eight flat but rimmed 4-ounce (120 mL) ovenproof dishes (the dishes won't be going in the oven, but they must be able to resist the heat of the torch for brûléeing).

2. In a saucepan, heat the cream on medium-low with the scraped seeds of the vanilla bean pod (and the pod, too, if you wish) and the lemon zest. If using vanilla bean paste, whisk it into the cream with the zest. Heat the cream for about 5 minutes, watching so that it doesn't boil over.

3. Bring a second saucepan filled with 1 inch (2.5 cm) of water to a gentle simmer over medium-low heat. In a metal bowl, whisk the egg yolks, sugar, and lemon juice together. Place the bowl on top of the saucepan of simmering water and whisk the egg mixture until it has doubled in volume and is a pale buttery colour, 3–4 minutes. Remove the bowl from the saucepan of water.

4. While whisking, slowly pour the heated cream into the whipped egg mixture and return the entire mixture to the saucepan, stirring with a wooden spoon or silicone spatula over medium heat until the custard thickly coats the back of a spoon, about 4 minutes. Pour the custard through a sieve and then pour it slowly over the berries, stirring the berries slightly just to ensure they are fully coated and covered. Cool the custards for 15 minutes, then chill, uncovered, until set, at least 4 hours and up to a day.

5. To serve, sprinkle each custard with a thin layer of sugar. Carefully ignite a kitchen butane torch and caramelize the sugar by moving the torch back and forth over the custard, about an inch or two away from it. Sprinkle another thin layer of sugar over the first layer and torch it, repeating another two times or until the desired caramel layer is achieved. Serve immediately.

I like to use a flat-bottomed dish for this crème brûlée so that the berries sit in a single layer, enveloped by the custard.

• • • • • • • •

The reason you can't bake berry crème brûlée in the oven is because the berries would cook and become a sloppy mess under the custard. This technique of making a sabayon, a fluffy mixture of whipped eggs with sugar, keeps the brûlée light in texture so it doesn't weigh down the berries.

This recipe will leave you with 10 unused egg whites. You can store these in an airtight container in the fridge for up to a week or the freezer for up to 3 months. Thaw when you are ready to use them for a recipe, like my Angel Food Cake (page 108) or Meringue Mushrooms (page 224). To measure out a single egg white from the container, it's easiest to use a scale—a single egg white will weigh 1 ounce, or 30 grams.

Classic Passion Fruit Pavlova

*A Pavlova is a meringue dessert that has a crunchy exterior, but yields to a soft,
marshmallow-like interior. Topped with cream and passion fruit,
I find I appreciate it best in wintertime, when it's like a taste from the tropics.*

Serves 6 to 8 • Prep 30 minutes • Bake 90 minutes

Meringue

4 | 4	egg whites, at room temperature
1 cup | 200 g	granulated sugar
1 Tbsp | 7 g	cornstarch
¾ tsp | 4 g	cream of tartar
1 tsp | 5 mL	pure vanilla extract

Assembly

1 cup | 250 mL	whipping cream
½ tsp | 2 mL	finely grated lemon zest
1 Tbsp | 15 mL	fresh lemon juice
3 Tbsp | 36 g	granulated sugar
½ tsp | 2 mL	pure vanilla extract
2 | 2	ripe passion fruits

1. Preheat the oven to 275°F (135°C). Using a marker, trace a circle 8 inches (20 cm) across on parchment paper, then flip the paper over, ink side down, onto a baking tray.

2. Whip the egg whites, first on low speed, and then, once the whites are foamy, increase the speed and slowly pour in the sugar while whipping. Continue to whip the whites on high speed until they hold a firm peak when the beaters are lifted. Stir the cornstarch and cream of tartar together and fold them into the meringue by hand, then fold in the vanilla.

3. Dollop the entire meringue into the centre of the drawn circle and spread using a spatula, creating an upward "swoosh" from the base to create lines going up (this gives the Pavlova a pretty shape).

4. Bake the Pavlova for 60–90 minutes. It will still seem soft on the outside when warm, but if it does not cool to have a crunchy exterior (press gently with your finger near the bottom to check this), you can return it to the oven for an additional 15–30 minutes (the outdoor temperature and humidity affect the baking time—the meringues take longer if it is humid or warm outside). If the Pavlova begins to brown (check after 20 minutes), crack open the oven door and then continue baking. Cool the Pavlova completely on the baking tray on a cooling rack.

5. To assemble, whip the cream to a soft peak and fold in the lemon zest, lemon juice, and then the sugar. Gently lift the Pavlova (using the bottom of a removable-bottom tart pan to do this works well) onto your serving plate, then spoon the whipped cream over top, spreading it, but not quite to the edges. Cut the ripe passion fruits in half and scoop out the seeds and juice, spooning this over top of the cream. The Pavlova meringue can be baked hours ahead, but the final product should be assembled right before serving.

The addition of that small amount of cornstarch is all that it takes to separate a crunchy meringue like Birds' Nests (page 212) from a fluffy, soft-centred Pavlova, as the cornstarch holds in moisture. That's what inspired me to start putting cornstarch in my chocolate chip cookie recipe years ago, to guarantee a soft centre in my cookies every time.

This recipe makes great use of any leftover egg whites that you may have from another recipe (such as Classic Vanilla Bean Crème Brûlée, page 211).

Meringue Mushrooms

These cute meringues are a classic garnish for a yule log, but can also be used to decorate a torte or any dessert platter or plated dessert, particularly at holiday time.

Makes about 12 mushrooms • Prep 30 minutes • Bake 45 minutes

2 | 2	**egg whites, at room temperature**
¼ tsp | 1 g	**cream of tartar**
½ cup | 100 g	**granulated sugar**
1 ½ oz | 45 g	**semisweet chocolate or coating chocolate, chopped**
	cocoa powder, for dusting

1. Preheat the oven to 275°F (135°C). Line a baking tray with parchment paper.

2. Whip the egg whites and cream of tartar first on low speed, then once the whites are foamy increase the speed and slowly pour in the sugar while whipping. Continue to whip the whites on high speed until they hold a firm peak when the beaters are lifted.

3. Spoon the meringue into a piping bag fitted with a large plain tip. Pipe the stems of the mushrooms onto the prepared baking tray by pulling the bag upward while piping out the meringue (pipe two or three extra, in case they tip when baking). Pipe 12 caps by keeping the piping tip low to the tray to create the mushroom cap shape. If the caps have a point to them from lifting the piping bag, tap them down with a finger dipped in icing sugar.

4. Bake the meringues for about 45 minutes (the outdoor temperature and humidity affect the baking time—the meringues take longer if it is humid or warm outside). There will be no visible change in colour—they should remain white—or any other visual cue to tell you they are ready, but they should be dry to the touch once cooled to room temperature. If they still feel sticky to the touch once they are cooled, they should be returned to the oven to dry further.

5. Melt the chocolate in a metal bowl placed over a saucepan of barely simmering water, stirring gently until melted.

6. To assemble, dust the tops of the mushroom caps lightly with cocoa powder. Use a skewer to poke a small hole in the underside of each cap. Use a small, thin brush to paint chocolate on the underside of each mushroom cap. Insert the pointed stem end in the hole you made and set the meringue back on the baking tray until the chocolate has set. The mushrooms can be made up to 2 days in advance and stored in an airtight container.

Once you realize how creative you can get with piping meringue shapes, your imagination is your only limit. Think ghosts, snowmen, flowers, and more.

• • • • • • • •

You can tell when you reach a firm peak (also called stiff peak) with your meringue when you lift the beaters. The meringue that pulls away from the beaters as you lift them out of the bowl should stand upright. If those whites curl or droop at all, keep whipping them.

Coating chocolate is used for dipping and assembling sweets. When melted, it is smoother than melted chocolate chips and sets up quickly at room temperature. It is not necessarily top-quality chocolate, but when only a little is needed and you do not want to go through the process of tempering chocolate (see Classic Florentine Cookies, page 56) it does the trick. Coating chocolate can be found at stores that sell craft and candy-making supplies.

Coconut Marshmallows

These homemade marshmallows are tender and delicate—a far cry from the store-bought versions. I love the addition of coconut, but you can get creative by adding an extract or a colour of your choosing.

Makes 36 marshmallows • Prep 40 minutes plus setting • Cook 15 minutes

1 ½ Tbsp | 8 g	**unflavoured gelatin powder**
6 Tbsp | 90 mL	**cold water**
3 | 3	**egg whites**
1 ½ cups | 300 g	**granulated sugar**
2 tsp | 10 mL	**pure vanilla extract**
1 tsp | 5 mL	**pure coconut extract**
	equal parts icing sugar and cornstarch, mixed together (for dusting)
1 cup | 100 g	**sweetened flaked coconut, lightly toasted**
1 ½ cups | 270 g	**white chocolate chips, for melting**

1. Line an 8-inch (20 cm) square pan with parchment paper so that it comes up and over the sides. Using a piece of paper towel, lightly grease the parchment paper with vegetable oil.

2. Stir the gelatin powder with 6 Tbsp (90 mL) of cold water in a small dish and set aside.

3. Whip the egg whites in a large bowl using electric beaters or in a stand mixer fitted with the whip attachment on high speed until foamy.

4. Place the sugar in a medium saucepan with ¼ cup (60 mL) of water over high heat and bring it up to a full boil. Boil the sugar, without stirring, until it reaches a temperature of 240°F (115°C) on a candy thermometer. Carefully pour this into the egg whites while whipping on high speed (let the sugar syrup run down the side of the bowl, to avoid hitting the beaters and splashing and scalding you). Add the softened gelatin to the meringue and continue to whip on high speed until the meringue

cools to almost room temperature, about 5 minutes. Stir in the vanilla and coconut extracts. Scrape the marshmallow into the prepared pan and spread to level. Sift a layer of the icing sugar/cornstarch mixture over top and allow the marshmallow to cool until completely set, about 2 hours.

5. Line a baking tray with parchment paper. Dust a cutting board with the icing sugar-cornstarch mixture. Turn the marshmallow out onto the cutting board and cut it into 36 squares. Lightly dust all sides with the icing sugar-cornstarch mixture, tapping off any excess, and set on the prepared baking tray.

6. Melt the white chocolate chips in a metal bowl placed over a saucepan of barely simmering water, stirring gently until melted. Remove this from the heat. Dip each marshmallow a third to halfway into the white chocolate (it may take two dips to get the chocolate to coat evenly over the starch on the marshmallow). Shake off any excess chocolate (it should no longer drip) and then dip the marshmallow into the toasted coconut. Place the coated marshmallow back on the baking tray to set, and repeat with the remaining marshmallows. The marshmallows will keep in an airtight container for up to 2 weeks.

You can make a vegetarian version of marshmallows by using agar agar powder in place of the gelatin powder. The measures and method remain the same.

Torrone (Italian Nougat)

Torrone is a white, meringue-based nougat that is sweetened with a combination of sugar and honey. The base is made of Italian Meringue, which is a Foundation recipe within this recipe (see my note below).

Makes about 4 dozen pieces • Prep 30 minutes • Cook 20 minutes plus setting

3 | 3	egg whites, at room temperature
	pinch salt
2 cups + ¼ cup | 450 g	granulated sugar, divided
2 cups | 670 g	honey
2 cups | 320 g	blanched whole almonds, lightly toasted
1 cup | 120 g	shelled pistachios
2 tsp | 10 mL	finely grated orange or lemon zest
1 tsp | 5 mL	pure vanilla extract
	cornstarch, for dusting

1. Grease a 13- x 9-inch (33 x 23 cm) pan and line it with parchment paper so that the paper comes up and over the sides.

2. Whip the egg whites with the salt in a stand mixer fitted with the whip attachment on high speed until foamy and then gradually add ¼ cup (50 g) of sugar while whipping until the whites hold a soft peak when the beater is lifted.

3. In a large saucepan, bring the remaining 2 cups (400 g) of sugar and the honey to a boil over high heat, stirring constantly. Keep stirring and use a candy thermometer to gauge when the sugar reaches 280°F (138°C), at which point stop stirring (the sugar will no longer be at risk of boiling over) and continue boiling until the sugar reaches 315°F (157°C)—this takes about 4 minutes from when it hits 280°F (138°C). Remove the saucepan from the heat and stir the sugar until it cools to about 300°F (150°C), 1–2 minutes.

4. Turn on the mixer to high speed and carefully pour the hot sugar down the inside of the mixer (to avoid hitting the beaters and splashing and scalding you) onto the egg whites. Continue to whip on high speed until the meringue thickens and cools enough that it can be touched, about 4 minutes. When you first add the sugar, the meringue will inflate but then collapse a little as it continues to whip.

5. Remove the bowl from the mixer and stir in the almonds, pistachios, zest, and vanilla by hand. Dust your hands with cornstarch. Work quickly to scoop and spread the torrone into the prepared pan with your hands. Press it evenly into the pan and let it cool completely, 3 hours, before slicing.

6. To slice, tip the torrone onto a cutting board, peel away the parchment paper, and dust the torrone liberally with cornstarch. Use an oiled knife (wiped with vegetable oil or cooking spray) to cut the torrone into bite-sized pieces.

Sometimes a Foundation recipe isn't a standalone recipe, but a technique or baking method that is utilized within other recipes only. That is the case here, with the base of the torrone. This base is made of Italian Meringue, one of the three styles of meringue that pastry chefs learn to make. Sugar (and, in this case, honey) is boiled and then poured into the whipping egg whites, providing a volume and stability that can be used to create a candy, like this torrone, or to act as a base for other recipes such as an Italian Buttercream (page 150).

The torrone should be stored in a single layer—if stacked, it will stick and squish over time. To further prevent sticking, you can place a sheet of rice paper on the top and bottom of the torrone—just skip the dusting with starch so that the paper sticks onto the candy. You can find rice paper at stores that sell cake decorating supplies (often it's stored behind the counter, since it's fragile, so you may have to ask for it).

• • • • • • • •

While regular caramel should not be stirred as it cooks, the torrone sugar must be stirred as it begins to cook so that the honey doesn't boil over.

Classic English Trifle

This classic style of trifle layers a sponge cake with pastry cream and fresh berries. There's something inherently comforting about that sumptuous combination of cake, custard, and fruit—and even more so because you're permitted to eat it with a spoon! Trifles are ideal for a crowd, particularly in a buffet setting, since you can spoon out as much or as little as you wish.

Serves 12 to 16 • Prep 30 minutes • Bake/Cook 30 minutes plus chilling

1 | 1	recipe **Sponge Cake batter** (page 126)
1 | 1	**double recipe Pastry Cream** (page 86), chilled

Fruit and Assembly

1 ½ cups | 375 mL	whipping cream, divided
2 Tbsp | 25 g	granulated sugar
1 tsp | 5 mL	pure vanilla extract
4 cups | 1 L	assorted fresh berries (raspberries, blueberries, blackberries, sliced strawberries)
⅔ cup | 160 mL	berry jam
⅓ cup | 80 mL	cream sherry
¼ cup | 25 g	toasted sliced almonds

Sherry is a classic addition to an English Trifle, but you can replace it with apple or orange juice, for a family-friendly version.

• • • • • • •

If you don't own a trifle bowl (I don't know too many who do, or they received one as a wedding gift and it's buried deep in the back of a closet or long since given away), you can still assemble a grand trifle. Any glass flower vase with straight sides and an opening that you can fit your hand into, and that can hold at least 10 cups (2.5 L), will do the trick.

1. Preheat the oven to 350°F (180°C). Line a 17- x 11-inch (43 x 28 cm) baking tray with parchment paper, but do not grease it.

2. Spread the batter into the prepared pan. Bake the cake for about 25 minutes, until it is an even golden brown on top and springs back when gently pressed. Cool the cake completely in the pan on a cooling rack.

3. To get ready to assemble, find a glass vessel that can hold 10 cups (2.5 L). Whip the cream and fold one-third of it into the pastry cream. Add the sugar and vanilla to the remaining two-thirds of the whipped cream. In a separate bowl, toss the berries gently with the jam.

4. To assemble, turn the sponge cake out onto a cutting board and peel away the parchment. Depending on the size of your trifle dish, cut out three or four portions of the cake big enough to fit snugly into the dish. Place a layer of cake in the bottom of the dish and sprinkle or brush generously with the cream sherry. Top this with dollops of the pastry cream and spread it evenly. Spoon the berries over top and cover with a second layer of cake. Repeat this two or three times, until the cake portions, cream, and fruit have been used up. Top the trifle with the reserved whipped cream and sprinkle the top with toasted almonds. Chill the trifle until ready to serve. The trifle can be prepared 1 day in advance and refrigerated until needed.

Baked Apple Crème Brûlée

This crème brûlée is cinnamon-scented and baked inside an apple.
Coated with a thin layer of caramelized sugar, it is like a candy apple for adults.

Makes 4 individual desserts • Prep 45 minutes • Bake/Cook 45 minutes plus chilling

4 | 4	apples, firm variety such as Mutsu, Granny Smith, or Red Gala
1 ½ cups | 375 g	sour cream
6 | 6	egg yolks
6 Tbsp | 75 g	packed light brown sugar
1 tsp | 5 mL	pure vanilla extract
½ tsp | 2 g	ground cinnamon
⅛ tsp | 0.5 g	ground nutmeg
1 cup | 200 g	granulated sugar
1 Tbsp | 15 mL	lemon juice

1. Preheat the oven to 350°F (180°C).

2. Peel the apples about halfway down. Use a melon baller to scoop out the core of each apple (take care not to break through the bottom of the apples) and to scoop out extra apple flesh to make room for the custard, leaving a wall of apple about ¾ inch (1.5 cm) thick. Place the apples in a baking dish large enough to hold them without crowding.

3. In a large bowl, whisk the sour cream, egg yolks, brown sugar, vanilla, cinnamon, and nutmeg together and pour some into each apple, so that it comes up to the top but without spilling (you may have a little extra filling left, depending on how big your apples are). Pour boiling water around the apples to ½ inch (1 cm) up their sides and then loosely cover the dish with aluminum foil. You can insert toothpicks into the apples, if necessary, to keep the foil from touching the custard.

4. Bake the apples for 25 minutes, then remove the foil and bake for about another 10 minutes, until the custard is just set (it should jiggle just a little). Cool the apples in the pan on a rack, then remove to a plate to chill until set, at least 3 hours. A little juice may come out of the apples as they chill.

5. To finish, place the apples on a cooling rack placed over a parchment-lined baking tray. Bring the granulated sugar, lemon juice, and 3 Tbsp (45 mL) of water up to a boil in a saucepan over high heat. Continue to boil the sugar, without stirring and occasionally brushing the sides of the saucepan with water, until the sugar is an amber colour. Remove the saucepan from the heat and carefully spoon the hot sugar over the apples so that they are evenly and fully coated with a thin layer of the caramelized sugar. Let the sugar set for about 10 minutes, and then transfer the apples to a plate to serve. The apples can be made a day ahead and stored, refrigerated, until you are ready to dip them in the syrup. The apples should ideally be served just after the sugar has set, but this step can be prepared up to 2 hours ahead.

It is important to use a firm variety of apple so that the apple doesn't collapse as it bakes.

I use sour cream instead of whipping cream in this crème brûlée mixture. It has more body to it than cream, so it bakes in the centre of the apple well without dripping or leaking out.

Charlotte Royale

This classic moulded dessert uses slices of raspberry jelly roll cake to line a mould or even a glass bowl that is then filled with a silky vanilla Bavarian custard.

Serves 10 to 12 • Prep 1 hour • Cook 25 minutes plus chilling

1 | 1	recipe Classic Raspberry Jelly Roll (page 116)

Bavarian Custard

1 cup | 250 mL	milk
½ | ½	vanilla bean, seeds only, or 1 ½ tsp (7 mL) vanilla bean paste
4 | 4	egg yolks
⅔ cup | 140 g	granulated sugar
2 Tbsp | 10.5 g	unflavoured gelatin powder
1 ½ cups | 375 mL	whipping cream

1. Bring the milk up to a simmer in a saucepan over medium heat along with the scraped seeds from the vanilla bean. In a bowl, whisk the egg yolks with the sugar. Slowly pour the hot milk into the yolks while whisking constantly, then return the entire mixture to the saucepan. Cook the custard over medium heat, stirring constantly with a wooden spoon, until the mixture thickens and coats the back of the spoon, about 4 minutes. Strain the custard through a fine mesh sieve into a bowl.

2. Stir the gelatin with ⅓ cup (80 mL) of cool water and let it soften for a minute. Whisk this into the hot custard. Cool the custard completely to room temperature, then chill, uncovered, for about 15 minutes, so that it is cool to the touch but not starting to set.

3. Whip the cream to soft peaks and use a whisk to fold it into the cool custard. Assemble the charlotte while the custard is still fluid.

4. Line a 6-cup (1.5 L) bowl or charlotte mould with plastic wrap. Slice the jelly roll into ½-inch (1 cm) slices and line the entire bowl, pressing the jelly roll slices together as tightly as possible without altering their shape. Pour the Bavarian custard into the mould and place any remaining jelly roll slices on top. Cover the charlotte with plastic and chill for at least 4 hours to set.

5. To serve, invert the charlotte onto the serving plate and peel away the plastic wrap. Slice into wedges to serve. The charlotte is best enjoyed within a day of assembling.

This dessert is "old school," and while most pastry students learn how to make a
Charlotte Royale, you don't often see them in pastry shops. I have complete respect for
anyone who makes this dessert, as I appreciate the skill behind making its distinctive
Bavarian custard—a pastry cream that at the same time is like a mousse.

Chocolate Mousse Cups

These handmade chocolate cups are the perfect way to show off your skills as a pastry chef a little.

Makes 8 to 10 mousse cups • Prep 90 minutes • Cook 5 minutes plus chilling

1 | 1	recipe White Chocolate Mousse (page 100), chilled
8–10 | 8–10	mini balloons
4 oz | 120 g	bittersweet couverture/baking chocolate, chopped
	raspberries and/or bittersweet chocolate shavings, for garnish

The little balloons that are the ideal size for these mousse cups can be found at discount stores or at any place that sells party supplies. The ideal choice is water balloons (seriously, those balloons you fill with water and toss in the backyard!), as they are thinner than regular balloons and come away from the chocolate more easily.

. . . .

When I dip my balloon, I dip it at a slight angle, then lift and rotate before dipping at an angle again, continuing on. This creates a pretty tulip-like petal effect.

. . . .

It's important to allow the air to slowly escape the balloon once you poke a little hole. If the air escapes too quickly, the chocolate shell will shatter, so resist the urge to squeeze the balloon to speed things up.

1. Line a baking tray with parchment paper. Inflate and tie the mini balloons. Give them a little wipe with a damp cloth and allow them to dry.

2. Melt the chocolate in a metal bowl, placed over a saucepan of barely simmering water, stirring gently until melted. Remove the chocolate from the heat.

3. Dip the balloons halfway into the chocolate on an angle, and lift and rotate, dipping repeatedly, creating a tulip shape around the balloon. Shake off any excess chocolate and place each balloon on the prepared tray. Chill the balloons until the chocolate has set, about 30 minutes.

4. Use a pin to gently pop the balloon. Lift the balloon out of the chocolate cup and discard. Pipe white chocolate mousse into the cups and top with raspberries and/or chocolate shavings. Chill until ready to serve. The desserts are best eaten the day they are made and assembled.

Cheesecake Pops

Great for an hors d'oeuvre party, these two-bite lollipops are made with New York–style cheesecake and dipped into melted chocolate and decorated. You can get creative with the presentation—standing the pops upright in a long vase filled with coloured sugar makes them look like an edible bouquet.

Makes about 24 pops • Prep 90 minutes plus freezing and chilling • Cook 5 minutes

⅓ | ⅓	**Classic New York Cheesecake (page 118)**
24 | 24	**long lollipop sticks**
3 oz | 90 g	**bittersweet couverture/ baking chocolate**
3 oz | 90 g	**milk couverture/ baking chocolate**
3 oz | 90 g	**white couverture/ baking chocolate**
	dipping items: graham cracker crumbs, coloured sugar, pearl dust, and small sprinkles for decor

These pops are a great way to use those last few slices of cheesecake in the fridge. You can scoop and shape the pops and freeze them (before dipping in chocolate) for up to 3 months, wrapped in plastic wrap. Add the lollipop sticks if you like, so you can dip them in chocolate later on (or just pop them in your mouth when you need a cooling, creamy treat!).

1. Gently stir the cheesecake, crust and all, by hand with a spatula, until the crust has mixed with the filling. Use a small ice cream scoop or melon baller to scoop 1-inch (2.5 cm) balls of cheesecake and roll them in your hands to shape them more precisely. Insert a lollipop stick into each cheesecake ball and place them on a parchment-lined baking tray (if the cheesecake mixture seems too soft, you can freeze the scooped balls for 30 minutes before shaping and inserting the sticks). Freeze the pops for 1 hour, while you prepare the chocolate and accents.

2. Melt each type of chocolate in separate bowls.

3. Dip the pops in your choice of chocolate and then dip or sprinkle the accents on according to choice. The pops can be refrigerated, covered, for up to 4 days.

Double Chocolate Pear Trifle

This trifle is inspired by the classic dessert poires Belle-Hélène. Layers of rich chocolate cake are nestled between decadent white chocolate pastry cream and vanilla-poached pears. A chocolate ganache drizzled over the layers takes it over the top.

Serves 12 to 16 • Prep 2 hours • Bake/Cook 75 minutes plus chilling

Cake

1 ½ cups | 200 g	cake and pastry flour
1 ⅓ cups | 270 g	granulated sugar
½ cup | 60 g	Dutch process cocoa powder
¾ tsp | 4 g	baking soda
¼ tsp | 1 g	salt
½ cup | 115 g	cool unsalted butter, cut into pieces
½ cup | 125 mL	hot, strongly brewed coffee
½ cup | 125 mL	milk
1 tsp | 5 mL	pure vanilla extract
2 | 2	eggs, at room temperature

White Chocolate Pastry Cream

2 cups | 500 mL	milk
1 | 1	vanilla bean, seeds only, or 2 tsp (10 mL) vanilla bean paste
6 | 6	egg yolks
6 Tbsp | 75 g	granulated sugar
¼ cup | 30 g	cornstarch
3 oz | 90 g	white chocolate, chopped
2 Tbsp | 30 g	unsalted butter, cut into pieces

Vanilla-Poached Pears

5 | 5	Bartlett pears
3 cups | 750 mL	water
3 cups | 600 g	granulated sugar
¼ cup | 60 mL	fresh lemon juice
1 | 1	vanilla bean, seeds only, or 1 Tbsp (15 mL) vanilla bean paste

Ganache and Assembly

4 oz | 120 g	bittersweet couverture/baking chocolate, chopped
1 ½ cups | 375 mL	whipping cream, divided
2 Tbsp | 25 g	granulated sugar
1 tsp | 5 mL	pure vanilla extract
	dark chocolate shavings, for garnish

1. For the cake, preheat the oven to 350°F (180°C). Line a 17- x 11-inch (43 x 28 cm) baking tray with parchment paper, but do not grease the pan.

2. Sift the flour, sugar, cocoa powder, baking soda, and salt into a large mixing bowl or the bowl of a stand mixer fitted with the paddle attachment. Add the butter, cutting it in (if using a large bowl, use electric beaters) until the mixture is a fine crumble (like the texture of fine breadcrumbs) and no large pieces of butter are visible.

3. Stir the hot coffee, milk, and vanilla together and add it all at once to the flour mixture, blending on medium speed until smooth. Break the eggs into a small dish, stir them with a fork, and then add them to the batter, again blending on medium speed just until smooth (the batter will be very fluid). Pour the batter into the prepared pan, spreading it evenly, and bake for about 25 minutes, until a tester inserted in the centre of the cake comes out clean. Cool the cake in its pan.

Continued . . .

4. For the white chocolate pastry cream, heat the milk in a saucepan over medium heat with the vanilla bean seeds until just below a simmer.

5. In a bowl, whisk the egg yolks, sugar, and cornstarch together. Place the white chocolate and butter in a bowl, placing a fine mesh sieve over top.

6. Gradually whisk the hot milk into the egg mixture and then return it all to the saucepan. Whisk this constantly (switching to a spatula now and again to get into the corners) over medium heat until thickened and glossy, about 2 minutes. Pour this immediately through the sieve, whisking it through if needed, and stir in the white chocolate and butter. Place a piece of plastic wrap directly onto the surface of the custard, cool to room temperature, and then chill until ready to use.

7. For the poached pears, peel, halve, and core the pears and remove the stems. Bring the water, sugar, lemon juice, and vanilla bean seeds up to a full boil in a saucepan over medium-high heat. Add the pears. Place a piece of parchment paper cut to fit the saucepan (called a cartouche) directly on the surface of the liquid to cover the pears. Return the liquid to a gentle simmer over medium heat and simmer for 10 minutes. Remove the saucepan from the heat and let the pears cool to room temperature in the syrup before chilling until ready to assemble.

8. For the ganache, place the chocolate in a small bowl. Heat ½ cup (125 mL) of the whipping cream to a simmer in a saucepan over medium heat and pour this over the chocolate. Gently stir the mixture until the ganache is smooth and cool to room temperature. Whip the remaining 1 cup (250 mL) of cream with the sugar and vanilla and chill until ready to assemble.

9. To assemble, have ready a 12-cup (3 L) trifle bowl or glass vessel. Turn the chocolate cake out onto a cutting board, peel away the parchment paper, and cut three or four pieces of cake the size of your trifle bowl. Remove the pears from the vanilla syrup (saving the syrup) and cut them into ½-inch (1 cm) slices, saving one intact pear half for the top of the trifle.

10. Start by placing a layer of cake in the bottom of the bowl. Brush this generously with vanilla syrup and top with a layer of white chocolate pastry cream. Drizzle the cream with a little chocolate ganache and arrange some pear slices over top. Repeat this with the cake, syrup, cream, and pear until the cake layers are used, finishing with a layer of pear slices. Top this with the whipped cream and chocolate shavings. Slice the final pear half so that it fans out from the stem end and place this on top. Chill the trifle until ready to serve. The trifle can be prepared and assembled up to a day in advance.

There are a lot of steps to make this trifle, but one reason trifle is perfect for a special occasion or a crowd is that you can make it ahead of time. The cake, the custard, and the pears can be made 1 to 2 days ahead (you can even make the cake weeks ahead and freeze it), and you can fully assemble the trifle a day in advance of serving it.

Breads

In cooking school, a bread baker's apprenticeship followed a different path than a pâtissier's. Now the two schools of baking are blended in North America, but the skill sets and thinking remain distinct.

A pâtissier's kitchen is warm to start the day, but cools down for the decorating and assembling of desserts, and the pâtissier uses countless specialty tools. However, a bread baker's kitchen is warm all day (more precisely, all night, in order to have breads ready for the morning), the ovens are on all the time, lots of table space is used for the rising and shaping of doughs, and the baker's hands are their most important tools.

I have always found immense gratification in making bread by hand. It somehow feels important. We sometimes take bread for granted when we eat—a roll is placed off to the side of our dinner plate, or the fillings get all of the attention when we are eating a sandwich. But when you are kneading bread, and connecting with the texture of the simple ingredients under the palms of your hands, you can't disregard its significance as a cornerstone of our Western food culture.

Simple

Scrumptious

Sensational

Basic Buttermilk Biscuits

These are a simple, drop-style of biscuit that bakes up soft and delicate with an almost cake-like texture. They are ideal to serve alongside a bowl of soup or chili or in place of a roll at dinner.

Makes 18 biscuits • Prep 15 minutes • Bake 15 minutes

2 cups | 300 g	all-purpose flour
1 Tbsp | 12 g	granulated sugar
1 Tbsp | 9 g	baking powder
½ tsp | 2 g	baking soda
¾ tsp | 4 g	salt
1 ¼ cups | 310 mL	buttermilk
1 | 1	egg
¼ cup | 60 mL	vegetable oil

There are times when substituting buttermilk with regular milk (adding a splash of lemon juice) will work just fine, but in a simple recipe like this, where the buttermilk is a key ingredient, it's best to stick with the real deal.

• • • • • • • •

After you've made this recipe, any leftover buttermilk has other delicious uses. It can make the base for a fantastic (and low-fat) Caesar or ranch dressing, can be blended into fruit smoothies, or can make a fantastic marinade for chicken, even tandoori chicken, in place of yogurt.

• • • • • • • •

Unused buttermilk also freezes well, for up to 3 months. Once thawed, give it a good shake (it will have separated) and use it as needed.

1. Preheat the oven to 400°F (200°C). Line two baking trays with parchment paper.

2. In a large bowl, sift the flour, sugar, baking powder, baking soda, and salt together.

3. In a separate bowl, whisk the buttermilk, egg, and oil together. Add this to the flour mixture and stir just until blended.

4. Use a medium ice cream scoop or two tablespoons to drop batter (about ¼ cup/60 mL each) onto the prepared baking trays, leaving 2 inches (5 cm) between them. Bake the biscuits for about 15 minutes until they are a light golden brown and lift away from the parchment easily. Serve the biscuits warm from the oven, or reheated at 300°F (150°C) for 10 minutes. The biscuits are best enjoyed the day they are baked.

Indian Naan

Naan is traditionally baked on the walls of a tandoori oven, but you can easily make this bread at home using a cast iron frying pan. Once you see how easy it is to make authentic naan from scratch, you'll never buy it again!

Serves 6 • Prep 15 minutes plus resting • Bake/Cook 5 minutes

¾ cup | 180 mL	warm water (around 115°F/46°C)
2 ½ cups | 375 g	all-purpose flour
½ cup | 125 mL	plain yogurt (any fat %)
2 Tbsp | 30 mL	olive oil or vegetable oil
2 ¼ tsp | 8 g	instant dry yeast
½ tsp | 2 g	salt
	melted butter or ghee, for brushing
	sea salt and/or chopped cilantro, for sprinkling

A well-seasoned cast iron frying pan is best for cooking naan indoors. You can also grill it over high heat if you wish.

• • • • • • • •

When I'm making a curry for supper, I always plan a batch of fresh naan to go with it. I make the dough first, and by the time I chop all my vegetables and start the curry cooking, the dough has risen and is ready to roll and cook. Since they take no time to cook, a single recipe (six flatbreads) is done in a snap (but it's rare that all six ever make it to the table . . .).

1. Mix the water with 2 ¼ cups (340 g) of the flour and the yogurt, oil, yeast, and salt in a large mixing bowl and stir with a wooden spoon until it becomes too difficult to do so. Pour the remaining ¼ cup (35 g) of flour on a clean work surface and tip the dough out onto it. Knead the dough for about 3 minutes, turning it and working in all of the remaining flour. Place the dough in a bowl, cover it with plastic wrap, and let it rise on the counter for 1 hour.

2. Turn the dough out onto a work surface lightly dusted with flour and divide it into six pieces. Roll out each piece of dough into a rough circle (precision is not essential here) about 8 or 9 inches (20–23 cm) in diameter.

3. Heat a cast iron or other heavy-bottomed frying pan on high heat. Drop in a naan and cook for about 90 seconds, until browned in spots on the bottom. Use tongs to flip the naan over and cook for another 90 seconds, until the bubbles blister and turn toasty brown. Brush the naan with melted butter or ghee and sprinkle with salt and/or cilantro. Repeat with the remaining pieces of dough. Stacking the naan will keep it warm, or you can hold them in a 300°F (150°C) oven until ready to serve. The naan is best eaten the day it's cooked.

Easy Poppy Seed Bagel Bites

*These little bagel-like bites have a nice sweet edge, so are great for breakfast,
but they aren't too sweet, so they can also make a great hors d'oeuvre base for something
like little smoked salmon sandwiches or even burger sliders.*

Makes 48 bites • Prep 30 minutes plus resting • Bake/Cook 25 minutes

Dough

1 cup | 250 mL	**milk**
½ cup | 115 g	**unsalted butter**
1 | 1	**egg**
¼ cup | 50 g	**granulated sugar**
1 ½ tsp | 6 g	**instant dry yeast**
3 ½ cups | 525 g	**all-purpose flour**
½ tsp | 2 g	**salt**

Poppy Seed Syrup

2 Tbsp | 18 g	**poppy seeds**
½ cup | 125 mL	**milk**
¼ cup | 50 g	**granulated sugar**
1 Tbsp | 15 g	**unsalted butter**

1. For the dough, heat the milk and butter in a saucepan over low heat until the butter has melted and the milk is around 115°F (46°C) (no need to precisely measure the temperature—just above body temperature is a good gauge). Mix with the egg, sugar, yeast, flour, and salt in a stand mixer fitted with the dough hook on low speed until blended and then one speed higher, kneading until the dough is smooth and elastic. If mixing by hand, stir the dough with a wooden spoon until it is too difficult to do so, and then turn the dough out onto a clean surface and knead by hand until elastic, about 5 minutes. Place the dough in a bowl, cover with plastic wrap, and let it rise for an hour on the counter, until almost doubled in size.

2. Preheat the oven to 350°F (180°C). Line two baking trays with parchment paper.

3. Turn the dough out onto a clean, flour-free surface and divide it into four. Roll out a piece of dough into a rope about 12 inches (30 cm) long and cut it into 12 pieces. Shape each piece into a ball and place these on the baking trays, leaving about 2 inches (5 cm) between them. Cover the trays with tea towels and let the dough balls rest for 15 minutes.

4. Bake the bagel bites for 16–20 minutes until they brown just a little (they will not brown a lot). While they bake, prepare the poppy seed syrup. Bring the poppy seeds and milk up to a full simmer in a saucepan over medium heat and then whisk in the sugar and butter, simmering for just a few minutes. When the bagel bites come out from the oven, immediately place them in a large bowl (you may need to do one tray at a time). Pour the hot syrup over the bagel bites and toss well to coat. Transfer them to a cooling rack to cool and enjoy. The bagel bites are best enjoyed the day they are made, but will keep for up to 2 days in an airtight container.

*Unlike regular bagels, which are dropped into boiling water before they are baked,
these little bites are baked first and then softened with the hot liquid tossed with them
while they are warm. Boiling them first would make them too chewy.*

Classic Parker House Rolls

Buttery and soft, these are a real treat for Sunday supper, which is usually a roast in our house. I enjoy a couple with dinner, and then use another for a sandwich with leftovers later in the evening!

Makes 18 rolls • Prep 30 minutes plus resting • Bake 25 minutes

1 cup | 250 mL	milk
¼ cup | 60 mL	water
2 ¼ tsp | 8 g	instant dry yeast
1 | 1	egg, at room temperature
2 Tbsp | 25 g	granulated sugar
2 Tbsp | 30 g	unsalted butter, melted, plus extra for brushing
3 ¼ cups | 485 g	all-purpose flour
1 tsp | 5 g	salt

You can make the dough for these rolls ahead of time, and once they are shaped and put into the muffin pan, you can chill them overnight to bake the next day. Give them 90 minutes to come up to room temperature before you bake them.

1. Heat the milk and water in a saucepan over low heat until it reaches around 115°F (46°C) (no need to precisely measure the temperature—just above body temperature is a good gauge). Mix with the yeast, and then the egg, sugar, and butter in a stand mixer fitted with the hook attachment on low speed. Add the flour and salt and continue to mix until the dough comes together, about 3 minutes. If mixing by hand, mix the ingredients in a large bowl using a wooden spoon until it is too difficult to do so, and then turn it out onto a work surface and knead by hand until it feels smooth and elastic, about 5 minutes. Place the dough in a bowl, cover with plastic wrap, and let it rise for about 90 minutes on the counter, until doubled in size.

2. Turn the dough out onto a lightly floured work surface and roll it out into a 12-inch (30 cm) square. Brush the surface of the dough with melted butter. Cut the dough into nine squares and then cut each square in half to create 18 rectangles. Brush 18 muffin pan cups with melted butter. Twist each piece of dough around once and press into the muffin pan. Cover the pans loosely with plastic wrap and let rise for 30 minutes.

3. Preheat the oven to 350°F (180°C). Unwrap the rolls and bake for 15–20 minutes, until they are golden brown. The rolls are best served warm, but can be reheated for 5 minutes in a 300°F (150°C) oven. They are best enjoyed the day they are baked.

Classic Brioches

Brioche is a rich, buttery bread that is delicate and tender—almost cake-like in its airiness, but not at all sweet. Be careful—once you've made it once, it'll become your weekend staple.

Makes 6 brioche buns • Prep 40 minutes plus resting and chilling • Bake 30 minutes

6 Tbsp | 90 mL 2 Tbsp + 1½ cups | 335 g	milk all-purpose flour
1 Tbsp | 10 g	instant dry yeast
2 | 2	eggs, at room temperature
2 Tbsp | 16 g	icing sugar, sifted
¼ tsp | 1 g	salt
6 Tbsp | 90 g	unsalted butter, at room temperature
1 | 1	egg, whisked with 2 Tbsp (30 mL) of water, for brushing

1. Heat ¼ cup (60 mL) of the milk in a saucepan over low heat until it reaches around 115°F (46°C) (no need to precisely measure the temperature—just above body temperature is a good gauge). Remove from the heat and stir with 2 Tbsp (17 g) of the flour and the yeast and let sit for about 5 minutes.

2. Mix with the remaining milk and the flour, eggs, icing sugar, and salt in the bowl of a stand mixer fitted with the paddle attachment on low speed until blended, about 3 minutes. Add the butter while mixing and, once incorporated, switch to the dough hook attachment and beat until the butter is fully incorporated and the dough is smooth. If mixing by hand, mix the ingredients in a large bowl using a wooden spoon until evenly combined, about 6 minutes, then add the butter and increase your mixing action until the dough is smooth (it will be very soft). Place the dough in a large bowl, cover with plastic wrap, and let it rise for 30 minutes on the counter, then chill for at least 8 hours, and up to 24 hours.

3. To shape the brioche, turn the chilled dough out onto a lightly floured work surface and divide it into six. Shape each piece into a ball, flouring your hands and the dough as needed. Then shape each piece into a slight oblong shape, sort of like a snowman, with a head and body. Use your finger to poke a hole through the centre of the larger "body" of the brioche and poke the smaller ball through it. Place each piece in an oiled 4-inch (10 cm) brioche pan. Cover the pans with a tea towel and let rise for 90 minutes on the counter, until doubled in size.

4. Preheat the oven to 350°F (180°C). Brush the tops of the brioches with the egg wash, place the pans on a baking tray, and bake for about 25 minutes, until they are an even rich brown colour. Cool the brioches in the pans on a cooling rack for 15 minutes, then turn them out of the pans onto the rack to cool completely. The brioches are best enjoyed the day they are baked, but they will keep for 1 day in an airtight container, or can be frozen for up to 2 months.

Brioche dough is a very forgiving dough, so it's fantastic to try this if you've never made a yeast bread before. Once the dough is chilled, the set butter makes the dough easy to handle and even if you proof it for less or longer than the required time, the brioche will still bake up beautifully.

The technique for getting that knob on top of a classic brioche may seem funny, but it works. If you were to shape a little piece of dough and press it into the top, it would pop off during baking as the bread rises.

. . . .

Brioche pans are distinctively fluted and angled, and make for beautifully shaped loaves. However this recipe can also be baked in two 9- x 5-inch (2 L) loaf tins; the rising time will stay the same, but you should bake the loaves for an additional 10 minutes.

Rosemary Onion Focaccia

*This recipe is gratifying to make by hand. The dough is easy to mix and knead
and produces consistently delicious results. Focaccia is a great
rustic-style bread to make if you're new to the bread-baking world: it's not intended
to look pristinely perfect, so it's very forgiving to whatever shape it turns out.*

Makes two 15- x 10-inch (38 x 25 cm) breads
Serves 16 • Prep 30 minutes plus resting • Bake 25 minutes

Focaccia

2 ½ cups | 625 mL	warm water (around 115°F/46°C)
2 ¼ tsp | 8 g	instant dry yeast
2 Tbsp | 30 mL	extra virgin olive oil
½ cup | 75 g	semolina flour, plus extra for sprinkling on pans
5–5 ½ | 750– cups | 825 g	all-purpose flour
1 Tbsp | 15 g	coarse sea salt

Toppings

½ | ½	medium red onion, sliced
2 Tbsp | 30 mL	chopped fresh rosemary
3–4 | 45– Tbsp | 60 mL	extra virgin olive oil
	coarse sea salt

1. Mix the water with the yeast, then add the oil and semolina in a large mixing bowl using a wooden spoon until blended. Add the flour, 1 cup (150 g) at a time, stirring well after each addition until it becomes too difficult to do so. Turn the dough out onto a lightly floured work surface, add the salt, and knead by hand until all the flour has been worked in (you may not need the final ½ cup/75 g of flour) and the dough is smooth and elastic, about 10 minutes. Place the dough in a bowl, cover with plastic wrap, and let it rise for about 90 minutes on the counter, until doubled in size.

2. Turn the risen dough out onto a lightly floured surface again and divide it in half. Roll out each piece of dough into a rectangle measuring 15 x 10 inches (38 x 25 cm). Line two baking trays of this size (or a little larger) with parchment paper, and sprinkle each one with a little semolina. Lift the rolled dough pieces onto each pan, cover the trays with tea towels, and let rise on the counter for 45 minutes.

3. Remove the tea towels and use your fingertips to gently "dimple" the dough, cover again, and let rise for another 45 minutes.

4. Preheat the oven to 400°F (200°C).

5. Toss the red onion and rosemary in the olive oil to coat. Remove the tea towels from the trays and sprinkle the onion evenly over the dough, trying to coat as much of the dough as possible with the olive oil. Sprinkle with sea salt. Bake the focaccia for about 25 minutes, until it is a rich golden brown colour. Carefully remove the focaccia from the trays to cool (to prevent the bottom of the bread from going soft) and cool on a cooling rack to room temperature before slicing. The focaccia will keep for 1 day, or can be frozen, well wrapped in plastic wrap, for up to 2 months.

While this entire chapter on breads could be regarded as a collection of Foundation recipes, focaccia is a textbook example of the basic bread-making process. From the kneading to the proofing, rolling, and baking, it is a perfect recipe to become comfortable with bread making in general.

• • • • • • • •

If you're serving this bread to dinner guests, try to time it so that it comes out of the oven as your guests arrive—the smell of the onion caramelizing on the baking bread with hints of rosemary is just so appealing.

Classic Lemon Cranberry Scones
with Lemon Glaze

These scones have that gorgeous balance of cakey and flaky.
They aren't overly sweet and have just the right amount of richness.

Makes 8 large scones • Prep 15 minutes • Bake/Cook 25 minutes plus setting

Scones

3 cups | 450 g	all-purpose flour
¼ cup | 50 g	granulated sugar
1 Tbsp | 9 g	baking powder
¼ tsp | 1 g	salt
1 Tbsp | 15 mL	finely grated lemon zest
½ cup | 115 g	cold unsalted butter, cut into small pieces
½ cup | 125 mL	whipping cream
¼ cup | 60 mL	2% milk, plus extra for brushing
1 | 1	egg
1 tsp | 5 mL	pure vanilla extract
1 cup | 250 mL	fresh or frozen and unthawed cranberries

Glaze

1 cup | 130 g	icing sugar, sifted
1 ½ Tbsp | 22 mL	fresh lemon juice

The dough recipe for these scones is essentially neutral, so you can switch out the fruit to whatever you wish, or even bake them as plain. Some of my favourites include currants, raisins, blueberries, raspberries, and figs with walnuts.

· · · · · · · ·

I like to work my scone dough with my fingers so I can feel where I'm at with the butter during the process. When I'm cutting the butter into the flour mixture, I first rub the butter in with my fingertips. Once the big pieces of butter are broken down, I then switch the motion and flatten the butter and flour bits between the palms of my hands. Flattening the pieces of butter before the liquid has been added helps to build in the flakiness.

1. Preheat the oven to 375°F (190°C). Line a baking tray with parchment paper.

2. For the scones, sift the flour, sugar, baking powder, and salt into a large bowl. Stir in the lemon zest. Cut in the butter until the mixture is rough and crumbly but small pieces of butter are still visible.

3. In a separate bowl, whisk the cream, milk, egg, and vanilla together. Add this to the flour mixture and stir to just bring the dough together, turning it out onto a very lightly floured work surface to complete bringing it together with your hands. Flatten the dough out and press the cranberries into the dough, folding it over and flattening it out a few times to incorporate them.

4. Shape the dough into a disc about 10 inches (25 cm) across. Cut the disc into eight wedges and place them on the prepared baking tray, leaving about 2 inches (5 cm) between them. Brush the scones with a little milk and bake for 20–25 minutes, until the scones are lightly browned on top. Cool completely on the pan on a cooling rack before glazing.

5. For the glaze, whisk the icing sugar and lemon juice together and drizzle over the scones using the whisk or a fork. Let the glaze set for 1 hour before serving. The scones are best enjoyed the day they are baked.

Braided Egg Buns

This egg bun recipe is very much in the style of challah bread—the eggs come first, giving it its richness, tenderness, and gorgeous yellow hue.

Makes 12 buns • Prep 1 hour plus resting • Bake 25 minutes

¾ cup	180 mL	**milk**
2 ¼ tsp	8 g	**instant dry yeast**
2	2	**eggs, at room temperature**
1	1	**egg yolk**
¼ cup	60 mL	**vegetable oil**
¼ cup	50 g	**granulated sugar**
3 ¼ cups	485 g	**all-purpose flour**
½ tsp	2 g	**salt**
1	1	**egg yolk, whisked with 2 Tbsp (30 mL) milk, for brushing**
	sesame seeds and/or poppy seeds, for sprinkling

1. Heat the milk in a saucepan over low heat until it reaches around 115°F (46°C) (no need to precisely measure the temperature—just above body temperature is a good gauge). Mix with the yeast, then the eggs, egg yolk, oil, sugar, flour, and salt in a stand mixer fitted with the hook attachment on low speed, until it comes together. Then knead the dough for 3 minutes to achieve elasticity. If mixing by hand, mix the ingredients in a large bowl using a wooden spoon until it becomes too difficult to do so, then turn the dough out onto a lightly floured work surface and knead until it feels smooth and elastic, about 5 minutes. Place the dough in a bowl, cover with plastic wrap, and let rise for about 90 minutes on the counter, until doubled in size.

2. Turn the dough out onto a lightly floured work surface, roll it into a log, and cut it into 12 equal pieces. To create the braided buns, cut each piece of dough in half and roll out each half into a thin rope about 12 inches (30 cm) long. Place one rope of dough over the second, creating a cross. Make sure the ropes cross in the middle so that you have four evenly sized lengths. Bring the ends of the bottom (vertical) rope over the top rope, crossing over completely. Repeat this with the horizontal piece of dough and continue crossing the ropes over until you reach the ends of the dough (the bun will be about 4 inches/10 cm long). Tuck in the end pieces and place the bun on a parchment-lined baking tray. Repeat with the remaining buns, spacing them at least 2 inches (5 cm) apart on the tray. Cover the tray with plastic wrap and let the buns rise for about 45 minutes, until almost doubled in size.

3. Preheat the oven to 350°F (180°C).

4. Brush the buns with the egg wash and sprinkle them with sesame seeds and/or poppy seeds. Bake for 20–25 minutes, until a rich golden brown. The buns are best served warm, but can be reheated for 5 minutes in a 300°F (150°C) oven. They are best enjoyed the day they are baked.

This technique for braiding buns is significantly different from how you braid hair. In fact, it's a little simpler since you are only working with two lengths of dough, not three, and by starting with a cross first and overlapping each length of dough completely over itself, you get a bun that really sits tall and has a lot of dimension and character to it.

• • • • • • • •

You can bake this recipe as a full challah braided loaf (the ropes you start out braiding will be really long, at almost 3 feet/90 cm, but once braided the loaf will be just over a foot/30 cm)—just give it an extra 15 minutes to rise and then an extra 15 minutes of baking time.

Cranberry Chocolate Focaccia Twists

*A savoury focaccia dough is transformed into a breakfast bread
that isn't over-the-top sweet, but is still a nice treat.*

Makes 12 twists • Prep 40 minutes plus resting • Bake/Cook 20 minutes

Focaccia Twists

1 ¼ cups	310 mL	**warm water (around 115°F/46°C)**
1 Tbsp	15 mL	**extra virgin olive oil**
1 ⅛ tsp	4 g	**instant dry yeast**
¼ cup	38 g	**semolina flour**
2 ½–	375–	
2 ¾ cups	410 g	**all-purpose flour**
1 ½ tsp	7 g	**coarse sea salt**

Toppings

½ cup	70 g	**chopped dried cranberries**
3 oz	90 g	**semisweet chocolate chips**
	turbinado sugar and ground cinnamon, for sprinkling

Syrup

¼ cup	75 g	**honey**
3 Tbsp	45 mL	**water**
½ tsp	2 mL	**pure vanilla extract**

*Most recipes calling for yeast use instant dry
yeast. This yeast doesn't need to be dissolved
in water, although I usually add it to the water
needed for the recipe out of habit. If using
traditional yeast, add it to your water and let
it sit for 5 minutes to dissolve. If using fresh
yeast (harder and harder to find these days),
double the measurement by weight.*

1. Mix the water with the oil and then the yeast and semolina in a large bowl using a wooden spoon. Add the flour 1 cup (150 g) at a time, stirring well after each addition until it becomes too difficult to do so, then turn the dough out onto a lightly floured work surface and knead until all the flour has been worked in (you may not need the final ¼ cup/35 g of flour) and the dough is smooth and elastic, about 10 minutes. Place the dough in a large bowl, cover with plastic wrap, and let it rise for about 90 minutes on the counter, until doubled in size.

2. Turn the dough out onto a lightly floured work surface and roll it out to a rectangle measuring 16 x 12 inches (40 x 30 cm). Sprinkle half of the rectangle with the chopped dried cranberries and chocolate and fold the dough over the filling, pressing gently with your hands. Roll it out, just a little more, to seal in the additions. Cut the dough into 12 equally sized rectangles. Use a paring knife to make an incision through the dough at the centre of each piece. Twist the dough through the incision to create a twist and place these, 2 inches (5 cm) apart, on two parchment-lined baking trays. Cover the twists with a tea towel and let rise for 1 hour until almost doubled in size.

3. Preheat the oven to 375°F (190°C).

4. For the syrup, bring the honey, water, and vanilla just up to a simmer in a saucepan over medium heat and brush each twist generously with it. Stir the turbinado sugar with a little cinnamon and sprinkle this generously on top. Bake the twists for about 20 minutes, until they are an even golden brown. Allow the twists to cool on the pan on a cooling rack for at least 20 minutes before serving. The twists are best served the day they are baked.

Whole Wheat Pita

If you are getting into making bread from scratch, homemade pitas are a fun option—watching them puff up in the oven as they bake really shows you the magic of bread baking.

Makes 6 pita breads • Prep 25 minutes plus resting • Bake 6 minutes

1 ¾ cups	410 mL	warm water (around 115°F/46°C)
1 ½ tsp	5 g	instant dry yeast
1 ¾ cups	260 g	bread flour
1 ¾ cups	260 g	whole wheat flour
1 Tbsp	15 mL	extra virgin olive oil
1 tsp	5 g	granulated sugar
1 tsp	5 g	salt

Do be sure your oven is fully preheated before baking your pita breads. If the oven isn't hot enough, you won't get the pocket in the centre to puff up.

• • • • • • •

I love making garlic bread with leftover or day-old pita. I split the pitas in half (open the pocket fully), brush them with garlic butter, and sprinkle with salt and pepper. I then bake them at 375°F (190°C) until they are toasted and crispy and mmmmm . . . What a treat.

1. Mix the water with the yeast and then the flours, oil, and sugar in a stand mixer fitted with the dough hook attachment on low speed to incorporate, then increase the speed one level and knead for 5 minutes until the dough is smooth and elastic. If mixing by hand, mix the ingredients in a large bowl using a wooden spoon until it is too difficult to do so, then turn the dough out onto a clean counter and knead until it is elastic (add as little extra flour as possible while kneading), about 7 minutes. Place the dough in a large bowl, cover with plastic wrap, and let it rise on the counter for 1 hour, until almost a quarter bigger in size.

2. Turn the dough out onto a clean work surface and divide it into six (5 oz/150 g) pieces (using a scale is best for evenly sized pita). Shape the dough pieces into rounds (try to not use flour for dusting), cover with a tea towel, and let rest for 20 minutes.

3. With a rolling pin, roll out each piece of dough to a circle about 8 inches (20 cm) in diameter (if the dough springs back when rolling, just set them aside for 5 minutes and then roll them to the right size). Cover with a tea towel and let rest for 20 minutes.

4. Preheat the oven to 450°F (235°C). Place two baking trays in the oven to heat. Remove one baking tray from the oven, dust lightly with flour, and place two or three pita rounds on it. Immediately return the tray to the oven and repeat with the second tray. Bake the pita for 5–6 minutes (they will puff up like balloons!) and then carefully remove them (they will let off steam if pressed) from the tray to an open tea towel. Cover the pitas with the towel to deflate them and let them cool for a few minutes (this will soften them so they are tender and the pocket will open easily). The pita breads are best enjoyed the day they are made.

Soft Pretzels

Soft pretzels are a delicious bread treat. They have a distinctively tender but chewy outside layer from boiling the pretzels before baking them. Although they are altogether different from bagels, soft pretzels fall into the same family of boiled breads. This dough is pliable enough to make by hand—no mixer required.

Makes 12 soft pretzels • Prep 45 minutes plus resting • Bake/Cook 30 minutes

⅔ cup | 160 mL	water
⅔ cup | 160 mL	milk
3 Tbsp | 45 g	warm melted butter
1 Tbsp | 12 g	granulated sugar
1 ½ tsp | 5 g	instant dry yeast
3 ½ cups | 525 g	all-purpose flour
1 tsp | 5 g	fine salt
3 ½ Tbsp | 42 g	baking soda
2 | 2	egg yolks whisked with 2 Tbsp (30 mL) water, for brushing
	coarse salt, for sprinkling

1. Heat the water and milk in a saucepan over low heat until it reaches around 115°F (46°C) (no need to precisely measure the temperature—just above body temperature is a good gauge). Mix with the melted butter, sugar, and yeast in a large bowl using a wooden spoon. Add the flour and salt and stir until too difficult to do so (it is a dense dough), then turn it out onto a lightly floured surface and knead the dough by hand until it feels elastic and smooth, about 5 minutes. Place the dough in a large bowl, cover with plastic wrap, and let it rise for 90 minutes on the counter, until almost doubled in size.

2. Turn the dough out onto your work surface and divide it into 12 equal pieces. Using as little flour as possible, roll each piece of dough into a rope about 12 inches (30 cm) long. Drop the rope onto the table as an elongated "U," then twist the dough around twice, and place the ends over the bottom curve of the "U" to create the signature pretzel shape. Once you are happy with the shape, press down the ends gently to secure them. Line a baking tray (coated, not aluminum) with parchment paper and place the pretzels on the tray, leaving 2 inches (5 cm) between them. Cover the pretzels with a tea towel to rise again for 20 minutes, until a quarter bigger in size.

3. Preheat the oven to 350°F (180°C). Fill a stainless steel 16-cup (4 L) saucepan almost to the top with water and bring it to a full rolling boil over high heat. Add the baking soda (the water will foam briefly) and then carefully drop two or three pretzels into the water. Boil the pretzels for 90 seconds without turning. Lift them out with a slotted spoon and put them back on the baking tray. Repeat with the remaining pretzels, in batches.

4. Brush the boiled pretzels with the egg wash and sprinkle with coarse salt. Bake the pretzels for 20–25 minutes, until they are an even, rich brown. Soft pretzels are best enjoyed within 5 hours of being made.

The soft pretzels and pretzel buns that you see in commercial bakeries are boiled in water with added pretzel lye. This is an alkaline addition that is key to the colour and texture of the pretzels, but it is also highly caustic and not recommended for home use. Using baking soda in the boiling liquid creates an appropriate and, most importantly, safe alkaline liquid for the pretzels—the texture is virtually the same, although the colour will be a slightly lighter brown. This is also the reason that you need to use a non-aluminum, coated baking tray—to avoid a reaction between the baking soda liquid and the aluminum in the tray that could cause a blackening of the pretzels and an undesirable metallic taste.

• • • • • • • •

The reason soft pretzels are best eaten within such a small window isn't to do with the dough or the way they are cooked—the salt that coats the outside of the pretzels eventually causes them to dry out.

• • • • • • • •

I sometimes make pretzel knots instead of the twisted pretzel shape. After dividing the dough into 12 pieces, I just roll the dough and tie it into a single knot and then boil and bake as above.

Hot Cross Buns

*What sets these hot cross buns apart is the hot glaze that gets
poured over them right when they come out of the oven.*

Makes 12 buns • Prep 1 hour plus resting • Bake/Cook 35 minutes plus setting

Dough

¾ cup | 180 mL	2% milk
4 ½ tsp | 13 g	instant dry yeast
3 | 3	eggs, at room temperature
⅓ cup | 70 g	granulated sugar
½ cup | 125 mL	vegetable oil
3 ¾ cups | 560 g	all-purpose flour
1 tsp | 5 mL	finely grated lemon zest
¾ tsp | 4 g	salt
½ tsp | 2 g	ground cinnamon
¼ tsp | 1 g	ground allspice
¼ tsp | 1 g	ground nutmeg
¼ tsp | 1 g	ground cloves
⅓ cup | 45 g	dried currants
¼ cup | 25 g	diced mixed peel

Hot Glaze

½ cup | 100 g	granulated sugar
3 Tbsp | 45 mL	water
1 tsp | 5 mL	pure vanilla extract

Icing

¾ cup | 100 g	icing sugar, sifted
1 Tbsp | 15 mL	milk, plus extra if needed

1. For the dough, heat the milk in a saucepan over low heat until it reaches around 115°F (46°C) (no need to precisely measure the temperature—just above body temperature is a good gauge). Mix this with the other ingredients except the currants and peel in a stand mixer fitted with the hook attachment on low speed until it comes together, then increase the speed by one level and knead until the dough is smooth and elastic, about 5 minutes (the dough is soft and should stick to the bottom of the bowl). If mixing by hand, mix the ingredients in a large bowl using a wooden spoon until the dough comes together, then turn out onto a lightly floured work surface and knead until smooth. Toward the end of kneading, add the currants and mixed peel and knead in. Place the dough in a large bowl, cover with plastic wrap, and let it rise for 75–90 minutes on the counter, until doubled in size.

2. Grease a 13- x 9-inch (33 x 23 cm) baking pan.

3. Turn the risen dough out onto a lightly floured work surface and divide it into 12 evenly sized pieces. Shape each piece into a ball by rolling it between your hands while it remains on the work surface. Place the rolled buns on the prepared pan, leaving equal space between them. Cover the pan with plastic wrap and let the buns rise for 45 minutes.

4. Preheat the oven to 350°F (180°C). Uncover the buns and bake for 25–30 minutes, until they are a rich brown on top. While still hot from the oven, prepare the glaze.

5. For the glaze, bring the sugar, water, and vanilla up to a simmer in a small saucepan over medium-high heat, stirring until the sugar is fully dissolved. Brush this syrup over the still-hot buns, until it has all been used. Let the buns cool completely on the pan on a cooling rack.

6. For the icing, stir the icing sugar and milk together until thick enough for piping (add a few more drops of milk, if necessary). Pour this into a small piping bag fitted with a small plain tip and pipe crosses on top of each bun. Let the icing set for 1 hour before serving. The buns will, keep, well wrapped in plastic wrap, for 1 day.

Sometimes the cross that is put on top of each bun is made from a simple water/flour mixture, but I like to use icing for a little added sweetness.

These buns have to be in my Top Ten favourite baking smells. The combination of the yeast dough with the baker's spices (cinnamon, nutmeg, cloves, and allspice) is just divine.

Potato Parmesan Focaccia

This focaccia uses cooked potato in the dough. This results in a soft, remarkably tender bread that has an almost cake-like texture. Topped with thin slices of potato, it's a real showstopper.

Makes two 9-inch (23 cm) breads • Prep 50 minutes plus resting • Bake/Cook 50 minutes

1 ½ lb | 675 g	russet (baking) potatoes (2–4 potatoes)
1 ¾ cups | 430 mL	warm water (around 115°F/46°C)
2 ¼ tsp | 8 g	instant dry yeast
3 ¾ cups | 560 g	all-purpose flour
2 tsp | 10 g	coarse sea salt, plus extra for sprinkling
	extra virgin olive oil
1 tsp | 2 g	chopped fresh thyme
½ cup | 50 g	grated Parmesan cheese

1. Peel and dice 1 lb (450 g) of the potatoes and boil them in salted water until tender, about 10 minutes. Drain the potatoes well and push them through a ricer or mash by hand. Measure out 1 ½ cups (375 mL) loosely packed if pushed through a ricer, and 1 ¼ cups (310 mL) if mashed. Allow the potatoes to cool to just above room temperature.

2. Mix the water with the yeast, and then add the flour, cooled mashed potatoes, and salt to the bowl of a stand mixer fitted with the hook attachment, and mix on low speed until everything is blended. Increase by one speed and knead the dough until smooth and elastic (but it will still stick to the bottom of the bowl and even the sides slightly), about 4 minutes. If mixing by hand, mix the ingredients in a large bowl using a wooden spoon until the dough comes together, then turn it out onto a lightly floured work surface and knead until smooth and elastic (the dough will be soft), about 8 minutes. Place the dough in a bowl, cover with plastic wrap, and let it rise for 90 minutes on the counter, until doubled in size.

3. Grease two 9-inch (23 cm) pie plates. Turn the risen dough out onto a lightly floured surface, divide it in half, and roll out two circles, each 9 inches (23 cm) in diameter. Gently place the dough circles in the prepared pie plates. Cover the plates with tea towels and let the dough rise for 45 minutes until almost doubled in size.

4. Preheat the oven to 400°F (200°C). Peel the remaining potatoes and slice them thinly on a mandolin or through a food processor. Toss the potato slices with olive oil and a pinch of salt along with the thyme. Uncover the dough and dimple it gently with your fingers. Sprinkle an even layer of grated Parmesan over the dough and arrange the potato slices over top, overlapping one another. Top the potatoes with a generous, even layer of Parmesan. Bake the focaccia for 35–40 minutes, until the Parmesan cheese has browned evenly. Cool the focaccia for 10 minutes in their pans on a cooling rack, then carefully remove to the cooling rack to cool completely before serving. The focaccia are best enjoyed the day they are baked.

The cooked potato in the dough really adds to the bread's tenderness and its moist, soft consistency.

Crispy Seed Lavash

Lavash is a crispy, cracker-like flatbread, coated with seeds or spices.
I like including it in a bread basket to switch things up a bit.

Makes 16 pieces • Prep 40 minutes plus resting and chilling • Bake 20 minutes

1 cup | 250 mL	water
⅔ cup | 160 mL	milk
1 tsp | 4 g	instant dry yeast
1 Tbsp | 50 g	honey
2 cups | 300 g	bread flour
½ cup | 65 g	cake and pastry flour
½ cup | 75 g	whole wheat flour
⅓ cup | 50 g	semolina flour
1 Tbsp | 15 g	salt
	roasted, unsalted pumpkin seeds
	roasted, unsalted sunflower seeds
	poppy seeds
	sesame seeds
	salt and pepper

1. Heat the water and milk in a saucepan over low heat until it reaches around 115°F (46°C). Mix with the yeast, and then the honey, in a stand mixer fitted with the hook attachment on low speed. Add the four flours and salt and mix on low speed until the flour is incorporated, then increase the speed by one level and knead for about 5 minutes, until the dough becomes elastic and a little sticky. The dough will be very soft and definitely stick to the bottom of the bowl as it mixes. If mixing by hand, mix the ingredients in a large bowl using a wooden spoon until it becomes too difficult to do so, and then turn it out onto a work surface and knead for about 7 minutes. Place the dough in a large bowl, cover with plastic wrap and let it rise for 30 minutes on the counter (it won't change much in size), and then chill overnight.

2. Preheat the oven to 375°F (190°C). Line four baking trays with parchment paper (or prepare the lavash in batches).

3. Divide the dough into 16 evenly sized pieces and roll them into balls. Shape each piece of dough into an oval with your hands, so that it will fit through the rollers on the lowest setting of your pasta maker. Flour the dough generously (you will need lots of flour to coat the lavash as you roll it) to prevent sticking, and roll it through settings 1 through 4, flouring at each rolling, and rolling until the dough is a long oblong piece about 1/16 inch (1.5 mm) thick. Place the pieces on the baking trays, trimming them if needed so they fit. They can be placed very close together on the tray, but should not overlap.

4. Brush the lavash with a little water and sprinkle with your chosen assortment of pumpkin seeds, sunflower seeds, poppy seeds, sesame seeds, salt, and pepper. Bake for about 15 minutes until the lavash is a rich golden brown. Remove the lavash immediately from the baking trays, and transfer to a cooling rack to cool completely before breaking into pieces to serve. The lavash will keep in an airtight container at room temperature for up to 2 weeks.

A pasta roller really does make easy work of step 3, but if you don't have one,
you can roll the dough by hand, as thinly as possible. Don't worry too much about the shape,
since the lavash will be cracked into pieces to eat and enjoy.

Classic Bagels

Making bagels from scratch does take a bit of time (the dough needs to be made a day ahead), but is worth the effort. Including honey in the dough and in the water in which the bagels are boiled, gives them their signature, subtly sweet, taste.

Makes 12 bagels • Prep 1 hour plus resting • Bake/Cook 35 minutes

Sponge

2 ¼ cups | 550 mL	warm water (around 115°F/46°C)
1 tsp | 4 g	instant dry yeast
3 cups | 450 g	bread flour

Dough

¾ tsp | 3 g	instant dry yeast
2 Tbsp | 30 g	honey
2 ½ cups | 375 g	bread flour
1 Tbsp | 15 g	salt

Assembly

2 Tbsp | 30 g	honey
1 tsp | 5 g	baking soda
1 | 1	egg white, lightly whisked
	poppy seeds, sesame seeds, onion flakes, for topping

1. For the sponge, stir the water, yeast, and flour together in a large bowl or in the bowl of a stand mixer. Let this sit for 10 minutes.

2. For the dough, add the yeast, honey, flour, and salt to the sponge and mix using the dough hook on low speed until the dough comes together, then increase the speed by one level and knead the dough until it is smooth and elastic, about 7 minutes. If mixing by hand, mix the ingredients into the sponge using a wooden spoon until it becomes too difficult to do so, then turn it out onto a lightly floured work surface and knead by hand until smooth and elastic, for about 10 minutes. Place the dough in a large bowl, cover with plastic wrap, and let sit for 1 hour on the counter, and then chill overnight.

3. Turn the chilled dough out onto a work surface very lightly dusted with flour and divide the dough into 12 evenly sized pieces (if weighing, these will be 3 ½ oz/110 g each). Shape each piece of dough into a ball.

4. There are two styles of shaping the dough for baking, and the choice is yours:

   a) *Roll and twist*—for a bagel that sits taller and with a more defined hole, roll each ball of dough into a rope about 8 inches (20 cm) long and loop up the ends to overlap each other by about 2 inches (5 cm). Roll them together, with your hand in the middle of the bagel, place them on the baking trays (six per tray), cover them with a tea towel, and let them rest for 15 minutes.

   b) *Make a hole*—for a bagel that is a little flatter but also wider, use your thumb to poke a hole in the centre of the dough ball and roll it into a doughnut shape with your floured hand. Place them on the baking trays (six per tray), cover them with a tea towel, and let them rest for 15 minutes.

5. Preheat the oven to 425°F (220°C). Line two baking trays with parchment paper.

6. Fill a large stockpot halfway with water, set it over high heat, and bring the water up to a full boil. For every 10 cups (2.5 L) of water add 2 Tbsp (30 g) of honey and 1 tsp (5 g) of baking soda. Have your egg white and bagel toppings on hand. Using a slotted spoon, gently drop the bagels into the water one at a time, taking care not to overcrowd the water (add only three or four bagels at a time). Boil the bagels for 90 seconds to 2 ½ minutes (the longer the boil, the chewier the crust) and remove with the slotted spoon to place them back on the baking trays.

7. Brush each bagel with egg white and sprinkle with toppings as you wish. Bake the bagels for 20 minutes and then turn the oven off and open the door, leaving the bagels in there for 10 minutes more. Remove the bagels to a cooling rack to cool before eating. They can be eaten warm or left to cool completely and then toasted. The bagels are best enjoyed the day they are made, but are perfect for toasting for up to 2 days afterwards.

Even though the dough for bagels really isn't much different from a regular bread dough, my first bite of a bagel always leaves me amazed at how the texture and chewiness are unique. And toasted . . . Well, isn't that a bite of heaven?

· · · · · · · ·

I focus on the toppings you can put on top of your bagels, but you can also add ingredients to the dough: cinnamon, raisins, dried blueberries, etc.

· · · · · · · ·

One time I made this recipe while a little distracted, and I brushed the bagels with the egg white and sprinkled on the toppings before I had even boiled them. So I continued on, and guess what? The toppings stayed on and the bagels came out just fine.

Sauces and Décor

Sauces and décor are as important in the dessert world as they are in the savoury world. Sauces allow a pastry chef to bridge flavours on a plate that might not normally go together, and also allow for creativity in how a plate comes together. Décor elevates the beauty of a dessert but also leaves room for creative expression—it is how you add your personality to a dessert.

This chapter is not divided into the Simple, Scrumptious, and Sensational categories of the other chapters, as these recipes are all sensational ways to dress up almost any dessert. Some of the recipes here are quick to make, and some are more involved, but it is how you choose to use them that will elevate your desserts to sensational, no matter which accents you choose.

Homemade Butter

Making butter from scratch is easy if you have a food processor, and kids (of all ages) love watching the cream transform from liquid to solid!

Makes 2 cups (500 mL) • Prep 20 minutes

4 cups | 1 L	whipping cream
	sea salt (optional)

1. Blend the cream using a food processor fitted with the steel blade attachment on high speed until it thickens, and then separates into fat and liquid (about 3 minutes).

2. Remove the blade and scoop out the butter (you can discard the liquid or use it as buttermilk in other recipes). Place the bowl of soft butter into a bowl of ice water and squeeze out any excess liquid with your hands, or place the butter in cheesecloth and squeeze it out while in the cold water. Stir in salt to taste, if desired. You can store the butter, refrigerated, for up to 1 month.

Homemade butter is the next level if you're trying to impress your guests. Butter made from scratch is light and sweet, and is meant for spreading on breads and buns. Serve this butter with any of the breads featured in this book, or with my Basic Buttermilk Biscuits (page 249) or Classic Lemon Cranberry Scones (page 260).

· · · · · · ·

This is not butter you can use in baking, because you can't exactly know what the fat content will be (80% butterfat is the minimum needed for baking, the standard in butter here).

· · · · · · ·

To make a delicious Orange Honey Butter, beat 1 cup of Homemade Butter (recipe above) with 1 Tbsp (15 mL) finely grated orange zest and a drizzle of honey to taste. This is perfect on Basic Buttermilk Biscuits (page 249) or Classic Parker House Rolls (page 254).

· · · · · · ·

Part of the charm in making an "artisan" product like butter is the modest inconsistency in yield. The amount of butter you end up with depends on how much liquid you manage to squeeze out, and this is why homemade butter is meant for slathering onto bread and not for using as a baking ingredient.

Espresso Chocolate Sauce

This chocolate sauce is best served warm or at room temperature.
It is delicious with almost anything—from Classic New York Cheesecake (page 118)
to Classic Gingerbread Cake (page 107).

Makes about 1 cup (250 mL) • Prep 10 minutes • Cook 10 minutes

¼ cup | 60 mL	whipping cream
3 oz | 90 g	bittersweet couverture/baking chocolate, chopped
3 Tbsp | 45 g	unsalted butter
2 Tbsp | 25 g	packed light brown sugar
2 Tbsp | 30 mL	corn syrup
	pinch salt
2 Tbsp | 30 mL	brewed espresso coffee

1. Stir the cream, chocolate, butter, brown sugar, corn syrup, and salt together in a heavy-bottomed saucepan over medium-low heat until melted and smooth. Remove the saucepan from the heat, stir in the coffee, and serve warm or chill for later use. The sauce can be reheated to make it more pourable. The chocolate sauce will keep, refrigerated, until the expiry date of the cream you used to make it.

The shot of espresso added at the end intensifies the chocolate "kick."
You can, of course, omit it if you wish, and/or add your own flavour additions
(using extracts like orange, mint, or almond, or spirits like orange liqueur or Irish cream).

Toffee Sauce

This sauce is easier to make than a caramel sauce, and is intended to be
served with English Sticky Toffee Pudding (page 219), but it would go with any other dessert that
would suit a caramel-style sauce such as Pumpkin Pie (page 82) or any apple dessert.

Makes enough for 8 servings • Prep 10 minutes • Cook 10 minutes

¼ cup | 60 g	unsalted butter
½ cup | 100 g	packed dark brown sugar
¼ cup | 60 mL	whipping cream
½ cup | 75 g	raisins or lightly toasted walnut pieces
2 Tbsp | 30 mL	brandy

1. Melt the butter with the sugar in a saucepan, stirring over medium-high heat until bubbling. Stir in the whipping cream, add the raisins, and return to a simmer, stirring. Stir in the brandy (taking care in case it ignites). If preparing in advance, chill in an airtight container, and re-warm in a saucepan until fluid before serving.

If you'd prefer not to include brandy in this recipe,
use the same measure of lemon or orange juice in its place.

Bananas Foster

This is a dessert from New Orleans that would typically be prepared tableside with flourish and flair and then spooned over ice cream. I like to use it as a sauce, and it's especially decadent when served with my Chocolate Peanut Butter Whoopie Pies (page 53).

Makes about 1 ½ cups (375 mL) • Prep 15 minutes • Cook 8 minutes

¼ cup | 60 g	**unsalted butter**
½ cup | 100 g	**packed dark brown sugar**
	juice of ½ lemon
2 | 2	**bananas, sliced**
	pinch ground cinnamon

1. In a sauté pan over high heat, melt the butter with the brown sugar, stirring until it begins to bubble. Squeeze the lemon juice directly into the pan. Add the bananas and a pinch of cinnamon and stir just to warm the bananas. Remove the pan from the heat and serve immediately, ladled over ice cream or alongside whoopie pies.

I also make this with peaches in summer, or pineapple if my mood takes me that way. The idea is to just wing it—once you have the butter and sugar base down pat, you can get creative with the fruit you add, both the combinations and the amounts you use.

Caramel Sauce

Imagine the perfect slice of apple pie.
Now imagine it with a drizzle of classic caramel sauce.
What could be better?!

Makes about 1 cup (250 mL) • Prep 10 minutes • Cook 10 minutes

3 Tbsp | 45 mL	**water**
1 cup | 200 g	**granulated sugar**
1 Tbsp | 15 mL	**white corn syrup or lemon juice**
⅔ cup | 160 mL	**whipping cream**
2 Tbsp | 30 g	**unsalted butter**
1 tsp | 5 mL	**pure vanilla extract**
	pinch salt

1. Place the water, sugar, and corn syrup in a medium saucepan, and have the cream and butter measured and on hand. Bring the sugar up to a full boil over high heat without stirring and continue to boil, occasionally brushing down the sides of the pot with water, until the sugar turns a light amber colour, about 5 minutes. Remove the saucepan from the heat and whisk in the cream and butter, watching out for the steam and bubbling up of the caramel that happens at first. Once the bubbling subsides, whisk in the vanilla and salt. This can be used warm or cool.

Caramel sauce will keep, refrigerated, until the expiry date of the cream you used to prepare it. Simply warm it through before using.

Laurel Crème Anglaise

Crème anglaise is a custard that is used as a sauce, and it pairs wonderfully with almost all desserts: fruit, chocolate, spiced . . . The bay leaves add a beautiful and unexpected aroma.

Makes almost 1 ¾ cups (400 mL) • Prep 10 minutes • Cook 6 minutes plus chilling

1 ½ cups | 375 mL	10% cream (half-and-half)
2 | 2	bay laurel leaves
½ | ½	vanilla bean
3 | 3	egg yolks
¼ cup | 50 g	granulated sugar

Because you have to heat your cream to make this sauce, you've got a lovely opportunity to infuse a little flavour into it. Consider options like Earl Grey tea, a little orange zest, a sprig of rosemary, a slice of fresh ginger, or a cinnamon stick in place of the bay leaves.

. . . .

We normally associate bay leaves with savoury dishes like roasted chicken and stews, but they have such a subtle flavour that they are a beautiful companion to sweet dishes, especially chocolate and fruit desserts.

1. Place the cream in a small saucepan over medium heat and add the bay leaves and the scraped seeds and the pod of the vanilla bean. Bring this to just below a simmer.

2. In a small bowl, whisk the egg yolks and sugar. Remove the vanilla bean pod from the cream, add a little of the warm cream to the yolks while whisking, then gradually ladle in about half of the cream while whisking. Add this mixture back to the pot and continue to whisk on medium-low heat until it thickens enough to coat the back of a spoon, 3–4 minutes. Strain this through a fine mesh sieve into a bowl, cool to room temperature, and then chill completely until needed. The crème anglaise will keep, refrigerated, for up to 4 days.

Mango Coconut Salad

This is a colourful, fresh salad ideal for serving alongside
Green Tea Genoise Sponge Cake (page 111) or Classic New York Cheesecake (page 118).

Serves 6 • Prep 10 minutes

½ cup | 125 mL	**grated fresh coconut (grate it with a vegetable peeler)**
3 Tbsp | 45 mL	**icing sugar**
2 | 2	**ripe mangoes**
1 tsp | 5 mL	**finely grated lime zest**
1 Tbsp | 15 mL	**fresh lime juice**

1. Toss the coconut in a bowl with the icing sugar and let it sit for 5 minutes.

2. Peel and dice the mangoes and add them to the coconut. Toss these with the lime zest and juice. Chill until ready to serve. The salad is best served the day it is made.

If you have access to young coconut, scoop out the flesh and chop, slice, or grate it using a box grater, keeping the juices to toss with the mango.

• • • • • • •

If you have access to calamansi limes, a variety from the Philippines that tastes like a cross between a tangerine and a lime, they make a fragrant and delicious addition.

Piped Chocolate Garnishes

A decorative piping of chocolate makes for a pretty garnish on top of a tart, cake, or individual dessert. There are classic patterns to follow, and repetition and practice are the keys to success. It's just like learning to draw using chocolate.

Makes about 3 dozen • Prep 30 minutes • Cook 5 minutes plus chilling

2 oz | 60 g   **bittersweet couverture/baking chocolate, chopped**

It usually takes a few tries to make a parchment cone that holds in place and fits in your hand nicely. A parchment cone is to a pastry chef what a knife is to a chef—the fit is very personal. I can only hold and use one that I have made myself, and my pastry-making friends all feel the same way.

. . . .

To create a parchment pastry cone, cut out a large triangle of parchment paper (the right angle sides should be about a foot/30 cm long). Twist it into a cone shape, so that the three points of the triangle all meet at the wide top of the cone. Wiggle the points, shifting them so that the point at the bottom of the cone is closed (this is so that it won't leak as you fill it). Fold these three points together into the cone to secure its shape.

1. Line a baking tray with parchment paper and prepare a parchment pastry cone (see note).

2. Melt the chocolate in a metal bowl placed over a saucepan of barely simmering water, stirring until smooth. Remove this from the heat and pour the chocolate into the parchment pastry cone and snip off the tip of the cone.

3. On the prepared baking tray, pipe patterns and designs with the chocolate, making them 1–2 inches (2.5–5 cm) in size. Repetition is the best way to improve and create consistent designs. Chill the chocolate garnishes for 10 minutes to set, then peel them off the paper and use them to decorate your desserts.

Caramel Springs

These little coils of caramelized sugar can be used to decorate cakes or individual plated desserts. They do take a little practice to make—the key is to boil your sugar just until it starts caramelizing, and not turning a full amber colour. This provides a cooked sugar with more flexibility, which is easier to stretch and spiral.

Makes 12 to 24 springs • Prep 30 minutes • Cook 10 minutes plus setting

2 Tbsp | 30 mL	water
1 cup | 200 g	granulated sugar
1 Tbsp | 15 mL	glucose syrup or white corn syrup

1. Before cooking your sugar, line a baking tray with parchment paper, and have this ready with a few clean tablespoons, and a few wooden spoons with straight, unpainted handles. Lightly grease the handles with cooking spray or rub them with a paper towel sprinkled with vegetable oil.

2. Add the water, sugar, and glucose syrup to a small saucepan and bring to a boil over high heat, without stirring. Continue to boil, occasionally brushing the sides of the saucepan with cold water, until the sugar barely begins to colour. Remove the saucepan from the heat and allow the caramel to cool to the point where it no longer drips off a spoon in droplets, but can be pulled and stretched (be careful, it will be hot).

3. Dip a tablespoon in the caramel and hold a wooden spoon over the pot, letting the caramel slowly catch onto the handle of the wooden spoon. Slowly twirl the wooden spoon so that the caramel wraps around it, spiralling into a coil or spring. After about five to eight rotations, set the spoon aside to set for just a minute, then carefully twist and remove the caramel spring and set it aside. Repeat this with the remaining sugar. It does take a little practice to develop a rhythm and flow, so don't worry if a few springs break or aren't perfect—these can be crushed up and sprinkled onto desserts or ice cream. If the sugar becomes too hard to work with, put it back on low heat and stir just a little to re-melt it. The springs will keep, refrigerated, for up to 1 week in an airtight container.

Glucose syrup can be found where you find cake decorating supplies. I use it when making caramel garnishes because it adds stretch to the caramel while it's warm, and sets firmly, so the garnishes aren't overly fragile (but still enjoyable to eat without fear of losing a filling).

Caramel Hazelnut Spikes

These caramel-dipped hazelnuts make a lovely garnish for a plated dessert such as Crème Caramel (page 208). You'll need toothpicks, parchment paper, and an 8-inch (20 cm) round piece of Styrofoam (such as a foam cake round) for these.

Makes 24 • Prep 20 minutes • Cook 5 minutes plus setting

24 | 24	**toasted and skinned hazelnuts**
3 Tbsp | 45 mL	**water**
½ cup | 150 g	**granulated sugar**
1 Tbsp | 15 mL	**glucose syrup or white corn syrup**

1. Insert a toothpick in the side of each hazelnut. Place a sheet of parchment paper on your countertop and put the Styrofoam on top of it (you can elevate the piece of Styrofoam by putting it on a bowl or container, so that it sits 2–3 inches/ 5–7.5 cm above the parchment). Have a large metal bowl filled with ice water on hand.

2. Bring the water, sugar, and glucose syrup up to a boil in a saucepan over high heat without stirring. Boil the sugar, occasionally brushing the sides of the saucepan with water, until the sugar turns a light amber colour, about 5 minutes. Remove the saucepan from the heat and immerse the bottom of the pot in the ice water to halt the cooking. Gently swirl the pot until you see that the sugar is thickening.

3. Use the toothpick to hold a hazelnut as you dip it halfway into the sugar. Hold it above the saucepan for a few seconds to let the sugar drip off, then stick the toothpick into the Styrofoam so that the hazelnut rests about 6 inches (15 cm) above the parchment. As the caramel cools, the thread of caramel that comes down from the hazelnut will set. Repeat with the remaining hazelnuts, until all are dipped. If the sugar becomes too thick or sets up, reheat over low heat, stirring very gently before continuing. Once the hazelnuts are set, remove the toothpicks and store the "spikes" in an airtight container for up to 1 week.

Fondant Flowers

These pink-hued flowers make a lovely décor for a fondant- or buttercream-covered cake,
such as my Fondant-Covered Heart Cake (page 154).

Makes enough flowers to cover a large cake • Prep 1 hour plus setting

Fondant

½ lb | 225 g	**Rolling Fondant (page 163)**
	pink food colouring paste (page 155)
	icing sugar
	assorted flower cutters (found at bulk and craft stores)

Royal Icing

2 cups | 260 g	**icing sugar, sifted**
1 ½ Tbsp | 22 mL	**meringue powder**
3 Tbsp | 45 mL	**warm water**

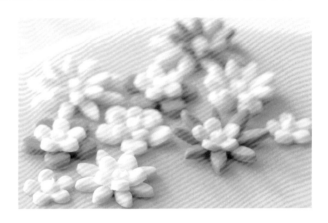

1. Divide the fondant into four equal pieces. Set one piece aside, wrapped in plastic wrap to prevent it drying out, for white flowers. Tint the other three pieces different shades of pink, using a toothpick to add paste colour a little at a time and kneading it in. Wrap each piece in plastic wrap and set aside until ready to roll.

2. Scatter icing sugar over a very clean work surface. Roll the first piece of fondant to about ⅛ inch (3 mm) thick, sprinkling with icing sugar as you roll to prevent sticking. Using different sizes of flower cutters, cut out flowers and place them on a parchment-lined baking tray. Continue with the other three pieces of fondant, giving you an array of different sizes of flower-shaped cut-outs.

3. For the royal icing, beat the icing sugar, meringue powder, and warm water together using electric beaters or in a stand mixer fitted with the whip attachment on low speed, increasing to high, until smooth and structured (you can always adjust the consistency by adding more icing sugar to thicken or water to loosen). Spoon the icing into a piping bag fitted with a small plain tip.

4. When you are ready to adhere the flowers to your cake, use the royal icing as glue. Place a small dot of icing on the back of the flower. Use a small dowel (usually supplied with the fondant cutters) or a bamboo skewer to press the flower on the cake, pulling the petals up slightly to form the shape of the flower. Continue with the rest of the flowers in whatever pattern you like. You can add texture and dimension to the flowers by placing smaller flower cut-outs in different shades on top of the base flower. With the icing, pipe a small dot in the centre of each flower. Allow at least 2 hours for the icing to set and store the cake according to the recipe instructions. The flowers can be made up to 3 days ahead and stored in an airtight container until needed.

Once the fondant flowers sit out in the air,
they will dry and become a little brittle.
This is handy for setting a bend or curve to
your flowers when you're freshly rolling,
cutting, and shaping them, but means if
you try to shape the fondant after about
1 hour, you'll find it cracks.

Homemade Marzipan

Once you realize how simple and tasty marzipan is when made from scratch, you'll never go back to pre-made.

Makes about 1 lb (450 g) • Prep 20 minutes • Cook 5 minutes

1 ¾ cups | 210 g	**ground almonds**
1 cup | 200 g	**granulated sugar**
¼ cup | 60 g	**honey**
2 Tbsp | 30 mL	**water**
1 tsp | 5 mL	**pure almond extract**

Once you try making this marzipan recipe from scratch, you will understand why I call it a Foundation recipe. Marzipan is a thing unto itself, but is also used as an ingredient in baking (such as in the Fondant-Glazed Petits Fours, page 163). What I love most about making marzipan myself is that I can use good-quality ingredients (I love the taste of honey in marzipan—too many pre-made marzipans don't use it), plus I can control how much almond extract I want to add. I like a little extract, but not too much as I don't want the taste of the extract to overwhelm my desserts.

1. Place the ground almonds in a food processor fitted with the steel blade attachment. Stir the sugar, honey, and water together in a small saucepan over high heat until they reach a full boil and the sugar has completely dissolved. Pour this into the food processor while it's running. Add the almond extract and blend until the marzipan comes together. While it's still warm, shape it into a log and wrap it tightly in plastic wrap. Leave it at room temperature to cool. Marzipan will keep, well wrapped, for up to 1 month, or can be frozen up to 3 months.

Marzipan Fruits and Veggies

Making fruits out of marzipan is a longstanding tradition, especially for the holidays. Here are some standard styles, from simple to more elaborate. To make all of them you'll need bamboo skewers and then an assortment of paring knives, marzipan tools (optional, but available at cake supply or craft stores if you choose to use them), small leaf cutters, and small paint brushes.

Makes 10 to 16 pieces • Prep 90 minutes

1 | 1   recipe Homemade Marzipan (page 295)

cocoa powder (for potatoes)

food colouring pastes, various colours (page 155)

raw whole wheat spaghetti (for stems)

whole cloves (for bottoms of pears and apples)

Potatoes

Shape a scant tablespoonful (15 mL) of marzipan between your palms into a potato shape. Use a bamboo skewer or other tool to make "eyes" in the potato and then roll it in a little cocoa powder (to replicate dirt), shaking off any excess.

Pumpkins

Add a little orange colouring paste to a spoonful of marzipan and knead the colour in. Shape the marzipan into a ball between the palms of your hands and then flatten it just a little on top. Use the back of a paring knife or a marzipan tool to press lines into the pumpkin. Add a little cocoa powder or brown colouring paste to a little more marzipan and shape it into a thin rope. Cut a little piece off and press it into the pumpkin to make the stem. Spiral the remaining piece around a bamboo skewer then carefully remove it and press it in near the stem to make a tendril.

Pears or apples

Add a little yellow or green (or both) colouring paste to a spoonful of marzipan and knead the colour in. Shape the marzipan into a ball between the palms of your hands. If making a pear, shape the marzipan to a pear shape. If making an apple, shape it into an apple shape. Use a small piece of raw whole wheat spaghetti as the stem and push a whole clove into the bottom for the blossom end. For added dimension, dilute a little contrasting food colouring (red or orange) in a little clear alcohol or water and brush on a "blush" to the fruit.

Leaves

Add a little green food colouring paste to some marzipan and knead it in. Roll out the marzipan as thinly as possible and cut out leaf shapes as desired. Use a bamboo skewer or the back of a paring knife to make vein marks on the leaves. You can bend and pinch the leaves to give them dimension and set them on a tray to dry, or press them into the other fruits as desired while still soft.

Allow the marzipan fruits to air dry for 12 hours, then store for up to 2 weeks in an airtight container.

This is definitely a case where you get to play with your food! Practice is key—and keep in mind that it takes a while for the marzipan to set, so if you're not happy with a shape, you can just squish it up and start again.

• • • • • • •

The potatoes are the easiest marzipan shapes to start with, and really look hilarious!

A Note to My British Readers

I know you'll be pleased to see that all of the recipes in this book include weighted measures to make life simpler. But while these measurements are listed on every page in the ingredient list, I've discovered in some of my work in the UK that you have different terminology for some ingredients, so I've listed the equivalents or appropriate substitutions here to keep you mixing, rolling, and baking with confidence.

Canadian	British
All-purpose flour	Plain flour
Chocolate: dark	Plain chocolate
Chocolate: semisweet or bittersweet	Dark or plain chocolate
Chocolate: unsweetened	Plain chocolate, 85% cocoa or higher
Cilantro and coriander	In North America, cilantro is the fresh herb and coriander is the dried version
Corn syrup	Golden syrup
Cornstarch	Corn flour
Food colouring paste	Food colour gel
Graham cracker crumbs	Digestive biscuit crumbs
Milk: 2%	Semi-skimmed milk
Pumpkin purée	Unsweetened, spice-free pumpkin pie filling
Quick-rise yeast	Fast action yeast
Skor bits	Daim bars (crushed)
Superfine sugar	Caster sugar*
Tapioca starch	Tapioca flour
Whipping cream	Double cream
White corn syrup	Light corn syrup
Zucchini	Courgette

*Caster sugar is a finer grind than granulated sugar, but within a recipe, the workability is the same. Since they are measured by weight, no adjustments need to be made.

Other equivalents

Molasses—You might need to shop around a little for molasses, but I know from personal experience that it is available. Avoid substituting treacle for molasses.

Pitted tart cherries—If fresh or frozen are not available, you can sometimes find jarred cherries. Be sure not to use cocktail, candied, or dried cherries, but Morello cherries will work just fine.

Rolling fondant—This can be found at specialty baking stores and online if you are not making your own (see page 163), or sugar paste can also be used.

Muffin tins—these are deeper than fairy cake tins, so don't be tempted use a fairy cake tin where I specify a muffin tin.

Acknowledgements

This delicious project never felt like work, thanks to all of the support and effort of the people involved. The love of my life, Michael, deserves an award for patience and for relinquishing the kitchen to days of testing and photos.

Lisa Rollo also has my never-ending respect and admiration for her work on recipe testing, photography, and overall organizing and coordinating on this book and the television series. Thank you for all you've done over the years—you are a treasured friend.

The television series that inspired this book is sheer joy to work on because of the fantastic team, and I owe thanks for this to Jennifer and Sylvie as producers and directors; Mia, Miss April and Amy on the food team; and Les and Julie for their big-picture thinking and determination. Ryan Szulc and Mike McColl did an incredible job reflecting the work through images and I thank you.

I also need to thank Dean Cooke for his support, advice, and work; Lindsay and Lesley for their fantastic editing (there is a trust between editor and author that is hard to describe); Scott for his stunning and inviting design; and Paige and everyone at Appetite and Random House who have demonstrated such commitment to the project.

And a big hug and my sincerest and heartfelt thanks go to Robert McCullough. We've been friends for so long and I value that each of us have stood by each other through thick and thin. I am so proud of you, and it is my honour to be under the Appetite banner.

Index